Contemporary Challenges in Mediatisation Research

This book focuses on key challenges related to conducting research on mediatisation, presenting the most current theoretical, empirical, and methodological challenges and problems, addressing ignored and less frequently discussed topics, critical and controversial themes, and defining niches and directions of development in mediatisation.

With a focus on the under-representation of certain topics and aspects, as well as methodological, technological, and ethical dilemmas, the chapters consider the main critical objections formulated against mediatisation studies and exchange critical positions. Moving beyond areas of common focus – culture, sport, and religion – to emerging areas of study such as fashion, the military, business, and the environment, the book then offers a critical assessment of the transformation of fields and the relevance of new and dynamic (meta)processes including datafication, counter-mediatisation, and platformisation.

Charting new paths of development in mediatisation, this book will be of interest to scholars and students of mediatisation, media studies, media literacy, communication studies, and research methods.

Katarzyna Kopecka-Piech is Associate Professor at Maria Curie-Skłodowska University in Lublin, Poland.

Göran Bolin is Professor of Media and Communication Studies at Södertörn University, Sweden.

Routledge Studies in Media Theory and Practice

Contemporary Challenges in Mediatisation Research

Edited by Katarzyna Kopecka-Piech and Göran Bolin

Routledge
Taylor & Francis Group
LONDON AND NEW YORK

First published 2023
by Routledge
4 Park Square, Milton Park, Abingdon, Oxon OX14 4RN

and by Routledge
605 Third Avenue, New York, NY 10158

Routledge is an imprint of the Taylor & Francis Group, an informa business

© 2023 selection and editorial matter, Katarzyna Kopecka-Piech and Göran Bolin; individual chapters, the contributors

The right of Katarzyna Kopecka-Piech and Göran Bolin to be identified as the authors of the editorial material, and of the authors for their individual chapters, has been asserted in accordance with sections 77 and 78 of the Copyright, Designs and Patents Act 1988.

British Library Cataloguing-in-Publication Data
A catalogue record for this book is available from the British Library

ISBN: 978-1-032-34681-6 (hbk)
ISBN: 978-1-032-34942-8 (pbk)
ISBN: 978-1-003-32459-1 (ebk)

DOI: 10.4324/9781003324591

Typeset in Sabon
by Newgen Publishing UK

Contents

Contributors

Göran Bolin is Professor of Media and Communication Studies at Södertörn University, Sweden. His research focusses on mediatisation, datafication, commodification and cultural production and consumption in digital markets. Among his publications can be mentioned *Value and the Media: Cultural Production and Consumption in Digital Markets* (2011), *Media Generations: Experience, Identity and Mediatised Social Change* (Routledge 2016) and *Digital Media and the Dynamics of Civil Society: Retooling Citizenship in New EU Democracies* (2021). He is a member of the Executive Board of ECREA and Chair of the Film, Media and Visual Studies section in *Academia Europaea*.

Deborah Chambers is Professor of Media and Communication Studies, Newcastle University, UK. Her research centres on media technologies in the home and in interpersonal communication with a focus on emerging technologies: AI, smart homes, mobile media, and social media. She collaborates on an EPSRC cybersecurity project, 'AGENCY: Complex Online Harms'.

Kirsten Frandsen is Professor of Media Studies at Aarhus University, Denmark. She has published intensively on the relationship between sport and media, including historical developments in sports journalism and sports broadcasting, production processes, television entertainment, digital media in sports and media sport audiences/users. Most recently she has published *Sport and Mediatization* (2020).

Tilo Grenz works at the Bertha von Suttner Private University, Austria. His research combines sociology of knowledge, dynamics of digital material and organisations. A particular focus is on the digital risk society and non-conventional forms of digital participation. Tilo further develops methods suitable for analysing the unfolding of sociotechnical events.

Rafael Grohmann is Assistant Professor of Media Studies with a Focus on Critical Data and Platform Studies, at the University of Toronto, Canada. He is Coordinator of the DigiLabour Research Lab, Principal Investigator for the Fairwork project in Brazil, Director of the Labor Tech Research

Network, and Coordinator of the Platform Cooperativism Observatory in Brazil.

Roman Horbyk is a Baltic Sea Foundation Postdoctoral Research Fellow with Södertörn University, Stockholm, Sweden. His research interests include mediatisation, transformation of journalism, fake news, mobile communication in war and conflict, conceptual history, postcolonial theory and sociolinguistics. Roman Horbyk is a winner of the 2022 Top Paper award at ICA.

Sigrid Kannengießer is Professor in Communication and Media Studies at the Institute for Communication Studies at the University of Münster, Germany. Her research focuses on digital media, sustainability and climate change, materiality of digital technologies, critical data practices, social movements and their media practices, and gender media studies.

Anne Kaun is Professor in Media and Communication Studies at Södertörn University, Sweden. Her research interests include media activism, media practices, critical studies of algorithms, automation and artificial intelligence. Together with Fredrik Stiernstedt, she is currently pursuing a larger project on the media history and media future of prisons, and is currently writing the book *Prison Media* under contract with MIT Press. She is also studying the democratic consequences of the automation of welfare institutions. Her research has appeared in, among others, *International Journal of Communication*, *New Media & Society*, *Media, Culture & Society* and *Time & Society*. In 2016, she published her book *Crisis and Critique*, and in 2020, *Making Time for Digital Lives*, co-edited with Christian Pentzold and Christine Lohmeier.

Katarzyna Kopecka-Piech is Associate Professor at Maria Curie-Skłodowska University in Lublin, Poland. She is the author of *Mediatization of Physical Activity: Media Saturation and Technologies* (Lexington Books 2019) and *Media Convergence Strategies: Polish Examples* (Astrum 2011), as well as the editor of *Mediatisation of Emotional Life* (Routledge 2022) and *COVID-19 as a Challenge for Media and Communication Studies* (Routledge 2022).

Knut Lundby is Professor Emeritus in Media Studies, Department of Media and Communication, University of Oslo, Norway. Lundby is Dr.Philos. with a dissertation on the sociology of religion. He is among the founding members of the research community on Media, Religion, and Culture. He has edited books on mediatisation and written on the mediatisation of religion. He also directed the CoMRel project on Engaging with Conflicts in Religious Environments.

Patrick McCurdy is Associate Professor at the Department of Communication, University of Ottawa, Canada. Taking an interdisciplinary approach, his research draws on media and communication theory, social movement studies and environmental communication, in order to study the media as a site and source of struggle.

Line Nybro Petersen, Ph.D., is Associate Professor in Media Studies, University of Copenhagen, Denmark. She is the author of *Mediatized Fan Play: Moods, Modes and Dark Play in Networked Communities* (Routledge 2022) and several journal articles and book chapters on mediatisation and play, ageing, fandom and religion.

Agnès Rocamora, Ph.D., is Professor of Social and Cultural Studies at the University of the Arts, London, UK. She has published widely on the field of fashion and on digital and social media.

Acknowledgements

The editors thank the Academia Europaea Wroclaw Knowledge Hub and the Wroclaw Academic Center – Municipality of Wroclaw for the organisational and financial support provided in connection with the realisation of this publication.

Introduction

Approaching the Challenges of Mediatisation

Katarzyna Kopecka-Piech and Göran Bolin

The concept of mediatisation has become increasingly popular since the turn of the millennium, to the extent that one can today speak of a specific field of mediatisation research. Although the concept itself can be traced back to at least the early 1970s (Bolin, 2014), or even the 1930s (Averbeck-Lietz, 2014), the early 2000s saw an exponential growth of it, as judged by a quick Google Ngram analysis. As the field is now "coming of age", and has been established as an approach in its own right, the question about its limits and challenges arises. This book is an attempt to systematise these challenges and point to areas where further theoretical and methodological refinement is needed.

Before we sketch the contours of these challenges, and how they are dealt with in the following chapters, we wish to give a short outline and historical overview of the field. In the next section we will therefore offer a brief characterisation of mediatisation research, and critically discuss mediatisation as a "sensitising concept", as a research programme, a research field, an approach, or a paradigm. We will then give a historical overview of how the concept and the field has developed over the past few decades until now, and what has shaped it in this way. We will account for the various approaches (the institutional perspective on mediatisation, the technological, and the cultural or social constructionist); and we will discuss ontological and epistemological differences. In the third section we will describe the main challenges and objections/criticisms to mediatisation studies defined so far, types of transformations that have been analysed, and which are neglected and marginalised.

Mediatisation in a historical perspective

Stefanie Averbeck-Lietz (2014) has traced the concept of mediatisation back to German sociologist Ernest Manheim (1933/1979), writing about public opinion in the 1930s. As a concept, mediatisation indicates change, development, and transformation. It thus has a clear temporal aspect to it, highlighting the processual. Friedrich Krotz, one of the pioneers of mediatisation research, also points to the processual nature of the concept and

DOI: 10.4324/9781003324591-1

argues that mediatisation is a "meta-process" on par with other grand theories such as globalisation, individualisation, industrialisation, and marketisation (Krotz 2001). Meta-processes should be understood as macro-level processes that impact on other processes on meso-levels or restricted regionally or locally. They are often understood in a linear temporal fashion and describe overarching forces that impact on culture and society as a whole, a "moulding force" in the words of Andreas Hepp (2011/2013), carrying its own inner dynamics and complexities (Bolin & Hepp, 2017).

So, how should one regard the concept of mediatisation, and what does it signify? Klaus Bruhn Jensen (2013) has pointed to the polysemic nature of the concept and argued that it is more of a "sensitising concept", borrowing from Herbert Blumer's (1954) distinction between "definitive" and "sensitising" concepts. A sensitising concept works as "a general sense of reference and guidance", according to Blumer (quoted in Jensen 2013, p. 206). This is a good thing, argues Jensen, because "a plurality of sensitising strategies holds the greatest promise" to support further theoretical development (Jensen 2013, p. 218). Jensen discusses this by positing two scholars against one another, representative of the two dominant strands or approaches to it: the institutional perspective represented by Stig Hjarvard (2013), and a more societally focussed perspective represented by Nick Couldry (2012).

The distinction between approaches that Jensen makes in this context is, in fact, indicative of the dominant way in which the field has gradually become understood and discussed, where the institutional approach is posited against a cultural or constructivist perspective.

Broadly, the *institutional* perspective approaches the process of mediatisation as a relationship between societal and cultural institutions, where media institutions – for example journalism – impact on other societal institutions – for example politics. The "mediatisation of politics" approach is by far the most common focus in mediatisation research from an institutional perspective, most likely because journalism and politics are clearly identifiable institutions in society, and because it is relatively easy to operationalise the theory of institutional mediatisation for empirical studies in this area. It is also an area that was focussed early on, by Scandinavian researchers such as Kent Asp (1990) and Jesper Strömbäck (2008). Theoretically, the institutional perspective has been elaborated in detail by Stig Hjarvard (2008, 2013), arguing for the benefits of conducting analysis on the meso-level. Even if the mediatisation of politics has been the most common focus of the institutional perspective, there are also other societal areas that have been studied. Hjarvard himself has, for example, also studied the mediatisation of children's play (Hjarvard, 2013, pp. 103ff), and there is also a subfield of research into the mediatisation of religion (Hjarvard & Lövheim, 2012; Lundby, 2021).

By contrast, the *constructivist approach* emphasises the role of the media in wider socio-cultural processes, and their co-variation with other meta-processes in society such as marketisation, globalisation, and individualisation. While the institutionalised perspective often works with shorter time spans, often placing the early phases of mediatisation after the Second World War, if not later, and also puts a strong emphasis on mass media institutions, the constructivist approach works with longer temporal perspectives, often pointing to the role of communication media in human life altogether. This means pointing to wider transformations in communication history, from chirographical culture to electronic media culture to the digital society of the present. And while the institutional approach often looks upon the media as an independent variable in the culture–society–media nexus, thus pointing to causal influences, the constructionist approach often emphasises the complexities of these processes (cf. Bolin & Hepp, 2017).

Although the institutional and constructivist approaches are by far dominant, there are also other ways in which mediatisation has been conceptualised in history. In the early 1970s, Jean Baudrillard (1971) was one of those who first theorised it. Rather than being inspired by organisational sociology or social constructivism, Baudrillard's influences came from anthropology, Marxism, and semiotics. His emphasis was thus not so much on the media as organisations, nor on their content structures, but on the *media as technologies* or communication channels. When mediated communication occurred, he argued, this prevented genuine dialogue from happening, and the media were merely engaging in "speech without response". The media – foremost the mass media but by extension all media technologies – by the nature of their technological operation, could only produce second-hand information about social reality, and hence only simulate genuine communication (Baudrillard, 1976/1993, p. 63).

There are, of course, benefits as well as downsides to all these ways of regarding mediatisation. On the beneficial side, an institutional approach can be much more easily operationalised into empirical studies, focussing on specific institutions either in the form of specific organisations or in specific institutionalised media domains such as journalism. This is also the case with the technological perspective, which also mainly focusses on mass media. On the other hand, their shorter historical perspectives make these approaches oversensitive to empirical change on the surface of things, while deep, fundamental societal change might be overlooked. The opposite is true of the constructivist perspective, which can often regard longer historical *durées*, but has far more difficulty in verifying change empirically and in detail.

As a *research programme*, then, the institutional analysis of mediatisation fits rather well, being easy to operationalise, and to delimit in concrete empirical projects. The other two are more similar to *research approaches* which look upon the general role of media technologies and forms in social and cultural processes. This is also close to how Sonia Livingstone and Peter Lunt (2014) conclude the handbook *Mediatization of Communication* (Lundby, 2014). It is of course possible to isolate individual communication technologies in order to study and lay bare their inner workings and how technologies of mediation impact on communicated messages, but it also becomes an empty exercise with a predicted outcome, since one can presuppose that each technological change does *something* with communication. But if one looks at communication as always already integrated in social processes, it is very hard to isolate them in order to study impact in any meaningful way. This makes the constructivist perspective more of a point of departure than a focus for analysis.

Critical questions for mediatisation research

Quite naturally, mediatisation research has been debated and criticised. Most elaborate of these criticisms is the one proposed by David Deacon and James Stanyer (2014), who propose three problems raised by mediatisation research based on a literature review of recent published journal articles on mediatisation: the presupposition of historical change without empirical qualification; the failure of establishing causality for change; and the conceptual construction of the concept itself. When it comes to the first of these criticisms, Deacon and Stanyer point out that inherent in the concept is a focus on change – something is mediatised that presumably was not before. Furthermore, there is an implied causal relationship where the media affects something in culture or society and changes this thing or phenomenon. This, they argue, makes mediatisation research "media centric" and risks overemphasising the importance of the media for social processes.

Second, most mediatisation researchers take their point of departure from how phenomena have become mediatised, but have a hard time establishing this empirically for the simple reason that they have not conducted comparative historical research. In fact, they argue that change is presumed rather than empirically validated.

Third, they argue that the concept itself has totalising ambitions and therefore lacks discriminatory power. If everything is mediatised, then what explanatory value does the concept have? To prove their argument, the authors ask the question, "if you removed the word mediatisation completely from each article, how many of these articles would still make sense?" Their answer is that only a small fraction of articles stand this test, while most of them would do well without the concept.

This criticism provoked a lively debate that while at the same time as it acknowledged (some) of the critique, also qualified the agenda for mediatisation research. The most constructive of these was perhaps Ekström et al. (2016) who called for future mediatisation research agenda to include three tasks: *historicity*, *specificity*, and *measurability*. The first of these concerns is perceived of as a lack of historical awareness of mediatisation research and they point to the fact that research so far has "hypostasized the existence of mediatisation and then focused on analyzing the contemporary effects of this taken-for-granted process" (Ekström et al., 2016,

p. 1098). This criticism, which is largely in line with the one proposed by Deacon and Stanyer (2014), asks for better historical analysis and more thorough historical comparative research. One could argue that such an historical analysis has also been made in some instances. Bolin (2016), for example, in his analysis of media and generations, has explicitly addressed this question and used the concept of generation in seeking to analyse long-time social change across generations as well as cross-culturally (see also Bolin, 2017).

Second, Ekström et al. (2016) argue that mediatisation research needs to be more specific when it comes to which media technologies are studied, in which specific contexts, and at which specific transformative pace. Most mediatisation research makes too many sweeping generalisations regarding these matters, and if change is to be established, there needs to be much better empirical detail about how change occurs. One might also add that the depth of change needs to be taken into consideration. Arguably, a view on society from a modernisation perspective would presuppose change, but change can also be on the surface, while deeper structures might be stable. For example, take the changes introduced when the Soviet Union collapsed. Many of the former states within the Soviet bloc had state-run mass media. When the communist system collapsed, as Colin Sparks (1998) has argued, most of them turned into commercial enterprises or public service companies. There was thus a clear change in organisational structure. However, these organisations were populated by the same "nomenklatura" as had run them during Soviet times, which meant that the social power structures remained intact. This makes Sparks conclude that although there was change at the organisational level, there was stability when it came to the social power distribution.

Third, it is argued that in order to establish change, there has to be some sort of qualifier that can determine whether change indeed has occurred or not. This can, the authors suggest, be in the form of empirical studies of specific sub-domains of mediatisation, focusing on more delimited parts of the overarching process of mediatisation in order to create indicators of change (Ekström et al., 2016, pp. 1102ff).

It is against the background of such debates that the contributors to the present volume discuss the forms of mediatisation across diverse societal domains, and the challenges facing mediatisation research in the contemporary media landscape.

The scope, the aim and the content of the book

The book focuses on the key challenges related to conducting research on mediatisation. Taking its point of departure from the current situation in the field, it concentrates on the under-representation of certain topics and aspects; and critically examines the methodological, technological, ethical, and other dilemmas. The aim is to further consider the main critical objections formulated against mediatisation studies and to exchange critical positions, which enriches research in this area and makes it possible to correct and develop the concept and theory.

The book consists of reflection on the following fields: politics and public life, religion, sport and physical activity, business, culture, home and family life, fashion, the military and warfare, the environment, work and labour, as well as such processes as datafication, platformisation and de-mediatisation.

The book presents the most current theoretical, practical, and methodological challenges and problems, and it identifies gaps and deficiencies in the research on mediatisation, regarding the temporal and spatial dimensions of mediatisation, the problematic nature of particular approaches, and the contradictions and paradoxes of research on mediatisation as well as underrepresented areas.

Furthermore, it explores the implications of the "heterogeneity, contradictions and ambiguities" (Nybro Peteresen, in this volume) of mediatisation studies. Responding to "increased quantity and complexity", it shows the greatest challenges that researchers face. Through the book, some elements of mediatisation theory are "critically unpacked" (Rocamora, in this volume), and some of the fields framed by mediatisation gain a new perspective.

In Chapter 1, Line Nybro Petersen considers the theoretical and empirical challenges relating to the heterogeneity of the field of mediatisation of culture. She argues for the necessity of identifying clearer sub-processes related to culture specifically. The chapter postulates, for example, a return to the "structures of feelings" concept of Raymond Williams (1977), inviting the reader to consider historical changes and draw out patterns of cultural experiences more broadly.

In Chapter 2, Knut Lundby discusses three aspects of the mediatisation of religion: globalisation, conceptualisation, and generalisation. The author asks the following questions: What are the gendered aspects of the mediatisation of religion in the world? How will datafication and machine learning affect the mediatisation of religion? What might insights into the mediatisation of religion mean for religious studies? The author continues with a theoretical discussion of how the concepts of "mediation" and "mediatisation" of religion should be understood. He considers the conditions under which the mediatisation of religion occurs and explores the dimensions of mediatised religion in time and space.

In Chapter 3, Kirsten Frandsen begins a discussion of the current challenges of conducting mediatisation research in sport. She discusses the following challenges in applying a mediatisation perspective to this field: Why is the concept of mediatisation not easily accepted by researchers in the field? How can we analyse such processes and explain the exact role of media without falling into mediacentrism? The author also asks about the role of the media–sport nexus in political contexts, and the impact of social and mobile media and technology on sport, everyday life, and practices of athletes and sport organisations.

In Chapter 4, Agnès Rocamora focuses on the mediatisation and datafication of fashion, and the transformation of everyday life into digitised, quantified data organised by algorithms. She engages in a dialogue with three fields of study: Bourdieuian field theory; mediatisation theory; and theories of datafication – all considered through the lens of contemporary developments in fashion. Drawing on van Dijck and Poell's (2013) notion of a "logic of social media", the author looks at the idea of a logic of digital media. The chapter asks questions such as: To what extent is the mediatisation of the fashion field supported by the correspondence between the logic of digital media and the logic of fashion? How can looking at the example of the fashion field help us to critically analyse the idea of deep mediatisation and vice versa?

In Chapter 5, Sigrid Kannengießer and Patrick McCurdy start from the premise that mediatisation science has largely ignored the socio-ecological effects and environmental impacts associated with mediatisation processes. By pointing to the resources and energy required for mediatisation and the e-waste it produces, they show that mediatisation implies a complex material dimension that must be acknowledged to address the socio-ecological challenges mediatisation raises. The authors argue that mediatisation research must acknowledge the relationship between mediatisation and climate change in order to better understand and make visible these problematic interdependencies and contribute to the development of solutions. Analysis of the relationship between mediatisation and climate change shows that the focus should be on energy production.

Tilo Grenz's Chapter 6 on the mediatisation of business starts from the premise that the analysis of the relevance of companies and corporate actors to the overall mediatisation process was initially somewhat abbreviated, in which mediatisation was often equated with success-oriented media use or media development, such that mediatisation has become another trend similar to the "platform metaphor". At the same time both human and non-human agencies, interests, and routines combine in increasingly volatile processes of mediatisation. One of the greatest challenges of mediatisation studies – theoretically, methodologically, and empirically – is to account for these recent dynamics. This chapter argues that by addressing these challenges, mediatisation research becomes a central resource in the analysis of the digital risk society. In addition, he argues for a strong process-based approach to case study analysis and discusses recent approaches to so-called real-time mediatisation research.

In Chapter 7, Roman Horbyk examines the field of military, war, and media from a contemporary mediatisation perspective. The question is how the military is adapting to a "mediatised" environment; how the military is increasingly using the media, in the context of issues such as legacy war coverage, military media management, and information warfare. According to the author, mediatisation has been under-utilised in the study of how new media and communication technologies blend into actual combat. This represents the second major challenge to the mediatisation of military research, coinciding with the need for more empirical field research. The lack of connection to a key concept in current military theory, hybrid warfare, and media weaponisation is also discussed.

In Chapter 8 Deborah Chambers explores the concept of mediatisation to assess the relationship between the macroprocesses and microprocesses of domestic mediatisation. She asks: How do macroprocesses configure and impose domestic media forms and meanings, and how do domesticators negotiate and interpret these dynamics in the "doing" and "making" of domestic life? Eliseo Verón's sociosemiotic approach is applied, and the term "mediatising agents" is developed to emphasise the role of social actors; and the term "mediatising nexus" is introduced to measure the parameters of domestic media adoption. The new dynamic, dubbed "confluent mediatisation", emphasises media convergence as the sequential integration of technical facilities and the accelerating displacement of redundant media equipment.

Rafael Grohmann's Chapter 9 aims to explore the connections and dialogues between mediatisation studies and platform labour studies. Grohmann considers platformisation (Poell, Nieborg & Van Dijck, 2019) to be the most prolific feature of contemporary mediatisation, affecting work at different levels, such as the mechanisms of rentier capitalism (Murdock, 2017; Sadowski, 2020), the datafication of labour (Mejias & Couldry, 2019; Chen & Qiu, 2019), algorithmic management (Mateescu & Nguyen, 2019; Woodcock, 2020), and the use of social media and other digital infrastructures by workers to organise themselves and build alternatives (Soriano et al., 2020; Hepp, 2020). The chapter discusses these aspects, highlighting the role of media and communication in each of these transformations. The chapter concludes with a research agenda for a better understanding of the platformisation of work from the perspective of a mediatisation approach.

In Chapter 10, Anne Kaun begins her analysis with historical approaches to explore the implications of media beyond simple media effects. However, she notes that for some time there has been a growing interest in the process of datafication, which is defined as the transformation of all aspects of our lives into data (Mayer-Schönberger & Cukier, 2013; van Dijck, 2014). For the author, it seems that datafication has emerged as a new bandwagon concept that is attracting more and more researchers within media and communication studies, very much like mediatisation studies before. This chapter attempts to answer the question of whether we are witnessing a shift from mediatisation research towards datafication research. At the same time, the chapter asks what datafication researchers can learn from mediatisation studies and how the two processes and approaches to studying them fundamentally differ.

In Chapter 11, Katarzyna Kopecka-Piech discusses rather exclusionary perspectives on de-mediatisation, juxtaposing them with concepts such as counter-mediatisation (Jansson), de-mediatisation (Grenz), digital disconnection (Syvertsen; Jansson & Fast), or desaturation of media technologies (Kopecka-Piech). The chapter redefines de-mediatisation and presents a small number of studies on voluntary disuse that fit within the framework of mediatisation studies, and explores existing research on voluntary non-use broadly conducted outside the mediatisation paradigm to identify key assumptions of the research agenda of de-mediatisation within it. The author considers suggestions for specific research approaches that are necessary for the coherent and complementary development of (de)mediatisation studies.

References

Asp, K. (1986). *Mäktiga Massmedier*. Stockholm: Akademilitteratur.

Asp, K. (1990). Medialization, Media Logic and Mediarchy. *Nordicom Review* 11(2): 47–50.

Averbeck-Lietz, S. (2014). Understanding Mediatization in "First Modernity": Sociological Classics and Their Perspectives on Mediated and Mediatized Societies. In Knut Lundby (ed.) *Mediatization of Communication*. Berlin & Boston: De Gruyter Mouton, 109–130.

Baudrillard, J. (1968). *Le système des objets*. Paris: Gallimard.

Baudrillard, J. (1970/1998). *The Consumer Society. Myths and Structures*. London: Sage.

Baudrillard, J. (1971). Requiem pour les media. *Utopie* 4: 35–51.

Baudrillard, Jean (1972/1981). *For a Critique of the Political Economy of the Sign*. St Louis MO: Telos.

Baudrillard, J. (1976/1993). *Symbolic Exchange and Death*. London: Sage.

Blumer, H. (1954). What Is Wrong with Social Theory? *American Sociological Review* 19: 3–10.

Bolin, G. (2014). Institution, Technology, World: Relationships between the Media, Culture and Society. In Knut Lundby (ed.) *Mediatization of Communication*. Berlin & Boston: De Gruyter Mouton, 175–197.

Bolin, G. (2016). *Media Generations: Experience, Identity and Mediatised Social Change*. London & New York: Routledge.

Bolin, G. (2017). Generational Analysis as a Methodological Approach to Study Mediatised Social Change. In Sakari Taipale, Terhi-Anna Wilska & Chris Gilleard (eds) *Digital Technologies and Generational Identity: ICT Usage Across the Life Course*. London & New York: Routledge, 23–36.

Bolin, G. & Hepp, A. (2017). The Complexity of Mediatization: Charting the Road Ahead. In Olivier Driessens, Göran Bolin, Andreas Hepp & Stig Hjarvard (eds) *Dynamics of Mediatization: Institutional Change and Everyday Transformations in a Digital Age*. London: Palgrave, 315–332.

Couldry, N. (2012). *Media, Society, World. Social Theory and Digital Media Practice*. Cambridge: Polity.

Deacon, D. & Stanyer, J. (2014). Mediatization: Key Concept or Conceptual Bandwagon? *Media, Culture & Society* 36(7): 1032–1044.

Deacon, D. & Stanyer J. (2015). "Mediatization and" or "Mediatization of"? A Response to Hepp et al. *Media, Culture & Society* 37(4): 655–657.

Ekström, M., Fornäs, J., Jansson, A., & Jerslev, A. (2016). Three Tasks for Mediatization Research. Contributing to an Open Agenda. *Media, Culture & Society* 38(7): 1090–1108.

Hepp, A. (2011/2013). *Cultures of Mediatization*. Cambridge: Polity.

Hepp, A. (2020). *Deep Mediatization*. Cambridge: Polity.

Hepp, A., Hjarvard, S. & Lundby K. (2015). Mediatization: Theorizing the Interplay between Media, Culture and Society. *Media, Culture & Society* 37(2): 314–324.

Hjarvard, S. (2008) The Mediatization of Society: A Theory of the Media as Agents of Social and Cultural Change. *Nordicom Review* 29: 105–134.

Hjarvard, S. (2013). *The Mediatization of Culture and Society*. London & New York: Routledge.

Hjarvard, S. & Lövheim M. (eds) (2012). *Mediatization of Religion: Nordic Perspectives*. Göteborg: Nordicom.

Jensen, K. B. (2013). Definitive and Sensitizing Conceptualisations of Communication. *Communication Theory* 23: 203–222:

Krotz, F. (2001). *Die Mediatisierung kommunikativen Handelns. Der Wandel von Alltag und sozialen Beziehungen, Kultur und Gesellschaft durch die Medien*. Wiesbaden: Westdeutscher Verlag.

Krotz, F. (2007). The Meta-process of "Mediatization" as a Conceptual Frame. *Global Media and Communication* 33: 256–260.

Krotz, F. (2009). Mediatization: A Concept with Which to Grasp Media and Societal Change. In Knut Lundby (ed.), *Mediatization. Concept, Changes, Consequences*. New York: Peter Lang, 21–40.

Livingstone, S. & Lunt, P. (2014). Mediatization: An Emerging Paradigm for Media and Communication Research? In Knut Lundby (ed.) *Mediatization of Communication*. Berlin & Boston: De Gruyter Mouton, 703–723.

Lundby, K. (2008). *Digital Storytelling, Mediatized Stories. Self-Representations in New Media*. New York: Peter Lang.

Lundby, K. (2009a). Introduction: "Mediatization" as a Key. In Knut Lundby (ed.) *Mediatization. Concept, Changes, Consequences*. New York: Peter Lang, 1–18.

Lundby, K. (2009b). Media Logic: Looking for Social Interaction. In Knut Lundby (ed.), *Mediatization. Concept, Changes, Consequences*. New York: Peter Lang, 101–119.

Lundby, K. (ed.) (2014). *Mediatization of Communication*. Berlin & Boston: De Gruyter Mouton.

Lundby, K. (2021). *Religion i medienes grep: Medialiserting i Norge*. Oslo: Universitetsforlaget.

Manheim, E. (1933/1979). *Aufklärung und öffentliche Meinung: Studien der zur Soziologie der Öffentlichkeit*. Leipzig/Brno/Prag: Rudolph M. Rohrer.

Mazzoleni, G. & Winfried, S. (1999). "Mediatization" of Politics: A Challenge for Democracy? *Political Communication* 163: 247–261.

Schulz, W. (2004). Reconstructing Mediatization as an Analytical Concept. *European Journal of Communication* 19(1): 87–101.

Sparks, C. (1998). *Communism, Capitalism and the Mass Media*. London: Sage.

Strömbäck, J. (2008). Four Phases of Mediatization: An Analysis of the Mediatization of Politics. *International Journal of Press/Politics* 133: 228–246.

Part I

Questions for Established Domains

1 Challenges in Research on the Mediatisation of Culture

Line Nybro Petersen

Introduction

This chapter considers the theoretical and empirical challenges of research into the mediatisation of culture, specifically challenges related to the heterogeneity of the field and the problem of identifying clearer sub-processes related to culture as a field of research. The chapter seeks to answer the question of how we might overcome these challenges in future research into mediatisation of culture, through a discussion of previous debates in the field and by proposing a possible path for future mediatisation research. The proposed path considers what Raymond Williams calls *structures of feeling* (1977) and what Ben Highmore (2017), more recently, labels *cultural moods*, in order to detect patterns and transformations in the structures of cultural experiences. In a special issue of the *Journal of Media and Communication Research* on the mediatisation of culture (2013), Hjarvard and I opened by drawing on Raymond Williams' (1958 [1989]) notion of culture as ordinary, as a way of emphasising the importance of understanding cultural artefacts and cultural practices in their social and material contexts. In the special issue, the articles analysed a wide range of cultural experiences, from digitalised journalistic practices to buying organic food online and listening to audiobooks. This focus on a diverse set of material objects, representations or practices not only embodies the problem of researching processes of cultural change, but may also, as I will argue at the end of this chapter, provide us with a way of thinking about mediatisation research in a way that allows it to have value and relevance without attempting to do everything at once. Ben Highmore reminds us of this quandary in cultural research more broadly: "While cultural historians and literary critics might seek to grasp the world as divided up into certain separate entities (religion, leisure, family, politics and so on), this is not how the world is experienced" (Highmore, 2017, p. 23). Studies of cultural changes as it relates to media, then, ought to consider how culture is experienced as practices and texts.

The first part of this chapter discusses objections to mediatisation theory put forth by Ekstrøm et al. (2016), while the second part of the chapter returns to Schulz's (2004) early contribution to mediatisation studies and

DOI: 10.4324/9781003324591-3

the problem with sub-processes of change in the context of culture. The third part of this chapter pays attention to the ongoing discussions of the concept "media logic" (Altheide and Snow, 1979) and social interaction (Lundby, 2009). And finally, the chapter brings these observations together and concludes by returning to Raymond Williams, but this time to his concept "structures of feeling" (1977), which invites us to consider historical changes and draw out patterns of cultural experiences more broadly. The idea of considering feelings in mediatisation research is not new. Ekstrøm et al. suggest we think about if and how "different areas of practice become reliant on media and to explore *how people feel* about such transformations" (Ekstrøm et al., 2016, p. 21, my emphasis). Similarly, Jansson (2018) asks: "How does it feel to live with mediatisation?" (p. 35) while also drawing on Williams' concept of structures of feeling. Along with Ben Highmore's (2017) notion of cultural moods, research might identify structural changes in the responses to changes in cultural experiences and representations, and reveal patterns in the processes of the mediatisation of culture.

The problem of synthesising research in the mediatisation of culture

Culture is, as we are reminded by referencing Williams in the early stages of mediatisation studies, "a whole way of life" (Hjarvard and Petersen, 2013, p. 1) and research into the mediatisation of culture faces the predicament of having to pay attention to how the specificities of their empirical data relate to a complex whole. As such, the mediatisation of culture is unique, and distinctly different from the other areas of research discussed in this book, as it contains all of them and can be contained by all of them. Jansson (2018) also draws on Williams' holistic approach to culture to underpin the interrelation between culture and everyday life. It seems clear that research into the mediatisation of culture is to a large degree shaped by heterogeneity, contradictions, and ambiguities, which opens up the research in this field to critique that mediatisation serves as an analytical orientation, rather than cultural processes that reveal empirically identifiable patterns across the cultural field. While other sub-fields within mediatisation studies, perhaps most notably the mediatisation of politics (Strömbäck and Esser, 2014), have established valuable sub-processes for understanding mediatisation, research into the mediatisation of culture faces challenges due to theoretical and empirical dispersion. The heterogeneity of the field is, in part, driven by technological and distributional developments, which afford a higher degree of participation – the result of which is that "the character of mediatization becomes increasingly multifaceted" (Jansson, 2018, p. 36). And, in part, by the theory of mediatisation itself, which seems to promise both reflections of transformations in the *longue durée* and empirically based meso-level observations of specific cultural practices and representations. When researching mediatisation of culture, the researcher navigates a theoretical and empirical space that is at once concerned with historical (and technological) developments, theoretical multidimensional analysis, context-sensitive phenomena and "interrelating influences" (Hepp, Hjarvard and Lundby, 2015) between different cultural spheres. At the same time, the researcher is also navigating processes of cultural transformation and media-centred "moulding forces" (Hepp, 2013; see also Hepp, 2009) that take place in relation to cultural institutions, cultural artefacts *and* cultural experiences. As a meta-theory, mediatisation is "resting in part upon empirical evidence, but which [is] not empirically verifiable in [its] entirety" (Hepp, 2013, p. 49). Ekstrøm et al. (2016) have addressed the "too grand claims as to mediatization's status as a unitary approach" (p. 2) and suggest abandoning the notion of mediatisation as a meta-theory and instead considering meso-processes of mediatisation, which lend themselves more readily to empirical studies. Ekstrøm et al. emphasise how mediatisation is a "a concept that holds great potential to constitute a space for synthesized understandings of media related social transformations" (2016, p. 1), but the problem of synthetisation requires interdisciplinary collaboration, and research into "processes in culture and everyday have been dispersed on insufficiently communicating disciplines and with many unresolved theoretical issues" (2016, p. 2). Instead, Ekstrøm et al. suggest three tasks for those researching mediatisation. First, they call for historicising research, for studies that are longitudinal or cross-temporal, which may be a way of accommodating Livingstone and Lunt's critique that a theory proposing to identify transformations of the *longue durée* should consider historical perspectives (2015), since mediatisation is concerned with: "the effects of the media on a domain of society that is historically separate from the media, and it recognizes that these effects work in a complex manner over a considerable period of time, usually decades or centuries" (Livingstone and Lunt, 2015, p. 706). In this line of thinking, our object of research is not media in and of themselves, but rather their influence on other social and cultural domains.

Sitting on the border between, on the one hand, culture as artefacts and their representations, and on the other, culture as lived experience and social interactions, mediatisation balances studying the role of media technologies in people's lives with studying people living with media as part of culture. In addition, discussions within the field of mediatisation theory have emphasised the aspiration to consider historical perspectives – more specifically, the need for media researchers to conduct historical research in order to argue for mediatisation theory's key argument about processes of cultural change. In practical terms, this leaves research into mediatisation of culture with an unbearably large task, one that seems to miss the opportunity to see the potential of mediatisation research into contemporary phenomena as manifestations of cultural change. Conducting historicising research raises a number of pragmatic problems associated with research that stretches over decades. Instead, Bolin has researched intergenerational aspects, in order to capture changes in the experience of living with media across several decades (2016, 2016a). By considering media memories for different generations and across geographic boundaries, Bolin is able to argue how the role of media has changed over time. In addition, Hepp et. al. (2017) discuss media generations in the context of elderly people, in order to point to the processes through which this age-group appropriate media use and position themselves "in contrast to younger media generations" (2017, p. 109). Deacon and Stanyer (2014) offer a strong critique of mediatisation theory, suggesting, for example, that: "much mediatization research depends on a presumption rather than a demonstration of historical change" (Deacon and Stanyer, 2014, p. 1037), thus reflecting other critiques directed at mediatisation theory (as mentioned above). Rather than committing to the notion that mediatisation research must always be historical, or that studies in this field must have a research design that directly investigates historical processes of change (although doing so is certainly valuable), mediatisation research should commit to being in dialogue with historical and social research, and draw on the knowledge that this research generates about cultural and social change. Incidentally, this would solve another of Deacon and Stanyer's points of critique, namely that research in mediatisation needs "to include other possible conditions as drivers of changing communicative practice including non-media factors" (Deacon and Stanyer, 2014, p. 1034). However, I think this has largely been the practice of existing research into mediatisation of culture. A commitment to consulting existing historical and sociological studies means that research into the mediatisation of culture need not rely on presumptions of historical change, but may in qualified ways describe these processes while accounting for the role of the media in these processes. In this context, the task of the researcher seems clearer: in dialogue with other fields of research, and with existing knowledge of the historical and social developments, to explore the role of media in these contexts and how the presence of media contributes to processes of change.

Second, Ekstrøm et al. (2016) call for increased attention to specificity, since processes of mediatisation "unfold differently in different domains and may influence each other across domains in different, uneven and asymmetric ways" (2016, p. 15). It is precisely because mediatisation theory, importantly, understands processes of change as context- and domain-specific that research in this field has become so diverse and multifaceted (and interdisciplinary) that it calls into question the concept's usefulness as a distinct field of research. This also sometimes leads us to assume that mediatisation is present everywhere, and that any processes of cultural change can be understood under the umbrella of mediatisation. This problem reminds us of a central point: the concept of mediatisation is being applied as a meta-concept both to describe global changes in relation to the influence and omnipresence of media (which are linear), and to describe highly localised cultural transformations (which are often distinctly non-linear in character), which means that individual research efforts have insufficient opportunities to synthesise and evaluate findings across the field. As a consequence, research into mediatisation of culture remains fragmented. How can research in media-centred processes of cultural change, on the one hand, capture the diversity of media influence, and on the other, contribute to the overall field in a way that allows us to see patterns and changes across domains, media technologies and time? Ekstrøm et al. propose that research should emphasise specificity – either by limiting the scope of the research to a single medium and singular social context, by engaging in comparative studies, or by mapping the role of media more broadly in a specific social practice (Ekstrøm et al., 2016). It strikes me that much research in mediatisation of culture is already concerned with this task of specificity, but also that processes of change in the context of mediatisation are rarely the result of changes in a singular medium, but rather a consequence of media convergence and the ubiquity of media technologies in cultural industries and everyday practices alike.

Finally, Ekstrøm et al. suggest that mediatisation research is concerned with measurability, as the quantification of mediatisation processes is a way of "granting the validity of the term" (2016, p. 18). Quantitative analyses, they argue, give us the opportunity to "work retrospectively" (p. 19) to determine the extent to which media influences other cultural institutions. Ekstrøm et al.'s proposed task for mediatisation research gives us helpful tools with which to think about the framing of our research question and research design. However, in the context of researching mediatisation of culture, there is still a need to consider how the field can overcome issues stemming from the heterogeneity of the field, of the transformative processes researched, and the diverse interdisciplinary and theoretical positions applied.

Grasping sub-processes of cultural transformations

As a concept, mediatisation has come to indicate processes of change in which media plays a central role. However, the focus on "change" also brings with it methodological and empirical challenges. How can we argue for processes of change if we cannot empirically validate what came before the phenomenon on which we are focusing in our research? Can analysis of a singular moment in time, a single dataset of contemporary tendencies, indicate processes of cultural change? I will argue that it can, in that analysis of mediatisation of culture is concerned with the interplay between culture and media, and it is this interplay and its consequences that constitute transformative processes. For example, if we consider the interplay between religion and media, it is clear that media has both changed the conditions for operating in a cultural context for institutionalised religions, but also that media adapts religious narratives, symbols and rituals and subsumes them to a media logic, thus changing the form, content and function of the ways in which religion is present in culture (Petersen, 2010, 2012; Hjarvard and

Lövheim, 2012). It is in the negotiated and dual relationship between institutional religion and folklore and media as institutions that these transformations of religion in culture become visible. Research in mediatisation of culture is concerned with the relationship between media and communication technologies and specific cultural forms, in the context of societal transformations. It explores the conditions that shape these processes of change and the consequences we can observe in relation to these processes (Hepp, Hjarvard and Lundby, 2015). In the context of mediatisation of religion, such consequences may appear as changes in the form, content, and function of any given cultural phenomenon as it intersects with media and communication technologies. Mediatisation theory provides a particular analytical frame or lens through which to understand cultural change. What unifies the diverse and multifaceted (in terms of theoretical and methodological approaches) research into mediatisation of culture, then, is the questions we ask; the task we set out to solve.

Winfried Schulz (2004) proposed four sub-processes of social change – *extension, substitution, amalgamation,* and *accommodation* – in an attempt to make the concept of mediatisation more readily available to analytical research:

> Four processes of change represent different aspects of mediatisation. First, the media extend the natural limits of human communication capacities; second, the media substitute social activities and social institutions; third, media amalgamate with various non-media activities in social life; and fourth, the actors and organizations of all sectors of society accommodate to the media logic.
>
> (Schulz, 2004, p. 98)

These four processes rather effectively describe the role of media in cultural settings in a way that allows us to think about mediatisation as a meta-concept and understand how media contributes to social change in the context of culture. However, empirical studies of mediatisation processes demonstrate that processes of change are considerably more nuanced and non-linear, and it is precisely in these nuances that this research has value. It seems that while thinking along the lines of Schulz's analytical framework might guide our research question and inform our understanding of media's role in society in a broader sense, these categories are insufficient as explanatory tools in a meso-level empirical analysis. Schulz also points to three functions of media communication. First, the relay function serves to bridge temporal and spatial distance; second, the semiotic function formats and encodes messages and narratives for consumption; and third, the economic function standardises media products and is tied to division of labour (Schulz, 2004). Schulz mainly discusses mass media, but the question of division of labour seems even more relevant in a media landscape shaped by digital networked communities and digital platforms that are entirely dependent on their users producing and sharing content. These functions, as suggested by Schulz, offer an orientation to research in mediatisation of culture, in that our task is to consider the functions of media in everyday cultural practices and consumption.

Bridging the gap between media logic and social interaction

In recent decades, certain theoretical concepts or approaches have come to dominate discussions of mediatisation and been the centre of much debate. Specifically, this section focuses on the concept of media logic (Altheide and Snow, 1979, Petersen, 2017), the adjacent concept of (digital) affordances (Gibson, 1979; Shaw, 2017) and the notion of social interaction (Lundby, 2009), while also considering some of the critiques of mediatisation. Hjarvard places media logic at the very centre of mediatisation: "mediatisation is the process whereby society to an increasing degree is submitted to, or becomes dependent on, the media and their logic" (Hjarvard, 2009, p. 160). For Hjarvard, media logic is a "conceptual shorthand" (2013, p. 17) for media institutions' *modus operandi*. In this understanding, media logic consists of the (formal and informal) rules and (material and symbolic) resources that guide the institutional, aesthetic and technological ways of operating in the media (ibid.). In a study from 2017, I investigated the production processes of a Danish TV programme aimed at elderly audiences (Petersen, 2017). It became clear that the production crew were navigating both a limited set of recourses and a range of formal and informal rules about how television programmes "should be" or have the possibility of being, which in turn shaped the programme's representations of elderly people and the ways in which it addressed its audience. Adhering to a mantra of "good TV" and a general aim of offering "conviviality", the programme's narrative and structure were shaped in ways that did not always conform with the production team's vision, but were in line with what was considered to work well on TV (ibid.). As a result, we might say that an underlying logic of the media operates in distinct ways in media production, and in turn "influences the nature and function of social relations, as well as the relationship between sender, content, and recipient of communication" (Hjarvard, 2013, p. 17). In this way, media logic allows us to consider the properties that are specific to a given media technology, institution or format, since the concept enables reflection on media's internal structures and ways of operating. The concept of media logic has been criticised for suggesting a singular logic (Couldry, 2012; see also Lundby, 2009) that is more akin to a market logic (i.e. wanting to distribute a good to as many consumers as possible) or, in early critiques, that mediatisation as a "catch all" concept is "not suitable to contain the heterogeneity of the transformations in question" (Couldry, 2008, p. 379). However, Altheide and Snow (1979), who coined the term media logic, specifically emphasise the need to take into account formats, genres, etc. when investigating the logics at stake. In mediatisation research, we are interested in the ways in which media intervenes in social interactions, and how this intervention shapes and transforms the social interaction. Hjarvard (2013) includes Gibson's (1979) concept of affordances to accommodate media's contribution to the structuring of social interaction. For Gibson, the concept of affordances captures the potential uses of any object. In this sense, affordances are not only embedded in the intentions of the object's designers, but are constantly negotiated between object and user. In media studies, we are often concerned with digital affordances. Adrianne Shaw (2017) considers the different approaches to digital affordances users might have by drawing on Stuart Hall's notion of encoding/decoding (1991 [1973]). In line with Hall, Shaw identifies three different uses of interactive media technologies: dominant, negotiated, and oppositional. Affordances as a concept allows us to draw attention to the ways in which media users engage with media, and how media in turn structures this engagement.

As a response to Hjarvard's focus on media logic, Knut Lundby (2009) suggests that it is more useful, or more pertinent, to consider social interaction as a key object of interest in mediatisation research: "Instead of ascribing the changes to a 'media logic', one may in concrete ways describe and analyse how these transformations take place. How media interfere in patterns of social interaction will be central" (Lundby, 2009, p. 113). According to Lundby, there is a risk that media logic as a concept may hide these "patterns of interaction" (ibid., p. 117). By placing emphasis on social interaction, in turn, there seems to be a risk of paying insufficient attention to the media-specific consequences of mediatisation, although Lundby calls for mediatisation studies to "develop new concepts and new tools to get hold of how various media-uses shape and change social interaction" (ibid., p. 117). Rather than discarding media logic, I suggest that we embrace the dual interest of mediatisation processes as being concerned with both the specificities of media institutions and technologies and the practices of social interaction, and instead attempt to bridge the theoretical gap between these two analytical viewpoints. Hjarvard leaves us with this invitation: "the notion of 'media logic' also serves as a useful reminder of the necessity of further theoretical work on how to understand the coupling between media characteristics and social practices" (Hjarvard, 2013, p. 18). In the following and final section of this chapter, I suggest that we might theoretically capture this coupling by considering cultural moods.

Cultural moods as manifestations of processes of cultural change

So where does research into mediatisation of culture go from here? Rather than attempting to accommodate the grand claims of mediatisation as a meta-process, I suggest, along the lines of Hjarvard (2013) and Jansson (2018), that we think of mediatisation in two distinct ways: first, as a phenomenon that can be identified as processes of change in the *longue durée*; and, second, as an analytical framework for investigating processes of change related to the role of media as it intersects with other cultural fields in people's everyday lives. As such, our research need not always consider historical perspectives, but these perspectives can very well be informed by existing interdisciplinary research, historical or otherwise. In the broad definition of culture, and in the call for an interdisciplinary approach, lies the indication that research into the mediatisation of culture will always be a bricolage of methodological, empirical, and cross-disciplinary approaches. Perhaps, in acknowledgement of this circumstance, we might seek paths forward that do not attempt to mitigate these conditions for research, but instead ensure that research into mediatisation of culture is unified (or has a direction) in the questions it asks and the analytical lens it applies to the object of study, rather than in its theoretical, empirical or methodological approaches. In the following, I will suggest that one potential path forward for research into mediatisation of culture might be to return to Raymond Williams and his understanding of culture as it relates to processes of change in the interrelatedness of media (technologies and industries) and culture (practices and expressions). Williams' concept of *structures of feeling* is concerned with the formation and emergence of new structures in a cultural domain. In other words, structures of feeling offer us insight into processes of change: "The idea of a structures of feeling can be specifically related to the evidence of forms and conventions – semantic figures – which, in art and literature, are often among the very first indications that such a new structure is forming" (Williams, 1977, p. 133). In labelling culture as ordinary and, in his later work, in formulating "structures of feeling" to his understanding of the cultural domain, Williams allows us, as researchers of cultural processes of change, to stay *in the moment* and consider the lived social experience, as opposed to a constant view of the *longue durée*. By considering this concept of structures of feeling, researchers into the mediatisation of culture are invited to ask, as Jansson (2018) does: "What senses of frustrations, stress, alienation, emptiness and dependence does mediatisation give rise to? And what new opportunities for social and cultural transformation emerge from within mediatisation itself?" (Jansson 2018, p. 35). Here, we must clarify what is meant by "feeling". Structures of feeling is not to be understood as personalised, private feelings, but as structures of feeling that manifest in the social domain across cultural expressions, institutions, and everyday practices. Changes in structures of feeling, then, are manifestations of cultural change. Williams says: "At the same time they are from the beginning taken as *social* experience, rather than as 'personal' experience or as the merely superficial or incidental 'small change' of society" (Williams, 1977, p. 131). He continues: "Such changes can be defined as changes in structures of feeling. The term is difficult, but 'feeling' is chosen to emphasize a distinction from more formal concepts of 'world-view' or 'ideology'" (Williams, 1977, p. 132). In this sense, Williams' structures of feeling has more in common with Martin Heidegger's concept of "*stimmung*" or attunement (Heidegger, 2010 [1953]): "Being attuned is not initially related to something physical, it is itself not an inner condition which then in some mysterious way reaches out and leaves its mark on things and persons" (Heidegger, 2010 [1953], p. 133).

Paddy Scannell also draws on Heidegger and a phenomenological approach to understanding media in society in *Radio, Television and Modern Life* (1996). He refers to the production processes of radio and television in order to understand how programmes come into being in a relationship with the everyday practices of the broader population. In his book, Scannell identifies different feelings or moods that shape different periods of cultural media production, beginning with "intentionality": "Intentionality is not to be understood in some psychological sense (as what the programme-makers have in mind). It is what is shared between participants as a precondition of any kind of social interaction (including the kind that broadcasting represents)" (Scannell, 1996, p. 16). In this sense, "intentionality" for Scannell is akin to Heidegger's attunement or Williams' structures of feeling. It is a directedness (or, in Heidegger's terms, "thrownness") in our way of being part of culture, which manifests in both cultural representations and cultural practices. As Williams argues:

Not all art, by any means, relates to a contemporary structures of feeling. The effective formations of most actual art relate to already manifest social formations, dominant or residual, and it is primarily to emergent formations (though often in the form of modification or disturbance in older forms) that the structures of feeling, as solution, relates.

(Williams, 1977, p. 134)

As mediatisation researchers, then, we are paying attention to emergent formations, cultural disturbances and modifications, as these processes carry with them the potential for transformations in the structures of feeling, changes in the lived social experience of a culture. In this sense, analysis of mediatisation need not be, but can certainly be, anchored in historical analysis. Rather, it is the disturbance itself, the disruption of form, the new emergence of cultural texts, material, and experiences brought on by the presence of media and digital technologies that signify change, and these changes demand our attention so that that we might understand the role of media in these processes. Williams reminds us: "it is more adequate to the actual range of cultural evidence: historically certainly, but even more (where it matters more) in our present cultural process" (Williams, 1977, p. 133).

Ben Highmore (2017) draws on both Heidegger and Williams, and emphasises how Williams' phrase is vague in that both "structure" and "feeling" lend themselves to a range of properties and characteristics. Instead, he argues: "In this, 'structures of feeling' is an abstraction, just like 'culture'; it is fundamentally tensile in quality and will always require clarification as it tries to apprehend the empirical" (Highmore, 2017,

p. 22). As we embark on research into mediatisation of culture, we would do well to be reminded of Highmore's words – perhaps the problems of researching processes of change arise out of a frustration that "culture" itself cannot readily be pinned down as one thing. Instead, we must continue to insist that researching mediatisation of culture will always require a clarification, a contextualisation, as it relates to its field of study, as noted by Ekstrøm et al. (2016). As such, the seemingly dispersed efforts and diversity of thought in mediatisation research are not solely a bug, they are also a feature. Cultural moods, for Highmore, are "an orchestration of cultural feeling" (2017, p. 43). He reminds us that we can "often give social and political names to" (p. 139) how it feels to live in a culture. Are our collective anxieties tied to the risk of terrorism or economic instability? Are our pleasures drawn from global narratives or more private forms? Cultural resources, their distribution and content shape the ways in which culture discloses itself to us, the ways in which we experience culture, and the ways in which we give meaning to cultural texts and practices. It is in this context that the role of media is at the centre of research into the mediatisation of culture.

By considering cultural moods in the infrastructure of society, we, as researchers, can bring attention to the synthesis between media and culture. Culture and media are deeply intertwined, in that media produces, distributes and is concerned with culture, and culture is often experienced or engaged with via media institutions and media technologies. For Highmore (2017), cultural moods are collective, historical, material, social, and a form of labour. They are the available register of experience and expression in any given culture. In this sense, cultural moods cut across cultural institutions and everyday practices, since cultural moods are both of these. Or, more precisely: "moods are embedded in cultural forms (in narrative and musical genres, for instance, or in institutional protocols and conventions) and [...] these forms often have technological delegates that perform mood work (dimmer switches, corporate furniture, customer feedback forms, and so on)" (Highmore, 2017, p. 2). Cultural moods manifest as we stand in line for Covid-19 testing or vaccinations. Moods become material on the music festival site, with its rituals and playfulness. Digital and social media are in themselves technological delegates of cultural moods that perform mood work through embedded gifs, emojis and filters in everyday conversations between family members or in larger, interest-based communities (Petersen, 2022). In digital fan communities, this mood work becomes visible. Fans textually poach and appropriate their fan object (a sports team, a TV series or a celebrity) in order to engage playfully with others. The fans' expressions of enthusiasms or deep textual investigations of their favourite cultural text contribute to establishing specific cultural moods. In the area of political culture on social media, we might detect a change in cultural moods as fans' playful practices infringe on political discourse and the way in which voters, politicians, and the media engage. In the US, protesters dress up in costumes from *The Handmaid's Tale* (2017–) to protest against abortion legislation. In Myanmar and Thailand, protesters use the hand signal from the book and movie series *The Hunger Games* (2008–12 and 2012–15, respectively) to demonstrate allegiance with the people over corrupt governments (Petersen, 2022). Political culture is increasingly in dialogue with fans' usage of popular culture as part of participatory practices. This cultural shift is visible precisely because it manifests in cultural moods that are both material and a form of labour performed by the participants and by inanimate, social, and historical objects: "The world of feeling that is generated by a generation is produced within circumstances that are inherited from the past" (Highmore, 2017, p. 156), but, as Highmore puts it "we don't just repeat the tones of the past" (ibid.). In this sense, historicity is built into contemporary cultural moods, but is different from these moods and thus indicates processes of change. Cultural moods is a useful concept, because they invite us to consider "the synchronising of humans and machines, bodies and tools, people and techniques" (Highmore, 2017, p. 10). They help us to consider media logic, digital affordances (Hjarvard, 2013), and social interaction (Lundby, 2009) in the same breath, while also serving as manifestations of cultural change. In a sense, cultural moods are what bind together notions of media logic and everyday experiences.

As researchers in mediatisation studies, we are no longer discussing *if* media plays a role in processes of cultural transformation, since this seems an obvious point. The presence and everydayness of media and digital technologies have changed the way we experience culture and will continue to do so. Rather, we are investigating the ways in which these changes take place in a range of cultural contexts, covering a range of experiences. What unifies the research in this field is the underlying, sometimes unarticulated question that it sets out to answer: What is the role of media in the context of processes of cultural change? Perhaps it is in the structures of feeling, or, as Highmore more precisely puts it: cultural moods, that the consequences of mediatisation of culture reveal themselves to us?

Bibliography

Altheide, D. & Snow, R. (1979). *Media Logic*. California: Sage.

Bolin, G. (2016). *Media Generations: Experience, Identity and Mediatised Social Change*. Abingdon: Routledge.

Bolin, G. (2016a). The Rhythm of Ages: Analysing Mediatisation through the Lens of Generations across Cultures. *International Journal of Communication* 10: 5252–5269.

Couldry, N. (2008). Mediatisation or Mediation? Alternative Understandings of the Emergent Space of Digital Storytelling. *New Media and Society* 10(3): 373–391.

Couldry, N. (2012). *Media, Society, World: Social Theory and Digital Media Practice*. Cambridge: Polity.

Deacon, D. & Stanyer, J. (2014). Mediatisation: Key Concept or Conceptual Bandwagon? *Media, Culture & Society* 36(7): 1032–1044.

Ekstrøm, M., Fornäs, J., Jansson, A. & Jerslev, A. (2016). Three Tasks for Mediatisation Research: Contributions to an Open Agenda. *Media, Culture & Society* 38(7): 1090–1108. https://doi.org/10.1177/0163443716664857

Gibson, J. (1979). *The Ecological Approach to Visual Perception*. Boston: Houghton Mifflin.

Hall, S. (1991 [1973]). Encoding, Decoding. In S. During (ed.) *The Cultural Studies Reader*. London: Routledge, pp. 90–103.

Heidegger, M. (2010 [1953]). *Being and Time*. Translated by Joan Stambaugh. Albany: State University of New York Press.

Hepp, A. (2009). Differentiation: Mediatisation and Cultural Change. In K. Lundby (ed.) *Mediatisation: Concept, Changes, Consequences*. New York: Peter Lang, pp. 139–158.

Hepp, A. (2013). *Cultures of Mediatisation*. Cambridge, MA: Polity Press.

Hepp, Andreas, Berg, Matthias & Roitsch, Cindy (2017). A Processual Concept of Media Generation: The Media-Generational Positioning of Elderly People. *Nordicom Review* 38, Special Issue 1: 109–122.

Hepp, A., Hjarvard, S. & Lundby, K. (2015). Mediatisation: Theorizing the Interplay between Media, Culture and Society. *Media, Culture and Society* 37(2). https://doi.org/10.1177/0163443715573835

Highmore, B. (2017). *Cultural Feelings: Mood, Mediation and Cultural Politics*. Abingdon: Routledge.

Hjarvard, S. (2009). Soft Individualism. In K. Lundby (ed.) *Mediatization*. New York: Peter Lang, 159–177.

Hjarvard, S. (2013). *The Mediatisation of Culture and Society*. Abingdon: Routledge.

Hjarvard, S. & Lövheim, M. (2012). *Mediatisation and Religion: Nordic Perspectives*. Göteborg: Nordicom.

Hjarvard, S. & Petersen, L. (2013). Mediatisation and Cultural Change. *Journal of Media and Communication Research* 54: 1–7.

Jansson, A. (2018). *Mediatisation and Mobile Lives: A Critical Approach*. Abingdon: Routledge.

Livingstone, S. & Lunt, P. (2015). Mediatisation: An Emerging Paradigm for Media and Communication Studies. In K. Lundby (ed.) *Mediatisation of Communication. Handbooks of Communication Science* (21). Berlin: De Gruyter Mouton, pp. 703–724.

Lundby, K. (2009). Media Logic: Looking for Social Interaction. In K. Lundby (ed.) *Mediatisation: Concept, Changes, Consequences*. New York: Peter Lang.

Petersen, L. (2010). American Television Fiction Transforming Danish Teenagers' Religious Imaginations. *Communications* 35(3): 229–247.

Petersen, L. (2012). Wicked Angels, Adorable Aliens. Ph.D. dissertation. University of Copenhagen.

Petersen, L. (2017). Generation Conviviality: The Role of Media Logic in Television Production for Elderly Audiences. *Nordicom Review* 38, Special Issue 1: 25–38.

Petersen, L. (2022). *Mediatized Fan Play: Moods, Modes, and Dark Play in Networked Communities*. Abingdon: Routledge.

Scannell, P. (1996). *Radio, Television and Modern Life*. Oxford: Blackwell.

Schulz, W. (2004). Reconstructing Mediatisation as an Analytical Concept. *European Journal of Communication* 19(1): 87–101. doi:10.1177/0267323104040696

Shaw, A. (2017). Encoding and Decoding Affordances: Stuart Hall and Interactive Media Technologies. *Media, Culture & Society* 39(4): 592–602.

Strömbäck, J. & Esser, F. (2014). Introduction: Making Sense of the Mediatisation of Politics. *Journalism Practice* 8(3): 245–257.

Williams, R. (1958 [1989]). Culture Is Ordinary. In R. Williams (ed.) *Resources of Hope: Culture, Democracy, Socialism*. London: Verso, pp. 3–18.

Williams, Raymond (1977). *Marxism and Literature*. Oxford: Oxford University Press.

2 Issues with Research on the Mediatisation of Religion

Knut Lundby

The mediatisation of religion is one of the specific domains of society, alongside the political field, which has been most thoroughly scrutinised in research on mediatisation. This chapter raises issues, i.e., problems, challenges, and questions, relating to the mediatisation research on religion that follows three lines: first, the missing and emerging *globalisation* – the global spread – of these ventures. Second, the *conceptualisation* of religion and of media. Third, the *generalisations* that usually occur in research on the mediatisation of religion.

Overview

An article outlining "The mediatization of religion. A theory of the media as agents of religious change", by the Danish media scholar Stig Hjarvard (2008a), is usually regarded as being the pioneering work in this particular field. He began from the three metaphors of media that were proposed by Joshua Meyrowitz (1993). The first being the media as *conduits*, which draws attention to what is covered, or transmitted, from the senders to the receivers. Second, by considering the media as *languages*, one focuses on the ways in which the media format and frame religious elements, i.e., the genres and modalities that they apply to religion. Third, with the metaphor of the media as *environments*, the research concentrates on the media systems, structures and power that encompass and direct the media representation and consumption of religion. As a whole "the media as conduits, languages and environments are responsible for the *mediatization of religion*", Hjarvard states (2008a, p. 13), adding that the media then "facilitate changes in the amount, content, and direction of religious messages in society, at the same time as they transform religious representations and challenge the authority of institutionalized religions. Through these processes, religion, as a social and cultural activity, has become mediatized" (Hjarvard, 2008a, p. 14).

Later, Hjarvard (2012) identified three forms of mediatised religion, namely, "religious media", "journalism on religion", and "banal religion". The former have their base in religious organisations, while journalism on religion basically applies a secular perspective. The third form is the

DOI: 10.4324/9781003324591-4

mixture of various religious symbols and traditions that is offered in the popular entertainment media. Hjarvard (2013, pp. 78–102) explicated his theory on the mediatisation of religion within a general argument on the mediatisation of culture and society. A particular focus in his works on religion has been on the loss of religious authority as a result of mediatisation (Hjarvard, 2016).

A debate published in *Culture and Religion* (2011), challenged Hjarvard's theory. David Morgan stated that "arguments for mediatisation need to be strongly qualified by historical evidence" (Morgan, 2011, p. 137). Gordon Lynch found that Hjarvard's theory "seems most relevant to societies characterised by the prevalence of non-confessional media institutions, declining direct public engagement with religious institutions and wider evidence of secularisation" (Lynch, 2011, p. 203). Alexandra Boutros, on the contrary, saw that in Hjarvard's theory there was limited use for analysis of "non-institutional or unofficial religions that have limited visibility in the public sphere" (Boutros, 2011, p. 185). Mia Lövheim challenged Hjarvard's definition of religion, asking for an understanding that "better acknowledges the complexities of modern religion" as well as "the agency of religious actors" in the shaping of media and modern society (Lövheim, 2011, p. 153). Lynn Schofield Clark proposed an alternative definition of mediatisation, as a process that "give(s) shape to how we think of humanity and our place in the world" (Clark, 2011, p. 167). Hjarvard himself pointed to the relationship between mediatisation and secularisation. At the level of society, he regarded mediatisation as being an integral part of secularisation. At the level of organisation and the individual, however, mediatisation "may both encourage secular practices and beliefs and invite religious imaginations typically of a more subjectivised nature" (Hjarvard, 2011, p. 119).

Stig Hjarvard is a proponent of an institutional approach to mediatisation. He regards an institution as being "an identifiable domain or field of social life that is governed by a particular set of formal and informal rules, displays a particular structure, serves certain social functions, and allocates resources for action in various ways" (Hjarvard, 2014a, p. 130). For the mediatisation of religion, the media, as an increasingly independent institution of their own, interfere with religion, as a generalised field in society. "Media logic" makes its way into the domain of religion. Religious institutions, and the religious field in general, to an increasing degree, "become dependent on the resources that the media make available" (Hjarvard, 2013, p. 17). There is no simple, mechanistic media logic operating, rather, there are encounters between the logics of the media institutions, the logics of religious institutions and the field of religion in general (Hjarvard, 2014b, pp. 212–216). The institutional perspective on mediatisation is "primarily focusing on the 'structuring influence' of the logics of media institutions for social interaction within other domains of society" (Lövheim & Hjarvard, 2019, p. 210) – here, within the domain of religion.

While researchers on this institutional track begin from a meso analytical level, scholars in the social-constructivist approach begin from below, in everyday communication and symbolic interaction. They observe how the various media are applied in a communicative construction of social and cultural reality (Hepp & Krotz, 2014). Nick Couldry and Andreas Hepp (2017) demonstrate the highly mediatised social construction of reality in contemporary modern societies. A range of "communicative figurations" are developed by the digital networked media (Hepp, Breiter, & Hasebrink, 2018). Kerstin Radde-Antweiler (2019) is a leading voice in the application of this approach to the domain of religion. In the steps of the communicative figurations approach, she asks, first, what is the specific "actors' constellation" in the religious field under study? Second, what is the particular thematic "frame of relevance" on religion?" Third, which ensemble of media are applied in the "communicative practices"? The three aspects make a changing media environment, a mediatised lifeworld, in which the understanding of religion is constantly redefined.

While this social-constructivist approach sees the mediatisation of religion through social *figurations*, the institutional approach asks for the mediatised *conditions* of contemporary religion (Lövheim & Hjarvard, 2019). Both are concerned with the influence and consequences of digital, networked media technology upon the social interaction and on the communication about religion.

These two contrasting theoretical approaches both appeared in Northern Europe, thus making the *globalisation* of research on the mediatisation of religion a pressing issue. The North European context may also limit the *conceptualisation* of religion and media, which is affected by both theoretical approaches. The possible *generalisations* in the research on the mediatisation of religion also depend on the geographical contexts of the studies, as well as on the understanding of religion and media.

Problems

The North European focus

The research on the mediatisation of religion has emerged in relation to the field of Media, Religion, and Culture Studies, which was initiated in Europe and the US (Lövheim, 2014). Since most of the research on the mediatisation of religion has been centred on Northern Europe, and in particular on Scandinavia (Hjarvard & Lövheim, 2012; Lundby, 2018), there is a need for studies from other parts of the world, and ones that go beyond Christianity (Clark & Gillespie, 2018).

This gap is slowly being filled (e.g., Martino, 2013; Radde-Antweiler & Zeiler, 2019). In general, the expansion of research on the mediatisation of religion implies encounters between different conceptions of modernity. Hjarvard's limitation of mediatisation to high modernity in 20th century

Europe (2008b) is challenged. Countries in Asia in particular, but also in Africa and Latin America, have followed their own paths to modernity. This, of course, has consequences for the understanding of mediatised religion.

The understanding of "religion"

"Religion" is a problem in this research, in so far as religion is a moving target. Leaving personal faith aside, there are various approaches to the scientific study of religion. The classic sociological distinction between substantive and functional definitions of religion (Berger, 1974; Knoblauch & Steets, 2018) appears over again in the research on the mediatisation of religion. Hjarvard carries a substantive understanding of religion, one that is not related to particular supernatural agencies, but to the capacity of the human mind "to imagine a metaphysical world" (Lövheim, 2011, p. 154). In contrast, Stewart M. Hoover applies a functional definition of religion, encompassing "the implicit power [of] religion and 'religion-like' symbols, practices, and conditions" (Hoover, 2009, p. 126). Radde-Antweiler is closer to the functional than to the substantive pole, underlining how religion, or religious symbol systems, "are constantly being redefined and renegotiated" in communicative practices "by different actors according to time and context" (Radde-Antweiler, 2019, pp. 212–213).

Functional understandings of religion may lead to loose conceptions of mediatised religion. The problem with substantive definitions of religion, on the contrary, is that a range of spiritual expressions may be overlooked and left aside. The "process of mediatization, and the practice of religion in a mediatized environment, goes well beyond the borders of institutional religion itself", the Brazilian scholar Luis Mauri Sa Martino (2013, p. 14) reminds us.

A further problem may arise from the kinds of religious studies that are applied in research on mediatised religion. While a sociological take on religion concentrates on social and cultural patterns, scholars in the field of the history of religion go deeper into the content and expressions of the various religious traditions. In mediatisation, such symbolic elements are remixed into media products. For the scholarly approach to such transformative processes, it still matters how detailed the analyses are that go into the content of the religious symbolism.

This aspect relates to the level of analysis. The three forms of mediatised religion that Hjarvard distinguishes all show "the public face of religion" (Hjarvard, 2012, p. 21). There is no direct link between such public religion and religion that is lived in groups and in individual lives, which may also be mediatised, i.e., more or less shaped through representations in the media, and interaction with the media. It's a problem of how to grasp this relationship between public and personal religion.

The over-generalisation of findings

The mediatisation of religion, like mediatisation in general, is regarded as a process that can be considered at a high level of abstraction. It has been termed a "meta-process", that is on a par with global connectivity, individualisation, and commercialisation. This implies "that mediatization must be understood as a long-term process that has, in each historical phase, a specific realization in each single culture and society" (Krotz, 2009, pp. 24–25). However, Krotz adds that this meta-process may consist of many sub-processes. "This is what must be studied in more detail by actual and historical mediatization research. But it does not mean that mediatization can be explained or understood only by reducing the overall process to some sub-processes which do not refer to one another" (Krotz, 2014, p. 153). The problem is the risk of over-generalisation while one tries to keep this balance between the overall and the specific aspects of mediatisation. This applies to the mediatisation of research on religion just as much as it does to other fields of mediatisation study.

Challenges

Variations in the mediatisation of religion beyond Northern Europe

The challenge is to develop research on the mediatisation of religion that is sensitive to religious and geographical contexts around the world. For *The Handbook on Religion and Communication*, I selected cases of research on mediatised religion that are both available and go well beyond Northern Europe, with its Christian and secular tradition (Lundby, 2023).

The variety in the mediatisation of religion depends partly on the geographical location, with its social, cultural, and political characteristics, and partly on the religious tradition in question. However, the understanding of mediatised religion in the global East and South also depends on the conceptualisation of mediatisation.

The Middle East

Orthodox Jews in Israel comprise a particular case of mediatised religion (Tsuria & Campbell, 2019). The *Modern* Orthodox, who make up one fifth of the Jewish population, try to balance the orthodox tradition of Judaism on the one hand, and the media and other benefits of modernity on the other (Cohen, 2012, pp. 96–107). The *Ultra*-Orthodox, however, try to avoid the modern media. This minority, which makes up 8 per cent of the Jews in Israel (Cohen, 2017, p. 114), may still apply various media for their own purposes. For example, rabbis created their own newspapers, which they could censor. Young members of the Chabad, an Ultra-Orthodox group, put up websites with the intention of strengthening internal cohesion within the Chabad community. However, the Chabad webmasters have also aimed to share their version of Judaism with people outside their own enclave. They have tried to "Chabadize" Judaism (Golan & Stadler, 2016, p. 85), thus mediatising their own strict tradition.

Tsuria and Cambell find the mediatisation approach useful but limited in relation to studies of Orthodox Judaism. The mediatisation perspective has to be complemented with studies of the way society shapes technology, and of how religious communities consciously take up its use, they argue (Tsuria & Cambell, 2019, pp. 202–203). They thus add the perspective from the approach of Religious Social Shaping of Technology (RSST, Campbell, 2010). "RSST argues that religious communities shape technology and mediatization claims that technology, as a social institution, shapes society" with its religious institutions, Tsuria and Campbell claim (2019, p. 192).

In Iran, where Shi'a Islam dominates, the annual commemoration of the tragedy at Karbala, in Iraq, is significant. The massacre of the grandson of the Prophet Muhammad and his family, initiated the split between Shi'a and Sunni Muslims. This Shi'a mourning, and procession, is called *Muharram*. While most religious Iranians still stick to traditional expressions of Shi'a Islam, many young Iranian believers take part in the *Muharram* through Instagram postings. The capabilities of Instagram make it possible for young Iranians "to mold the religious imagination and performances in accordance with the genres of popular culture and individual lifestyle" (Valibeigi, 2019, p. 187), and thus to mould a mediatised Shi'a identity. Narges Valibeigi found that Hjarvard's understanding of mediatisation fitted her analysis of young participants in the *Muharram*. She observes that the "traditional structure of the Iranian Shi'a community is under a perceptible transformation in the process of mediatization" (Valibeigi, 2019, p. 166).

Asia

The collection on *Mediatized Religion in Asia*, edited by Kerstin Radde-Antweiler and Xenia Zeiler (2019), opens doors to studies of the mediatisation of religion on this large continent.

Mediatised Islam is found in different forms and settings throughout Asia. Hew Wai Weng (2019) shares the story of how young Muslim preachers from China, where they are in a minority, gained popularity in the main cities of the Islam-dominated countries of Indonesia and Malaysia. Their radical-conservative message drew attention, not through Islamic training, but due to their media competence and their background in marketing. Their communication skills gave them authority. Their mediatised form of Islam was presented openly in online and offline events. Within China, on the contrary, where Muslim minorities are under the control of the government, the ultimate power of mediatisation resides with the Communist Party. Wai-yip Ho (2019) tells of the young Hui Muslims and their balancing act to keep a limited mediatised space of their own, which was finally closed down by the government.

Sikhism has its homeland in the Punjab region of India, where Sikhs are in the majority. Otherwise, the Sikh minority, consisting of no more than 2 per cent of the population of India, struggles to keep its identity in a Hindu dominated country. The Sikhs have a strong sense of religious and ethnic community, and are dispersed all over the world, in particular following migration, to countries within the former British Empire. They communicate on the internet and sometimes travel back to the Punjab. There is a global "Sikhscape", with narratives of a "Return" to the homeland (Ferraris, 2012). "Return" may also take place on the web, via YouTube or with smartphones. Global Sikhism is highly mediatised. The turban is the ultimate Sikh symbol, predominantly worn by men, but now taken up by Sikh women as part of their identity construction in exchanges on the internet (Jakobsh, 2015).

Asian Buddhism is also heavily mediatised. Buddhist ideas, themes and symbols have spread globally and, in particular, on the internet. Mediatisation is regarded as a "decisive process in the globalization of Buddhism" (Obadia, 2015, p. 347). It resonates with Western individualism. However, the roots are Asian. Attending a Buddhist ceremony with the Dalai Lama in Himalayan India, three scholars, Gregory Price Grieve, Christopher Helland, and Rohit Singh, observed an underlying Buddhist theory of communication. The Dalai Lama's readings from old Tibetan Buddhist philosophy were adapted to, and were shared on, the internet, and were thus mediatised. However, the ceremony in the Himalayas and the digital technology "mutually conditioned one another" (Grieve, Helland, & Singh, 2019, p. 140). A Buddhist theory of communication analyses media practices "as the mutual conditioning of two or more communicators" (Grieve, Helland, & Singh, 2019, p. 151), they argue. The three find this to be a "Buddhist reconditioning" of Hjarvard's theory of mediatised religion (Grieve, Helland, & Singh, 2019, p. 141). Lövheim and Hjarvard (2019) do not see such a contradiction. "The difference may be that Grieve, Helland, and Singh point to the circular conditions that are inherent to Buddhist ritual culture carried into mediatised forms by the digitalization, while Lövheim and Hjarvard point to the conditions for social interaction that are created through mediatization" (Lundby, 2023, p. 278).

Latin America

In Latin America, scholars of media, culture, and religion have a long tradition of mediatisation research that has been developed on their own ground, and which is published in Spanish and Portuguese. The works of Jesús Martín-Barbero on communication, culture, and hegemony (Martín-Barbero, 1993 [1987]) has been an inspiration, raising resistance to dominant power structures through the mobilisation of social movements. He changed the focus from the *media* as devices, to *mediations* as communication processes.

The further step that was needed to study the transformations arising from the concept of *mediatisation* became obvious (Gomes, 2017, p. 31). That concept had already been developed from the 1980s onwards, and with a Latin American twist, by Eliseo Verón (2014a, 2014b). He argued, not unlike the German scholar Friedrich Krotz (2009), that mediatisation is a long-term process throughout human history, from the very early use of tools in communication, and that it has been institutionalised in human societies. Verón (2014b), thus, distances himself from Hjarvard's take on mediatisation (Hjarvard, 2008b, p. 113), which is related to the Western context of high modernity in the 20th century.

Verón concentrated on "the sapiens' capability of semiosis", which expresses itself in the creation of "mediatic phenomena" as intermediaries. Mediatisation, then, is understood as "the long historical sequence of mediatic phenomena", from stone tools to the invention of writing, to printing, and so on through history (Verón, 2014a, p. 163). The mediatic phenomena are exteriorisations of the mental processes and preconditions of complex social systems. This is why mediatisation is so important, Verón (2014b) argues. He did not focus particularly on religion, but his approach obviously applies to religion. Verón's "semio-anthropological perspective" (Veron, 2014a) informs contemporary research on mediatisation in Latin America (Scolari & Rodríguez-Amat, 2018). In recent years, these scholars have sought active dialogue, in English, with European mediatisation researchers (Ferreira et al., 2020; Scolari, Fernández, & Rodríguez-Amat, 2021). Exchanges on the mediatisation of religion are part of this dialogue.

The Brazilian scholar Luis Mauro da Martino, who published *The Mediatization of Religion* (2013), stated that this transformative process "cannot be understood outside the political conflicts and instabilities of the region" (Martino, 2013, p. 21). Martín-Barbero depicted the relations between religion, media, and society in Latin America in terms of class conflicts. He reminds us that religion and the churches have "been a fundamental element in the historical memory of the people". The hegemonic Catholic Church, as a historical institution in Latin America, lost its ability "to challenge and inspire the urban masses, the youth, and the popular classes" (Martín-Barbero, 1997, p. 113) as its "mediatized Pentecostal competitors" won visibility with big investments in media communication (Martino, 2013, p. 50). On the way, the new charismatic forms of Catholicism and Pentecostalism "lost the capacity to make an independent criticism of power" (Martín-Barbero, 1997, p. 113).

The Catholic charismatic movement in Brazil has been imported from the US (Cleary, 2011). Their preaching and gatherings are as mediatised as their more commercialised Protestant Pentecostal competitors, offering their own interpretation of Catholicism, combined with a command of the media and the ability to create shows. These mass celebrations "were like any pop music festival" (Martino, 2013, p. 37).

The charismatic practices in Latin America demonstrate another form of mediatised religion compared to that which is dominant in Northern Europe, and they are analysed with a distinct Latin American perspective on mediatisation (Souza & Matos, 2017). Contemporary Pentecostalism in Brazil reorganises itself according to the developing mediatisation processes in society; believers tend to articulate their faith independently of declared denominations, on the internet, through defending conservative morality, and showing a greater concern with morality in society on the political right than with evangelism. This process of "Pentecostal semiosis", Souza and Matos (2017, pp. 49–50) conclude, puts this new Pentecostalism "into digital media's logics of production", and thus, under the "interpenetration to mediatization logics" (Souza & Matos, 2017, pp. 49–50).

Africa

Mediatised Pentecostalism has also been studied in an African context. The anthropologist and religious scholar, Birgit Meyer, followed transformations in Ghana from the 1980s, when the country was forced by international financial bodies to liberalise and to de-regulate its economy, including its media production. This commercialisation stimulated a video-film industry which fitted a charismatic Pentecostalism that promised health, success, and prosperity to people who were not well-off. These churches in Ghana engaged with the latest available media technology at the time. They were inspired by the American mega-churches but appeared to be genuinely African (Meyer, 2012). Pentecostal video-films mixed their charismatic expressions and promises with "old gods, witchcraft, and new spirits" in Ghanaian popular culture (Meyer, 2004, p. 96). This convergence "contributed significantly to the emergence of a pentecostally infused" public culture (Meyer, 2004, p. 92). Initially, Meyer termed these changes "mediatization" (2004, p. 105), but later turned to "mediation" as her key term.

"Mediation" versus "Mediatisation" in the understanding of religion

In the institutional, as well as in the social-constructivist approach, "mediation" is the ongoing communication process with media (Hjarvard 2014a; Hepp & Krotz, 2014, p. 3). However, in the realm of religion, "mediation", as used by scholars of anthropology and religious studies, has been taken as the concept with which to grasp the inner transformation of religion in its encounters with modern media. Key statements are Jeremy Stolow's "Religion *as* Media", instead of "Religion *and* Media" (Stolow, 2005), and Birgit Meyer and Annelies Moors' view of "religion as a practice of mediation". They advise us "to explore how the transition from one mode of mediation to another, implying the adoption of new mass media technologies, reconfigures a particular practice of religious mediation" (Meyer & Moors, 2006, p. 7).

The media activities within prosperity Pentecostalism informed Birgit Meyer's understanding of media as being intrinsic to religion: Religion "cannot be analyzed apart from the forms and practices of mediation that define it" (Meyer, 2004, p. 94). She applies a wide concept of "media", ranging from spirit mediums to computers (Meyer, 2013, p. 8). The use of media technologies invites a rearticulation of religion that "necessarily implies some kind of transformation, which entails shifts of its position in relation to the state and the market, as well as the shape of the religious message, structures of authority, and modes and moods of binding and belonging" (Meyer, 2009, p. 2). She finally skipped the concept of mediatisation altogether. For Birgit Meyer, the transformative capacity is inherent to the mediation of religion.

Researching cases of religion and media in Asia, the social anthropologist Patrick Eisenlohr argues that it is necessary to ask for the conception of the relationship to the divine in the tradition being studied. This, for him, is the "religious mediation". He does not leave aside the concept of mediatisation but finds it necessary to look at "the processes of interaction between human actors and the divine, along with the institutions and authorities that sustain them" (Eisenlohr, 2017, p. 870). The transformative capacity, then, lies with the inner religious mediation, as well as with the structural aspects of religion in its application of communication technologies. Eisenlohr (2017) illustrates this in studies of religious television in Asia, shown on one satellite channel, based on Salafist Sunni Islam, and on another television network that is based on Shi'a theology. The latter sticks so strictly to Shi'a teaching that Eisenlohr did not find any real transformation in this religious mediation. In contrast, the Sunni channel applies new genres and TV forms to such a transformative extent that Eisenlohr regards this as a case of mediatised religion.

Eisenlohr relates the transformative capacity to the concept of mediatisation, but argues that first one needs to understand the inner mediation with the divine. Meyer defines religion through its mediation, and the changing forms of mediation also explain the transformation of religion.

I have tried to sort out the various conceptions of media and the transformations of religion (Lundby, 2013). Meyer studies transformations through mediations. It is the materiality of the media that may trigger the change from mediations into transformations (Lundby, 2013, p. 191). I argue that the "mediation perspective gives priority to the forms of *religion*, while the mediatization approach gives priority to the forms of the *media*". From a mediation perspective, then, the "transformation of religion is seen from inside the mediation practices" of the actual religious tradition, "while the mediatization perspective sees transformations of religion from outside, through the media-saturated environment" (Lundby, 2013, p. 200).

Nuances in the processes of the mediatisation of religion

A further challenge is to establish the nuances in mediatised religion. The term "mediatisation of religion" so easily invites sweeping generalisations.

Mediatisation implies transformations. A general distinction is that between those transformations that occur gradually over time. However, there may also be sudden breaks that change the course of development, and, in that sense, signal a forthcoming transformation. This distinction goes back to the sociological contrast between changes through small adjustments (Mahoney & Thelen, 2009) and radical disruptions (Pierson, 2004).

I was confronted with further nuances when I wrote a history of the mediatisation of religion over the last 50 years in my home country of Norway (Lundby, 2021). I studied a range of cases on religion and media through the phases of the acceleration in general mediatisation since 1970. I had to admit that there are several dimensions of the mediatisation of religion in time and space that should be considered, among them the distinctions between *actual* and *potential*, *intended* and *unintended*, as well as *profound* versus *superficial* mediatisation of religion.

As Lövheim and Hjarvard (2019) state, there is a need to be more specific about the *conditions* under which the mediatisation of religion occurs.

Questions

From my reading of the current situation in the mediatisation of studies of religion, I want to briefly raise the following questions for further research:

What are the gender aspects of the mediatisation of religion?

Marina Franchi (2020) points out that mediatisation processes have profoundly gendered consequences, in particular for the empowering and disempowering of people's lives. However, the gender aspects of mediatisation are under-researched. Franci refers primarily to the mediatisation of politics, but the lack of gender studies on the mediatisation of religion is just as pressing. She mentions Mia Lövheim's work (2016) on how mediatisation can change religion when it comes to gender roles and gendered relations. Lövheim is a pioneer in addressing the gendered aspects of mediatised religion (see also Lövheim 2015; 2021). Another contribution has been made by Mona Abdel-Fadil and Louise Lund Liebmann (2018). More studies are needed, not just from Northern Europe, but also from other parts of the world.

How will datafication and machine learning affect the mediatisation of religion?

There has been almost no research on how datafication (Couldry & Hepp, 2017) and algorithmic machine learning affect the mediatisation of religion. An exception is that of the Latin American scholar Jairo G. Ferreira, who formulates hypotheses about polarisation, mediatisation, and algorithms. He refers to a "cosmological perspective" as part of his reflection on mediatisation (Ferreira, 2020, p. 301). Another example is Lynn Schofield

Clark and Angel Hinzo's study (2019) of mediatisation and the sacred in "digital survivance" among indigenous people in the US.

The overall question is how surveillance capitalism (Zuboff, 2019), with its "colonization of human life" (Couldry & Mejias, 2019) influences the mediatisation of religion around the globe. Dan M. Kotliar takes issue with "data orientalism". He is concerned that "the power of algorithms perpetually flows back and forth – between East and West, South and North". It's not just about the influence of a few big American tech companies. These algorithms are actually "developed in various geographical locations and used in highly diverse socio-cultural contexts" (Kotliar, 2020, p. 919). He thus attempts to grasp the algorithmic construction of the non-Western Other, with reference to Edward Said's book *Orientalism* (1995).

What might insights into the mediatisation of religion mean for studies of religion?

The final question I want to raise concerns what the research findings on mediatisation mean for religious studies, i.e., the sociology of religion, the history of religions, and the like. In general, the answer to this question is that religion cannot be taken as a subject for study without considering how mediation, and the transformations resulting from mediatisation, become part of the subject itself.

Conclusions

On *globalisation*, there appear to be great variations in the mediatisation of religion as one moves beyond the Northern European cradle of this research. Asian, African, and Latin American examples demonstrate that mediatisation of religion relates to political and cultural characteristics and different forms of modernity.

These global distinctions partly rest with different *conceptualisations* of religion and of media. This emerges in the discussion of whether the concept of "mediation of religion" or of "mediatisation of religion" best captures the transformations. In my sociological perspective, mediatisation of religion is the preferred term.

On *generalisation*, this chapter has demonstrated the need for more nuanced analyses of mediatised religion, which also relates to the distinction between the institutional and the social-constructivist approaches to mediatisation of religion. This antagonism may, after all, be a matter of choice. Which approach is best suited to the analytical task ahead?

Bibliography

Abdel-Fadil, M., & Lund Liebmann, L. (2018). Gender, Diversity and Mediatized Conflicts of Religion: Lessons from Scandinavian Case Studies. In K. Lundby (Ed.),

Contesting Religion. The Media Dynamics of Cultural Conflicts in Scandinavia (pp. 281–298). Berlin: De Gruyter.

Berger, P. L. (1974). Some second thoughts on substantive versus functional definitions of religion. *Journal for the Scientific Study of Religion, 13,* 125–134.

Boutros, A. (2011). Gods on the move: The mediatisation of Vodou. *Culture and Religion, 12* (2), 185–201.

Campbell, H. A. (2010). *When Religion Meets New Media.* London: Routledge.

Clark, L. S. (2011). Considering religion and mediatisation through a case study of *J+K's big day* (The J+K wedding entrance dance): A response to Stig Hjarvard. *Culture and Religion, 12* (2), 167–184.

Clark, L. S., & Gillespie., M. (2018). Globalization and the Mediatization of Religion: From Scandinavia to the World. In K. Lundby (Ed.), *Contesting Religion. The Media Dynamics of Cultural Conflicts in Scandinavia* (pp. 315–331). Berlin: De Gruyter.

Clark, L. S., & Hinzo, A. M. (2019). Digital survivance: Mediatization and the sacred in the tribal digital activism of the #NoDAPL movement. *The Journal of Religion, Media and Digital Culture, 8* (1), 76–104.

Cleary, E. L. (2011). *The Rise of Charismatic Catholicism in Latin America.* Gainesville: University Press of Florida.

Cohen, Y. (2012). *God, Jews and the Media: Religion and Israel's Media.* London: Routledge.

Cohen, Y. (2017). The media challenge to Haredi rabbinic authority in Israel. *ESSACHESS – Journal for Communicaation Studies, 10* (2), 113–128.

Couldry, N., & Hepp. A. (2017). *The Mediated Construction of Reality.* Cambridge: Polity.

Couldry, N., & Mejias, U. A. (2019). *The Costs of Connection. How Data Is Colonizing Human Life and Appropriating It for Capitalism.* Stanford, CA: Stanford University Press.

Eisenlohr, P. (2017). Reconsidering mediatization of religion: Islamic televangelism in India. *Media, Culture & Society, 39* (6), 869–884.

Ferraris, F. (2012). Narratives of "Return"? Travels to Punjab in the Contemporary Transnational Sikhscape. In K. A. Jacobsen & K. Myrvold (Eds.), *Sikhs Across Borders. Transnational Practices of European Sikhs* (pp. 87–104). London: Bloomsbury.

Ferreira, J. G. (2020). Hypotheses about Polarization, Mediatization, and Algorithms. In J. Ferreira, A. F. Neto, P. G. Gomes, J. L. Braga & A. P. da Rosa (Eds.), *Mediatization, Polarization, and Intolerance (Between Environments, Media, and Circulation)* (pp. 301–320). Santa Maria-RS: FACOS-UFSM (Universidade Federal de Santa Maria).

Ferreira, J., Neto, A. F., Gomes, P. G, Braga, J. L., & Rosa, A. P. da (Eds.) (2020). *Mediatization, Polarization, and Intolerance (Between Environments, Media, and Circulation).* Santa Maria-RS: FACOS-UFSM (Universidade Federal de Santa Maria).

Franchi, M. (2020). Mediatization. In K. Ross (Ed.), *The International Encyclopedia of Gender, Media, and Communication.* Hoboken, NJ: Wiley.

Golan, O., & Stadler, N. (2016). Building the sacred community online: The dual use of the Internet by Chabad. *Media, Culture & Society, 38* (1), 71–88.

Gomes, P. G. (2017). *From Media to Mediatization. An Evolving Concept.* Vale do Rio dos Sinos, Brasil: Editora Unisinos.

Grieve, G. P., Helland, C., & Singh, R. (2019). Digitizing Tibet. A Critical Buddhist Reconditioning of Hjarvard's Mediatization Theory. In K. Radde-Antweiler, & X. Zeiler (Eds.), *Mediatized Religion in Asia. Studies on Digital Media and Religion* (pp. 139–161). New York: Routledge.

Hepp, A., Breiter, A., & Hasebrink, U. (Eds.) (2018). *Communicative Figurations. Transforming Communications on Times of Deep Mediatization*. Cham, Switzerland (Open Access): Palgrave Macmillan.

Hepp, A., & Krotz, F. (2014). Mediatized Worlds: Understanding Everyday Mediatization. In A. Hepp & F. Krotz (Eds.), *Mediatized Worlds: Culture and Society in a Media Age* (pp. 1–15). Basingstoke: Palgrave.

Hew, W. W. (2019). On-Offline Dakwah: Social Media and Islamic Preaching in Malaysia and Indonesia. In K. Radde-Antweiler & X. Zeiler (Eds.), *Mediatized Religion in Asia. Studies on Digital Media and Religion* (pp. 89–104). New York: Routledge.

Hjarvard, S. (2008a). The Mediatization of Religion: A Theory of the Media as Agents of Religious Change. In S. Hjarvard (Ed.), *The Mediatization of Religion* (pp. 9–26). Northern Lights. Film & Media Studies Yearbook. Bristol: Intellect.

Hjarvard, S. (2008b). The mediatization of society. A theory of the media as agents of social and cultural change. *Nordicom Review, 29* (2), 105–134.

Hjarvard, S (2011). The mediatisation of religion: Theorising religion, media and social change. *Culture and Religion, 12* (2), 119–135.

Hjarvard, S. (2012). Three Forms of Mediatized Religion: Changing the Public Face of Religion. In S. Hjarvard & M. Lövheim (Eds.), *Mediatization and Religion. Nordic Perspectives* (pp. 21–44). Göteborg: Nordicom.

Hjarvard, S. (2013). *The Mediatization of Culture and Society*. London: Routledge.

Hjarvard, S. (2014a). From Mediation to Mediatization: The Institutionalization of New Media. In A. Hepp & F. Krotz (Eds.), *Mediatized Worlds: Culture and Society in a Media Age* (pp. 123–139). Basingstoke: Palgrave.

Hjarvard, S. (2014b). Mediatization and Cultural and Social Change: An Institutional Perspective. In K. Lundby (Ed.), *Mediatization of Communication* (pp. 199–226). Handbooks of Communication Science, *21*. Berlin: De Gruyter Mouton.

Hjarvard, S. (2016). Mediatization and the changing authority of religion. *Media, Culture & Society, 38* (1), 8–17.

Hjarvard, S., & Lövheim, M. (Eds.) (2012). *Mediatization and Religion. Nordic Perspectives*. Gothenburg: Nordicom.

Ho, W. (2019). Religious Mediatization with Chinese Characteristics. Subaltern Voices of Chinese Muslim Youths. In K. Radde-Antweiler & X. Zeiler (Eds.), *Mediatized Religion in Asia: Studies on Digital Media and Religion* (pp. 39–52). New York: Routledge.

Hoover, S. M. (2009). Complexities: The Case of Religious Cultures. In K. Lundby (Ed.), *Mediatization: Concept, Changes, Consequences* (pp. 123–138). New York: Peter Lang.

Jakobsh, D. R. (2015). Marking the Female Sikh Body: Reformulating and Legitimating Sikh Women's Turbaned Identity on the World Wide Web. In K. A. Jacobsen & K. Myrvold (Eds.), *Young Sikhs in a Global World. Negotiating Traditions, Identities and Authorities* (pp. 125–148). London: Routledge.

Knoblauch, H., & Steets, S. (2018). Sacred Canopies and Invisible Religions: The Dialectical Construction of Religion in Berger and Luckmann. In T. Hjelm (Ed.),

Peter L. Berger and the Sociology of Religion: 50 Years after The Sacred Canopy (pp. 85–101). London: Bloomsbury Academic.

Kotliar, D. M. (2020.) Data orientalism: On the algorithmic construction of the non-Western other. *Theory and Society, 49* (5–6), 919–939.

Krotz, F. (2009). Mediatization: A Concept with Which to Grasp Media and Societal Change. In K. Lundby (Ed.), *Mediatization: Concept, Changes, Consequences* (pp. 21-40). New York: Peter Lang.

Krotz, F. (2014). Mediatization as a Mover in Modernity: Social and Cultural Change in the Context of Media Change. In K. Lundby (Ed.), *Mediatization of Communication* (pp. 131–161). Handbooks of Communication Science, *21*. Berlin: De Gruyter Mouton.

Lövheim, M. (2011). Mediatisation of religion: A critical appraisal. *Culture and Religion, 12* (2), 153–166.

Lövheim, M. (2014). Mediatization and Religion. In K. Lundby (Ed.), *Mediatization of Communication* (pp. 547–570). Handbooks of Communication Science, *21*. Berlin: De Gruyter Mouton.

Lövheim, M. (2015). (Re)Making a Difference: Religion, Mediatisation and Gender. *Journal for Religion, Film and Media, 1* (1), 45–56.

Lövheim, M. (2016). Mediatization: Analyzing transformations of religion from a gender perspective. *Media, Culture & Society, 38* (1), 18–27.

Lövheim, M. (2021). Gender, Religion and the Press in Scandinavia. In K. Radde-Antweiler & X. Zeiler (Eds.), *The Routledge Handbook of Religion and Journalism* (pp. 62–75). London: Routledge.

Lövheim, M., & Hjarvard, S. (2019). The mediatized conditions of contemporary religion: Critical status and future directions. *Journal of Religion, Media & Digital Culture, 8* (2), 206–225.

Lundby, K. (2013). Media and the Transformations of Religion. In K. Lundby (Ed.), *Religion Across Media: From Early Antiquity to Late Modernity* (pp. 185–200). New York: Peter Lang.

Lundby, K. (Ed.) (2018). *Contesting Religion. The Media Dynamics of Cultural Conflicts in Scandinavia*. Berlin: De Gruyter.

Lundby, K. (2021). *Religion i medienes grep. Medialisering i Norge* [Religion in the grip of the media. Mediatization in Norway]. Oslo: Universitetsforlaget.

Lundby, K. (2023). Mediatization. In Y. Cohen, & P. Soukup (Eds.), *The Handbook on Religion and Communication* (pp. 273–286). Chichester: Wiley.

Lynch, G. (2011). What can we learn from the mediatisation of religion debate? *Culture and Religion, 12* (2), 203–210.

Mahoney, J., & Thelen, K. (2009). A Theory of Gradual Institutional Change. In J. Mahoney & K. Thelen (Eds.), *Explaining Institutional Change. Ambiguity, Agency, and Power*, (pp. 1–37). Cambridge: Cambridge University Press.

Martín-Barbero, J. (1993) [1987]. *Communication, Culture and Hegemony: From the Media to the Mediations*. Translated by E. Fox & R. A. White. London: Sage.

Martín-Barbero, J. (1997). Mass Media as a Site of Resacralization of Contemporary Cultures. In S. M. Hoover & K. Lundby (Eds), *Rethinking Media, Religion, and Culture* (pp. 102–116). Thousand Oaks, CA: Sage.

Martino, L. M. Sa. (2013). *The Mediatization of Religion: When Faith Rocks*. Farnham, Surrey: Ashgate.

Meyer, B. (2004). "Praise the Lord": Popular cinema and pentecostalite style in Ghana's new public sphere. *American Ethnologist, 31* (1), 92–110.

Meyer, B. (2009). From Imagined Communities to Aesthetic Formations: Religious Mediations, Sensational Forms, and Styles of Binding. In B. Meyer (Ed.), *Aesthetic Formations. Media, Religion, and the Senses* (pp. 1–28). New York: Palgrave Macmillan.

Meyer, B. (2012). Christianity in Africa: From African Independent to Pentecostal-Charismatic Churches. In E. K. Bongmba (Ed.), *The Wiley-Blackwell Companion to African Religions* (pp. 153–170). Malden, MA and Wiley Online Library: Wiley-Blackwell.

Meyer, B. (2013). Material Mediations and Religious Practices of World-Making. In K. Lundby (Ed.), *Religion Across Media. From Early Antiquity to Late Modernity* (pp. 1–19. New York: Peter Lang.

Meyer, B., & Moors, A. (2006). Introduction. In B. Meyer, & A. Moors (Eds.), *Religion, Media, and the Public Sphere* (pp. 1–25). Bloomington: Indiana University Press.

Meyrowitz, J. (1993). Images of media: Hidden ferment – and harmony – in the field. *Journal of Communication, 43* (3), 59–66.

Morgan, D. (2011). Mediation or mediatisation: The history of media in the study of religion. *Culture and Religion, 12* (2), 137–152.

Obadia, L. (2015). Buddhism: Modernization or Globalization? In B. S. Turner & O. Salemink (Eds.), *Routledge Handbook of Religions in Asia* (pp. 343–358). Abingdon: Routledge.

Pierson, P. (2004). *Politics in Time: History, Institiutions, and Social Analysis.* Princeton, NJ: Princeton University Press.

Radde-Antweiler, K. (2019). Religion as Communicative Figurations: Analyzing Religion in Times of Deep Mediatization. In K. Radde-Antweiler & X. Zeiler (Eds.), *Mediatized Religion in Asia: Studies on Digital Media and Religion* (pp. 211–223). New York: Routledge.

Radde-Antweiler, K., & Zeiler, X., (Eds.) (2019). *Mediatized Religion in Asia. Studies on Digital Media and Religion.* New York: Routledge.

Said, E. W. (1995) [1978]. *Orientalism: Western Conceptions of the Orient.* London: Penguin.

Scolari, C. A., Fernández, J. L., & Rodríguez-Amat, J. R. (Eds.) (2021). *Mediatization(s). Theoretical Conversations between Europe and Latin America.* Bristol & Chicago: Intellect Books.

Scolari, C. A., & Rodríguez-Amat, J. R. (2018). A Latin American approach to mediatization: Specificities and contributions to a global discussion about how the media shape contemporary societies. *Communication Theory, 28* (2), 131–154.

Souza, C. R. P. de, & Matos, R. de C. de A. (2017). Between no churched and cyber Pentecostals: Religious *modus vivendi* in the society under mediatization. *ESSACHESS – Journal for Communication Studies, 10* (2): 33–51.

Stolow, J. (2005). Religion and/as media. *Theory, Culture & Society, 22* (4), 119–145.

Tsuria, R., & Campbell, H. A. (2019). Understanding Jewish Digital Media in Israel: Between Technological Affordances and Religious-Cultural Uses. In K. Radde-Antweiler & X. Zeiler (Eds.), *Mediatized Religion in Asia. Studies on Digital Media and Religion* (pp. 190–207). New York: Routledge.

Valibeigi, N. (2019). Being Religious through Social Networks: Representation of Religious Identity of Shia Iranians on Instagram. In K. Radde-Antweiler & X. Zeiler (Eds.), *Mediatized Religion in Asia. Studies on Digital Media and Religion* (pp. 165–189). New York: Routledge.

Verón, E. (2014a). Mediatization Theory: A Semio-Anthropological Perspective. In K. Lundby (Ed.), *Mediatization of Communication* (pp. 163–172). Handbooks of Communication Science, *21*. Berlin: de Gruyter Mouton.

Verón, E. (2014b). Mediatization theory: A semio-anthropological perspective and some of its consequences. *MATRIZes, 8* (1), 1–8.

Zuboff, S. (2019). *The Age of Surveillance Capitalism. The Fight for a Human Future at the New Frontier of Power*. London: Profile Books.

3 Rivalling Concepts, Huge Gaps, and Analytical Complexities

Diverse Challenges in Researching the Mediatisation of Sport

Kirsten Frandsen

Sport and sports events have been mentioned time and again in theoretical discussions about mediatisation and used by pioneering and leading scholars to briefly illustrate the contemporary and historical impact of media and theorising the relationship between media and society (Bolin, 2014; Hepp, 2012; Krotz, 2009; Schultz, 2004). However, despite the fact that sport is an obvious example for many, none of these scholars have consulted existing research about the relationship between media and sport. This may well be unfortunate, because in some ways the niche community of media and sport scholars have been early-movers in applying the kind of interdisciplinary research and exploring interrelations and transformations spurred by changes in the media environment which now constitute the agenda among mediatisation scholars.

The possible value of consulting this body of literature is indicated indirectly by Bolin (2014), who actually uses the Olympic Games as a popular and well-known example to illustrate how the integrated character of media in modern society makes it difficult to analyse their role as "imposing themselves on a supposedly previously unmediated phenomenon" (Bolin, 2014, p. 189). In this way, he illustrates an important ontological and epistemological point, namely that media and sport have always shaped each other, and sports and events in some cases are born as mediatised phenomena. Arguing for more clarification of the role of media in socio-cultural transformations, Bolin also states that mediatisation should be seen as "communicative quality". In emphasising that the role of media (1) is difficult to analyse because of their integrated character, (2) also lies in their materiality, and (3) lies in their ability to produce sign commodities, he actually points out that this integrated character, economy, and technology are all parameters which have to be taken into consideration when theorising how media interrelate with other social domains and contribute to socio-cultural transformations. These points are key issues which will be touched upon in different ways in the following exploration of current challenges in mediatisation research on sport.

The scholarly community inquiring into the media and sport nexus has welcomed the agenda now set by mediatisation scholars, but also regards

DOI: 10.4324/9781003324591-5

the concept and approach with a certain amount of reservation or even indifference. The field of research is currently growing and becoming more established, with a substantial rise in both the number of research publications and the number of higher education programmes focusing on media and sport. Nevertheless, the concept of mediatisation has only been gaining ground in English-language publications since 2010.[1] Contributions which explicitly apply mediatisation as a key concept and approach have been surprisingly limited in number, with few of them shifting the dominant focus away from the big sports events and big professional, commercialised male sports with an international or global reach.

We will explore the intricate background for this mixed and somehow inert response by taking different perspectives. First, we take a closer look at the ontologies and conceptualisations which have shaped the field historically, and the present state of the field, where emerging new dispositions reflect how mediatisation evolves in sport, seeming to draw research in this field in other epistemological directions. Second, we turn our attention to existing mediatisation research, which is clearly dominated by a continued focus on big professional sports and sports events and therefore leaves a lot of significant gaps. Mediatisation is a growing theme, and both diachronic and synchronic perspectives have been applied. Even so, mediatisation appears to be no easy concept or approach to embrace in a field dominated by interest in empirical studies and perhaps even a sense of caution regarding more widespread use of "obtuse continental theory" (Wenner, 2015b, p. 215). Finally, we touch upon a central analytical challenge in implementing mediatisation theory in empirical research in analytical cases which are affected a great deal by commercialisation and globalisation.

Rivalling frameworks in the field

Without denying a range of challenges which mediatisation theory poses to scholars engaged in empirical studies, we start elsewhere by reviewing the theoretical conceptualisations of the interrelationships between media and sport presented by pioneering and leading scholars in the field. Because in this field, the concept of mediatisation is strongly rivalled by already established field-sensitive notions of these relationships. Strikingly, these now hegemonic frameworks were developed more than two decades ago, and they draw upon several of the same theoretical sources and ideas which have been brought to the table more recently by mediatisation scholars.

With a point of departure in North American and British works rooted in cultural studies in the mid-1970s, the field of media sport research started to take shape from the late 1980s onwards in particular. The rise of cultural studies "broke the ice for scholars to legitimately examine the nexus of communication and sport" (Wenner, 2015b, p. 248), and from the outset the analytical task was perceived as being interdisciplinary because "sport and media studies gained 'permission' to engage one other without apology"

(Wenner, 2015a, p. 629). For more than three decades, the American communications scholar L.A. Wenner has been a leading, pioneering figure, and his interests in exploring the relationship between media and sport was motivated and theorised in the late 1980s, drawing explicitly on Altheide & Snow's book *Media Logic* (1979), which includes a chapter on media and sport. In the anthology *Media, Sport and Society*, which was the first source to define the field more broadly, he paraphrases Altheide & Snow when arguing that mediated sports communication "forms the basis of a shared sports culture in America" and that "mediated sports culture is an inescapable reality, forming part of the context of every American's life" (Wenner, 1989, p. 16). Thus, besides describing American culture as a sports culture, he defines North American sport as a mediatised sports culture in which sports fans mainly engage with sports through media, and the social worlds and cultural frameworks of sports fans are basically shaped by mediated sports communication. These early conceptualisations, which are situated in a particular North American context characterised by highly commercialised media and sport systems, still seem very much in line with more recent general definitions of mediatisation as a process in which "media become *indispensable* to people's lives" (Jansson, 2018, p. 4), as their cultural frameworks and social worlds increasingly rely on mediated cultural products and the infrastructures of communication technologies (Jansson, 2002; Couldry & Hepp, 2017).

Whereas Wenner conceived of the integration of media into sport in 1989 by giving priority to a culturally oriented audience and fan perspective, S. Jhally takes another more generalising political economy perspective, including the media and sport industries as well. He conceptualises the relationship as follows: "as soon as we concentrate specifically on the subject of sports in capitalism it becomes apparent that we can talk *only* about a '*sport/media complex*' " (Jhally, 1989, p. 77). This conceptualisation of the relationship between media and sport as an *integrated complex* has been widely used ever since. Jhally rejects the idea of looking at media and sport as two distinct realms. He argues that there is no such thing as "pure sports" outside the influence of media; and as the quote above illustrates, he considers forces of the contextual capitalistic market superior to the powers stemming from media or sport. However, it could be argued that this conceptualisation of the interrelationship as a sport/media complex articulates the symbiotic and complex structure of the relationships of *some* media with *some* sports, in *particular* social-cultural contexts at a *particular* moment in history.

Jhally's conceptualisation remains relevant in the 21st century, as it points to the entangled structure of diverse third-party commercial interests which have increasingly come to characterise and co-structure a growing number of relationships between television broadcasters and a limited number of big male sports and big events. However, sport and media are mainly conceptualised as interrelated in a commodity structure within which they tend to be considered purely as instruments for market logics. Seen in a broader historical and social-cultural perspective, this tendency to foreground economic dynamics in the analysis is shaped by a particular empirical context, establishing the media–sport relationship as a black box concept which does not shed much light on the more precise role and power of media – regarded as socio-culturally situated institutions, organisations, and technologies.

By 1998 a somewhat similar conceptualisation, recognising the same kind of symbiosis, had been introduced by Wenner. However, his term "MediaSport" (Wenner, 1998) is less generalising, being dedicated specifically to conceptualising the particular commodified relationships between major sports events/leagues, large media organisations and corporate partners with global marketing interests. So besides the power of the market, Wenner adds globalisation as another important societal force which has shaped the relationships between big sports and big media in particular ever since the 1990s. Following this line of thought, and in a contribution in the same anthology, Whitson adds that the combined effects of commercialisation and globalisation can be traced in the "adoption of 'American' business practices and marketing strategies" by non-American sports organisations (Whitson, 1998, p. 58). Here Whitson indicates indirectly that internal processes of change in sports clearly involve media, something which has subsequently been described as a significant structure in current mediatisation processes, where media have become embedded elements inside other institutions (Borges, 2018; Hjarvard, 2013; Frandsen, 2016). Still, despite the obviously important role occupied by media in both internal and external processes of commercialisation and globalisation, their more precise contribution and power lacks substantial theoretical elaboration.

The Australian-based British scholar David Rowe acknowledges the integrated nature of the relationship between media and sport and the influence of societal forces of commercialisation and globalisation. However, he also contributes (1999) both substantial elaboration and refinement of the ontological understandings in the field. He conceptualises the relationship as a "media sports cultural complex" (Rowe 1999). Besides adding a historical and more pronounced cultural-theoretical perspective, Rowe stresses the role of media by putting the word "media" first in this concept. Building on cultural theories, he argues along some of the same lines as Bolin (2014), stating that the cultural perspective "signifies both the primacy of symbols in contemporary sport and the two-way relationship between the sports media and the great cultural formation of which it is part" (Rowe, 1999, p. 4). Without denying the powers of commercialisation and globalisation, he argues in favour of taking both production and reception of media texts into account in the analysis of the cultural power of sport, and when assessing the power balance between the two. Rowe roughly reiterates Wenner's thoughts from 1989, but he elaborates and connects them to commercialisation and globalisation, and he places them in a historical perspective drawing on Max Weber and Norbert Elias' conceptualisations of rational-isation and civilisation as important modern processes in sport: "Once elements of sport had become rationalized and industrialized, they necessarily entered into relations with other economic entities which acted as conduits, carrying sports culture far beyond its places of origin" (Rowe, 1999, pp. 23–24). Acknowledging the links between sport and media and commercial-isation, his cultural-theoretical routing establishes another, more nuanced perspective on the role of media and sport, which are not reduced to subor-dinate tools in processes of commercialisation and globalisation. According to Rowe, both sports organisations and media organisations are shaped by political and economic interests, but must also be regarded as powerful agents of change because of the specific ability of mediated sports to create value through the production and distribution of symbols. In seeing the integrated communicative quality of media and sport as important, Rowe is very much in line with Bolin (2014). But he takes the argument a step further by stating that "media sports texts are perhaps, then, at the leading edge of culturalization of economics" (Rowe, 1999, p. 70). Rowe draws on a wide range of theoretical inspirations from semiotics, cultural anthropology, postmodern cultural theory, consumption theory, and sociology, including a few of the same scholarly sources which have informed social constructivist mediatisation theories and many scholars who support culturally oriented mediatisation theories, as presented by Johan Fornäs, for instance (2014).

With the emergence of the internet and digital media, the media sport cultural complex remains an overarching and very inclusive key concept. Even though new terms such as "networked media sport", "sport as media" and a need for a "conceptual transition" (Hutchins & Rowe, 2012, p. 10) have also been articulated in order to grasp the way in which digital com-munication technologies in particular now underpin and change both the experience and practice of sport.

What we can take from this quick review of the conceptual legacies of the relatively few leading scholars who have engaged explicitly in theorising the media–sport–society relationship[2] is that they have been driven by a concern for the role of media in a broader social and cultural context "both *within* and *around* sport" (Wenner, 2015b, p. 251). In pursuing this aim, they have accumulated existing concepts and drawn on several of the same theories and ways of thinking as mediatisation scholars. These scholars also have a very similar background, being situated in Anglo-Saxon contexts which are characterised by long-running and shared (colonial) histories, as well as having highly liberalised, commercially oriented media and sport systems. Consequently, they share a great concern for the role of media in relation to processes of commercialisation and globalisation, whereas the role of media technologies (for instance) is only reflected on in more implicit or inco-herent ways. It is on the basis of this hegemonic but socio-culturally situated framework that the more recent theoretical elaborations of the concept of mediatisation obviously attract interest, while also leading to critique and being subject to both negations and adjustments when they are applied to empirical studies by some scholars in the field.

Mediatised sports – new epistemologies

As mentioned above, an increasing number of scholars are now involved in researching the media and sport nexus. The consolidation and growing legitimacy of the field is reflected in diverse initiatives during the last decade, such as the launching of several dedicated journals[3] and the establishment of various forms of interest groups and subsections at leading international mainstream communication conferences. One reason for this development is that sport has gained a higher status in society, while another reason relates to the increasing mediatisation of sport, requiring specialised knowledge and competences in communication within sports organisations and a corresponding increase in educational programmes to meet this need. Ironically, this development does not necessarily support mediatisation research. As Wenner has pointed out, a new tendency has emerged in the research field which takes the broader conceptualisations of the relationship between sport, media and society as a given and focuses on "the pragmatics of practice, strategies, and effectiveness in the sport communication market-place" (Wenner, 2015b, p. 253). This means that long-term and more fundamental socio-cultural questions regarding how "media acquire greater authority to define social reality and condition patterns of social interaction" (Hjarvard, 2013, p. 3), which are at the foreground of mediatisation research, are not immediately deemed relevant or theoretically interesting. Instead, the mediatisation of sport nourishes research questions rooted in applied epistemologies and more focused and specialised theoretical engagements with specific processes of mediation and their communicative effectiveness.

Wanted: diversity in terms of scope, context, and approach

The still rather limited body of English-language publications which have an explicit focus on the mediatisation of sport largely reflect and maintain existing biases in the field. The majority of these publications have focused on big sports events or big, highly professionalised, commercialised male sports and sports leagues in Europe, the USA, the UK or Australia. Historical transformations of the particular case of extraordinary megasporting events have been explored intensively in the anthology *Sport, Media and Mega-events* (Wenner & Billings, 2017), and analyses of various processes of mediatisation taking a case-analytical approach to sports like football, cricket, Formula 1 motor racing, rugby, American football and minor sports like BMX, volleyball, and recreational sports among young adults and e-sport have been published in English-language journals and books. In terms of their content, publications in other languages – especially German and other North European languages – reflect the same general pattern, focusing in particular on big events, men's football and a few other sports and the particular role of broadcast television operating in highly liberalised markets. However, a few studies from the European context add a little cultural diversity to the picture by exploring minor sports like skiing, beach volleyball and badminton, which are all interesting because they have had a less stable relationship with television broadcasters.

It is evident that one of the main challenges so far is to explore processes of mediatisation within a broader scope of social and cultural contexts and on a wider scale across cases. As one phenomenologically oriented analysis of the mediatisation of East African football fan culture (Skey & Waliaula, 2021) and accounts of the role of television in a North European context (Frandsen, 2014) illustrate, in some contexts processes of mediatisation may connect not only to commercialisation and globalisation but also to other types of societal forces, like politics and broader civil society movements. Hence, the exploration of processes of mediatisation within empirical contexts that are characterised not only by market-oriented, de-politicised liberal governance structures, but also by other political and economic dynamics and histories in media systems (Hallin & Mancini, 2004; Enli & Syvertsen, 2020), as well as in sports systems and local sports histories (Tokarsky et al., 2004; Petry et al., 2004; Tin et al., 2020), will bring important knowledge to the table.

Greater diversity to strengthen our understanding of the relationship between media and sport is not only a matter of geography. Both systematic and themed comparative approaches as well as more in-depth, historically oriented case studies are needed. Especially interesting cases for such exploration are traditional minor sports and recreational and amateur sports and their athletes, which have only been affected very indirectly (but still severely) by structural transformations related to broadcast television. The omnipresence of digital, mobile, and social media has put all these generally overlooked sports on the research agenda. Comparative approaches and in-depth analysis of this type of historically less mediatised cases are needed to bring more nuances to our understanding of mediatisation as a diversified process in sport, and the social significance and transformative power of mediated communication, now instigated by digital media technologies and their institutionalising processes (Hjarvard, 2014a). This is because on the one hand, their integration and use in different sorts of sporting cultures and organisational structures are informed to some extent by historically rooted practices, aims, and distinct values. But on the other hand, the communicative features of digital media – their affordances (Hutchby, 2001) – have an influence on "*which* patterns of social interaction become more dominant than others and *how* they are spelled out" (Hjarvard, 2014a, p. 131). Even though traditional sports all have to adhere to rules and ideals set by international or global governing organisations to some extent, they may still be culturally less homogenised by the processes of commercialisation and rationalising professionalisation, which have been distinct elements in the mediatisation process related to broadcast television and its globalisation. Sports which have only developed a rudimentary relationship with broadcast television (or no relationship at all) may be culturally more diverse or may have different types of engagement with other societal agents like local or national politicians, club members, NGOs or public authorities. The response of these marginalised sports to the opportunities and challenges emerging with digitisation could contribute a wider set of logics to the analysis of media transformation, helping not least to grasp the wider range of structural changes and complexities now involved in a new wave of mediatisation (Couldry & Hepp, 2017).

Digitisation emphasises the importance of avoiding totalising implications and the need for a more nuanced basis for a critical discussion of the wider societal effects of the mediatisation of sport. With a view to grounding such a debate, it may be important to avoid too many small single-case studies and take different approaches and address themes of structural importance across sports. One theme could be the implications of structures like differences in audiences and market size: are sports, organisations, and athletes located in small, national media markets, or in larger markets? Another interesting theme involves exploring and comparing processes across team-based or individualised sports. And a third very obvious theme in sport is gender. A historical gender bias in sport has been underpinned by media whose regular coverage has largely focused on male sports and been informed by male media professionals (Laucella et al., 2017; Cooky et al., 2021). As media coverage – and especially television coverage – establishes the grounds for enhancing revenues substantially (sponsorships and rights), the scant, irregular attention from television has had immense consequences for women in sports and for gendered identity formations both within and outside sport. Historically, media have sustained inequalities in sport, with women elite athletes having had more limited access to resources and processes of professionalisation, and with symbolic messages distributed by and through sport being characterised overwhelmingly by a masculine hegemony and by the fact that they serve masculine interests. A few mediatisation studies (Nölleke & Birkner, 2019; Nybelius, 2020) have included both male and female athletes in their empirical material, but have not engaged explicitly with questions related to gender. However, Johansen (2016) and Skey and colleagues (2017; 2021) all point to gender as an important factor in understanding the mediatisation of football fan cultures among children and young people in Northern Europe, and among adults in an East African context. With processes of digitisation, it is of great importance to explore the sturdiness of such a historical structure in a wider context. Digitisation affects everyone, and it saturates the everyday practices of female athletes, coaches, sports journalists and fans, shaping their professional and sporting careers. One big emerging question now is whether an increasingly diversified, networked, and technologically loaded media and sport environment can generate a dynamic which will change, modify, or perhaps even deepen such existing structures of neglect, polarisation, and inequality in sport.

Media are integrated, unsettled, negotiated

As the majority of work published on the mediatisation of sport takes big male sports and big sports events as its analytical objects, a couple of crucial analytical challenges can be identified. The first of these, as stressed by Bolin (2014), is that media are supposed to be (or have in fact been) an integrated element in some sports and big sports events right from the outset. Strictly speaking, this means that these events and sports have never been unmediated. They have been shaped to a varying extent by processes of self-mediatisation (Nölleke, Scheu & Birkner, 2020), with their organisers and social actors regarding media as important for the creation of public attention and exposure. Some sports and events are born mediatised phenomena, like Formula 1, road cycling, the Tour de France or e-sport (Finn, 2020; Frandsen, 2020), meaning that media organisations have organised them to pursue market and ideological goals, or relied on media technologies and mediated symbolic forms to bring the competition as a whole to an audience. Within various time frames, other male sports and big events have developed in tandem with media organisations and technologies, developing very tight relationships with particular media – from the second half of the 20th century broadcast television in particular. This tendency is illustrated by the Olympic Games (Tomlinson, 2017), professional football (Haynes & Boyle, 2017; Frandsen, 2020) and professional rugby (Bruce, 2017). If we stick to the idea that the main idea of mediatisation research is to understand the relationship between media and sport better, and especially to clarify the transformative role of media, many big sports events and big sports pose a particular analytical challenge. The whole idea of considering "the interrelation between the change of media and communication, on the one hand, and culture and society, on the other" (Hepp & Krotz, 2014, p. 5) presents an immediate and complex analytical challenge. This is because media have always shaped and/or become so embedded in a range of sports that they can only be separated from them analytically – and even that is a challenge.

The analytical challenge identified by Bolin is a more general problem shared across many social domains, and challenges some of the basic notions in mediatisation theory. This situation is compounded by the fact that owing to their relationship with the media, major sports and events have attracted the interest of a growing number of other social agents. They have evolved into "a dense matrix of intersecting tendencies and powers" (Gruneau & Compton, 2017, p. 41). The density of this matrix makes it difficult to establish the driving power behind the changes identified. As a result, in historical accounts the basic building blocks and key mechanisms of change in which media are actually core agents (by virtue of their institutional power, organisational needs, or technological characteristics) easily vanish. Instead, the wider structural and ideological implications of their presence and continued change seem to take priority. The intersection of both major trends and a growing number of institutional powers has grown since the advent of broadcast television. Historically speaking, television has spurred processes of commercialisation and later globalisation in sport; and in the 21st century this medium continues to have primary significance for big sports and big events – although a more multilayered media ecology is involved these days (Evens, Iosifidis & Smith, 2013; Haynes & Boyle, 2017; Hutchins & Sanderson, 2017). The historical, transforming role of television therefore has to be seen as a synergy between several transforming factors including the communicative, technological, and institutional features of television, and contextual, historical processes of economic growth and consumerism booming in Western Europe, North America and Australia from the mid-20th century (Frandsen, 2020; Haynes, 2017; Rowe, 1999). This also implies that in the case of big sports and big sports events in particular, the media–sport marriage has developed into an integral element in the interactions of other social domains with each other. Like the communication of commercial enterprises with the market or business partners through sponsorships; the communication of municipalities with their citizens, potential residents or tourists by co-organising sports events; and the communication of politicians with regional, national, or geopolitical contexts via national representation or the hosting of big international sports events.

This sort of complexity is addressed at the very foundational level in mediatisation theory, when emphasising that one important aspect of mediatisation is that media have become a semi-independent institution which is powerful not only owing to its relationships with other institutions, but also because it "provides a nexus between other cultural and social institutions" (Hjarvard, 2013, p. 3). So mediatisation is a social process which is not only a matter of media developments, but "also an outcome of technological, political and economic changes" (Hjarvard, 2013, p. 25). This may even imply that "the driving forces of change might not be the media at all" (Hepp & Krotz, 2014, p. 5), and in the digital age, which gives rise to more pronounced and complex processes of mediatisation, media will "gradually be integrated within various contexts and be influenced by the particular institutions and contexts in question" (Hjarvard, 2014a, p. 131). The complexities at hand are theorised by Hjarvard (2014b), using interinstitutional theory suggesting that society is made up of a range of different institutions which are interrelated: each institution is not living in isolation, but is constantly developed through influences stemming from other institutions.

Until now, leading media and sport scholars have been concerned primarily with the powers of the market, tending to see more or less shared commercial interests in both media and sports organisations as the main drivers behind the transformations of sport. More recently, theories about mega-events (Roche, 2000; Horne & Manzenreiter, 2006; Müller, 2015) have added to this holistic understanding of the intersecting forces in the matrix shaping big sports events when discussing mediatisation. Mega-events are "large-scale cultural (including commercial and sporting) events, which have a dramatic character, mass popular appeal and international significance" (Roche, 2000, p. 1). These events have attained multidimensional significance, being produced through a network of entangled local political, economic, and cultural interests. They are seen as having gained increasing significance, and media are absolutely crucial in this development as "an unmediated mega-event would be a contradiction in terms" (Horne & Manzenreiter, 2006, p. 2). In other words, it may be argued that the growing importance of mega-events is in itself a reflection of mediatisation.

In drawing on such concepts when discussing the mediatisation of big sports events, media/sport scholars have avoided the analytical pitfalls of being too media-centric and simplistic, acknowledging the complexities of inter-institutional forces at work in both sport and media. However, analytically they risk facing a new pitfall as the more exact role of media tends to be accounted for in more implicit ways. This is to the detriment of a more systematised and differentiated understanding of how media more precisely exert their influence on many levels using technical means, their organisational structure and expertise, and/or their institutionalising societal role. The more implicit notions of media reflect a certain anxiety with regard to simplistic understandings, a fear of overselling the role of media in social transformation, and not least a certain sociological reservation with regard to media determinism. In particular, the role of technology has been marginalised and only mentioned briefly in existing analyses of the mediatisation of big sports and events. However, as Hutchins and Rowe have already emphasised, this is a pattern which needs to be altered in the digital age if we really want to engage in "the difficult challenge of tracing the impact of fast moving social and technological change" (Hutchins & Rowe, 2012, p. 7).

In most of the cases and socio-cultural contexts that have been analysed, media and sport have been part of rather complex structures of interdependencies, including exceptionally strong processes of commercialisation and globalisation. Besides these mega-powers, sport is also entangled in other more localised social and cultural trends, like the development of tourism and environmental issues (Frandsen, 2017; Millington & Wilson, 2017). All these trends and processes of power merge in several contributions, meaning that the exact role of media is addressed in less detail; it is seen through the lenses of other themes or in balance with them. In the context of big sport events, which are well-suited to the analysis of long-term processes of mediatisation because of their historical consistency and ability to attract media attention, mediatisation theory generally seems to prompt scholars to negotiate the power of media relative to broader forces – especially those of a market increasingly operating on a global scale. But again, the more exact role of media somehow remains conceptually unsettled and relegated to be a matter of empirical investigation in studies where the role of media is illustrated – but often in implicit and less systematised ways. Even when media are regarded as central in "shaping and growing these events" (Billings & Wenner, 2017, p. 17), commodification and mediatisation are often regarded as "twin logics" (Real & Wenner, 2017, p. 202), and the various dimensions of the role of media *as* media are not explicitly conceptualised (as situated organisations, societal institutions, or technologies). In this way, the role of media remains implicit in the matrix, and mediatisation tends to be allocated the status of being an add-on to existing frameworks or a sub-force within a wider framework, with commercialisation being regarded as the dominant force: "In a very basic sense, Livingstone's (2009, p. 1) claim that there is now a 'mediatization of everything' synergizes with Debord's (1976/1995, p. 29) observations about our present society and the spectacle residing in a 'world of commodity' " (Billings & Wenner, 2017, pp. 12–13).

Final remarks: operationalisation

Until now the concept of mediatisation has formed a topical point of departure for both diachronic and synchronic approaches to sport. In general, the concept is thought of as very open theoretically and methodologically. In combination with the efforts made to eschew excessively simple understandings of big sports and events, this means that relatively few diachronic studies engage in more systematic elaborations specifying how the role of media is conceptualised and subsequently traced in systematic searches for empirical material. So far, more elaborate methodological reflections on how to implement mediatisation theory's rather abstract terms in analytical practice are relatively sparse in publications taking a historical approach. One underlying reason for this may be that established scholars have drawn largely on their existing expertise in media and used material from previous projects on media and particular sports and events. One main challenge for future research and emerging scholars in the field is to establish more interdisciplinary collaborations and transparency regarding the translation of mediatisation theory into systematic diachronic explorations. How can not only media but also structural social transformations, defined as changes in "human imaginations, relationships, and interactions" (Hjarvard, 2013, p. 3), be conceptualised, approached, and traced empirically in long-term studies which go beyond looking into the communication circuit itself? And how can such studies of partially invisible processes be accomplished in relation to highly professional sports, where for several decades it has become increasingly difficult for scholars to gain access to people and knowledge from the inside? These questions reveal some of the methodological challenges facing future mediatisation research. In a short-term analysis of the mediatisation of the International Skiing Federation from 2004 to 2013,

Nybelius (2020) has employed a model developed by German scholars involving the idea that the mediatisation of sport takes place through a series of steps (Dohle & Vowe, 2006; 2017), to guide her collection of relevant data. A few synchronic studies may also provide inspiration after identifying a missing link between the very generalised notions in mediatisation theories and particular fields of sport, engaging supplementary and more grounded concepts and frameworks to operationalise empirical investigations in a more systemised and transparent manner. Like Birkner and Nölleke, who have drawn on existing knowledge and frameworks from journalism studies and social media in their exploration of the mediatisation of professional football players and volleyball players (Birkner & Nölleke, 2016; Nölleke & Birkner, 2019). Similarly, Kopecka-Piech synthesises existing conceptualisations of media materialities into a concept of media saturation, covering an important aspect of mediatisation among recreational athletes (Kopecka-Piech, 2019); Ehrlén (2021) synthesises various concepts of community and social networks from both sociology, media, and sport studies into a concept of communality in her study of recreational athletes; and Frandsen (2016) engages concepts from the mediatisation of political organisations in her comparative study of sports organisations. No matter how productive are these efforts to solve the analytical challenge involved in translating the general concepts from mediatisation theory into analytical concepts or approaches which are more sensible to the select field of sport, it is also apparent that many of the theories utilised stem from the disciplinary field of media and communication studies. This reveals that sport has integrated various forms of mediated communication as part of a sports practice, and that the understanding of contemporary sport cultures therefore necessitates knowledge of media cultures. However, it may also indicate the presence of a related challenge for future research: it may be necessary to keep the door open to sports studies and sports sociology and seek advice in the conceptualisations of sport scholars regarding other conspicuous trends and themes permeating the field of sport. The interdisciplinary ambition which historically triggered both media and sport studies and more recently mediatisation research remains important – but may also be increasingly difficult to achieve as the two fields of media and sport studies have matured and become more self-reliant and established. However, instead of leaving the difficult job of bridging two fields of expertise to emerging young scholars, one future challenge involves engaging scholars from all levels in more collaborative processes and discussions across the increasingly specialised fields of both sports studies and media and communication studies.

Notes

1 In a German-language context, sport and mediatization have been an articulate theme since the 2000s, reflecting the fact that German scholars have been among the pioneers in mediatization research.

2 The relationship between media and sport has also been thoroughly theorized from other less societal-oriented or more media-oriented perspectives – for instance psychological perspectives on media audiences and semiotic perspectives on mediation.
3 Since 2012 three English-language and US-based journals, and one German-language and German-based journal have been launched.

References

Altheide, D.L. & Snow, R.P. (1979). *Media logic*. Sage.

Billings, A., & Wenner, L.A. (2017). The curious case of the megasporting event: Media, mediatization and seminal sports events. In L.A. Wenner & A. Billings (Eds.) *Sport, Media and Mega-Events* (pp. 3–18). London and New York: Routledge.

Birkner, T. & Nölleke, D. (2016). Soccer players and their media-related behavior: A contribution on the mediatization of sports. *Communication & Sport*, 4(4), 367–384. https://doi. org/10.1177/2167479515588719.

Bolin, G. (2014). Institution, technology, world: Relationships between the media, culture and society. In K. Lundby, *Mediatization of communication* (pp. 175–197). Berlin and Boston: DeGruyter.

Borges, F.V. (2018). Always together: How football clubs want constant connections with fans. *Athens Journal of Sports*, 5(4), 263–278. https://doi.org/10.30958/ajspo.5-4-2

Bruce, T. (2017). The Rugby World Cup experience: Interrogating the oscillating poles of love and hate. In L.A. Wenner & A. Billings (Eds.) *Sport, media and mega-events* (pp. 100–114). New York: Routledge.

Cooky, C., Council, L.D., Mears, M.A. & Messner, M.A. (2021). One and done: The long eclipse of women's televised sports, 1089–2019. First online March 24, 2021. *Communication & Sport*. https://doi:10.1177/21674795211003524

Couldry, N. & Hepp, A. (2017). *The mediated construction of reality*. Cambridge and Malden, MA: Polity Press.

Dohle, M. & Vowe, G. (2006). Der sport auf der "mediatisierungstreppe"? Ein modell zur analyse medienbedingter veränderungen des sports [Sport on the mediatization steps? A model for analyzing media conditioned changes in sports. *Merz, Sport und Medien*, 6, 18–28.

Dohle, M. & Vowe, G. (2017). Mediatisierung des sports. Mediatisierung des fussballs!? In Ihle, H. (Ed.) *Globales mega-event und nationaler konfliktherd* (pp. 31–45). Berlin: Springer.

Ehrlén, V. (2021). Communal pulse across media. Digital networked communication and communality in recreational sport cultures. Ph.D. dissertation, University of Jyväskyla.

Enli, G. & Syvertsen, T. (2020). The media welfare state: Why such a concept, what is it used for, does it have a future? *Nordic Journal of Media Studies*, 2, 37–45.

Evens, T., Iosifidis, P. & Smith, P. (2013). *The political economy of television sports rights*. London: Palgrave Macmillan.

Finn, M. (2020). From accelerated advertising to fanboost: Mediatized motorsport. *Sport in Society*, First online: DOI: 10.1080/17430437.2019.1710131

Fornäs, J. (2014). Culturalizing mediatization. In A. Hepp & F. Krotz (Eds.) *Mediatized worlds: Culture and society in a media age* (pp. 38–53). Basingstoke and New York: Palgrave Macmillan.

Frandsen, K. (2014). Mediatization of sports. In K. Lundby (Ed.) *Mediatization of communication* (Vol. 21 of *Handbook of communications sciences*) (pp. 525–543). Berlin: De Gruyter Mouton.

Frandsen, K. (2016). Sports organizations in a new wave of mediatization. *Communication & Sport*, 4(4), 385–400. https://doi.org/10.1177/216747951 5588185

Frandsen, K. (2017). Tour de France: Mediatization of sport and place. In L.A. Wenner & A. Billings (Eds.) *Sport, media and mega-events* (pp. 156–169). London and New York: Routledge.

Frandsen, K. (2020). *Sport and mediatization*. London and New York: Routledge.

Gruneau, R. & Compton, J. (2017). Media events, mega-events and social theory: From Durkheim to Marx. In L.A. Wenner & A. Billings (Eds.) *Sport, media and mega-events* (pp. 33–47). New York: Routledge.

Hallin, D.C. & Mancini, P. (2004). *Comparing media systems: Three models of media and politics*. Cambridge University Press.

Haynes, R. (2017). *BBC Sport in black and white*. London: Palgrave Macmillan.

Haynes, R. & Boyle, R. (2017). The FIFA World Cup: Media, football and the evolution of a global event. In L.A. Wenner & A. Billings (Eds.) *Sport, media and mega-events* (pp. 83–99). New York: Routledge.

Hepp, A. (2012). Mediatizatization and the "moulding force" of the media. *Communications*, 37, 1–28. DOI: 10.1515/commun-2012-0001

Hepp, A. & Krotz, F. (Eds.) (2014). *Mediatized worlds. Culture and society in a media age*. Basingstoke and New York: Palgrave Macmillan.

Hjarvard, S. (2013). *The mediatization of culture and society*. London and New York: Routledge.

Hjarvard, S. (2014a). From mediation to mediatization: The institutionalization of new media. In A. Hepp & F. Krotz (Eds.) *Mediatized worlds. Culture and society in a media age* (pp. 123–139). Basingstoke and New York: Palgrave Macmillan.

Hjarvard, S. (2014b). Mediatization and cultural and social change: An institutional perspective. In K. Lundby (Ed.) *Mediatization of communication* (pp. 199–226) Berlin/Boston: De Gruyter Mouton.

Horne, J. & Manzenreiter, W. (2006). An introduction to the sociology of sports mega-events. In J. Horne and W. Manzenreiter (Eds.) *Sports mega-events. Social scientific analyses of a global phenomenon* (pp. 1–24). Blackwell.

Hutchby, I. (2001). Technologies, texts and affordances. *Sociology*, 35(2), 441–456. https://doi.org/10.1177/S0038038501000219

Hutchins, B. & Rowe, D. (2012). *Sport beyond television. The internet, digital media and the rise of networked media sport*. New York and London: Routledge.

Hutchins, B. & Sanderson, J. (2017). The primacy of sports television: Olympic media, social networking services, and multi-screen viewing during the Rio 2016 games. *Media International Australia*, 164, 32–43. https://doi.org/10.1177/13298 78X17707065

Jansson, A. (2002). Spatial phantasmagoria: The mediatization of tourism experience. *European Journal of Communication*, 17(4), 429–443. https://doi.org/ 10.1177/02673231020170040201

Jansson, A. (2018). *Mediatization and mobile lives. A critical approach*. Abingdon and New York: Routledge.

Jhally, S. (1989). Cultural studies and the sports/media complex. In L.A. Wenner (Ed.) *Media, sports & society* (pp. 70–93). Newbury/London/New Delhi: Sage.

Johansen S. L. (2016). Being a football kid: Football as a mediatized practice. In A. Schwell, M. Buchowski, M. Kowalska & N. Szogs (Eds.) *New ethnographies of football in Europe: people, passions, politics* (pp. 161–175). Palgrave Macmillan.

Kopecka-Piech, K. (2019). *Mediatization of physical activity: Media saturation and technologies*. Lanham MD, Boulder CO, New York and London: Lexington Books.

Krotz, F. (2009). Mediatization: A concept with which to grasp media and social change. In K. Lundby (Ed.) *Mediatization. Concept, changes, consequences* (pp. 21–40). New York: Peter Lang.

Laucella, P., Hardin, M., Bien-Aimé, S. & Antunovic, D. (2017). Diversifying the sports department and covering women's sports: A survey of sports editors. *Journalism & Mass Communication Quarterly*, 94(3), 772–792. https://doi.org/10.1177/1077699016654443

Millington, B. & Wilson, B. (2017). The Masters golf tournament: Media mega-event, the environment and the emergence of Augusta National Syndrome. In L.A. Wenner & A. Billings (Eds.) *Sport, media and mega-events* (pp. 142–155). New York: Routledge.

Müller, M. (2015). What makes an event a mega-event? Definitions and sizes. *Leisure Studies*, 34(6), 627–642.

Nölleke, D. & Birkner, T. (2019). Bypassing traditional sports media? *Studies in communication and media*, 8(3), 287–310. DOI:10.5771/2192-4007-2019-3-287

Nölleke, D., Scheu, A. & Birkner, T. (2020). The other side of mediatization: Expanding the concept to defensive strategies. *Communication Theory*, 1–21. First online.

Nybelius, M.S. (2020). *Förhandling pågår: En studie av Internationella Skidförbudets (FIS) medialisering* [Ongoing negotiations: A study of the mediatization of the International Skiing Federation]. Malmö Studies in Sport Sciences, 35. Bokförlaget idrottsforum.org

Petry, K., Steinbach, D. & Tokarski, W. (2004). Sport systems in the countries of the European Union: Similarities and differences. *European Journal for Sport and Society*, 1(1), 15–21. https://doi.org/10.1080/16138171.2004.11687744

Real, M. & Wenner, L.A. (2017) Super Bowl: Mythic spectacle revisited. In L.A. Wenner & A. Billings (Eds.) *Sport, media and mega-events* (pp. 199–217). New York: Routledge.

Roche, M. (2000). *Mega-events and modernity*. London: Routledge.

Rowe, D. (1999). *Sport, culture and the media*. Buckingham and Philadelphia, PA: Open University Press.

Schulz, W. (2004). Reconstructing mediatization as an analytical concept. *European Journal of Communication*, 19(1), 87–101. https://doi.org/10.1177/0267323104040696

Skey, M. & Waliaula, S. (2021). A non-media-centric approach to mediatization: Digital orientations in the lives of football fans. *International Journal of Communication*, 15, 2059–2085.

Skey, M., Stone, C., Jenzen, O. & Mangan, A. (2017). Mediatization and sport: A bottom-up perspective. *Communication & Sport*, First online. https://doi.org/10.1177/2167479517734850

Tin, M.B., Telseth, F., Tangen, J.O. & Giulianotti, R. (2020). (Eds.) *The Nordic model and physical culture*. London and New York: Routledge.

Tokarsky, W., Steinbach, D., Petry, K. & Jesse, B. (2004). *Two players one goal?* Aachen: Meyer & Meyer Sport.

Tomlinson, A. (2017). Twenty-eight olympic summers: Historical and methodological reflections on understanding the Olympic mega-event. In L.A. Wenner & A. Billings (Eds.) *Sport, media and mega-events* (pp. 51–68). New York: Routledge.

Wenner, L.A. (Ed.) (1998). *MediaSport*. London and New York: Routledge.

Wenner, L.A. (Ed.) (1989). *Media, sports and society*. Newbury/London/New Delhi: Sage.

Wenner, L.A. (2015a). Assessing the sociology of sport: On the mediasport interpellation and commodity narratives. *International Review for the Sociology of Sport*, 50 (4–5), 628–633. https://doi.org/10.1177/1012690214560832

Wenner, L.A. (2015b). Communication and sport, where art thou? Epistemological reflections on the moment and field(s) of play. *Communication & Sport*, 3(3), 247–260. https://doi.org/10.1177/2167479515584781

Wenner, L.A. & Billings, A. (Eds.) (2017). *Sport, media and mega-events*. New York: Routledge.

Whitson, D. (1998). Circuits of promotion: Media, marketing and the globalization of sport. In L.A..Wenner (Ed.). *MediaSport* (pp. 57–72). London and New York: Routledge.

Part II

Advancement of Developing Fields

4 Deep Mediatisation and the Datafication of Fashion

Agnès Rocamora

Mediatisation has established itself as a significant notion for understanding contemporary social processes. It is a "sensitizing concept" that helps researchers interrogate the intensification of the influence of media technologies and institutions on various social spheres (Jansson, 2015, pp. 14–15; Hepp, 2020, p. 9). A meta-process, it "points to the changed dynamics and dimensionality of the (whole) social world in a media age" whereby the media increasingly mould practices and experiences (Couldry, 2014a, p. 231; Krotz, 2007; Hepp, 2013).

However, contexts of mediatisation need to be fully qualified to account for its dimension as a differentiated and historically situated process that is "domain specific" (Hepp and Hasebrink, 2018, p. 23; Landerer, 2013; Strömbäck and Dimitrova, 2014). The Bourdieuian notion of field allows for this qualifying and contextualising. In this conceptual chapter, I focus on the field of fashion, also concentrating on digital media the better to interrogate the differentiated nature of mediatisation (sections I and II). In doing so, I bring Bourdieu's field theory in dialogue with mediatisation theory, contributing to the small body of work that has started drawing conceptual links between the two theories. I do so through the notion of logic, turning, in particular, towards the recent literature on deep mediatisation as a new stage of mediatisation (sections I and II).

At the core of deep mediatisation is datafication, the process whereby everyday practices and experiences are increasingly turned into data. Drawing on critical data studies scholarship, a body of research that generally fails to engage with mediatisation theory, I explore manifestations of the datafication of fashion, and discuss datafication as a key logic of the field of fashion (section III). In dialogue with Bourdieu's conceptual framework, I reflect on the role of data as capital and on that of algorithms as key players and gatekeepers of the field of fashion (section III).

I Mediatisation of the field of fashion

A mediatised society is a society submitted to "the media and their logic" (Hjarvard, 2009, p. 160). Here Hjavard is drawing on a concept, "media

DOI: 10.4324/9781003324591-7

logic", at the heart of mediatisation scholarship (see e.g., Barnard, 2018; Couldry, 2008; Couldry and Hepp, 2013; Deacon and Stanyer, 2014; Strömbäck, 2008). The term was developed by Altheide and Snow (1979, p. 240) in their eponymous book, to refer to "a form through which events and ideas are interpreted and acted upon". It is that which shapes individual and collective agents' everyday experiences and practices and is a taken-for granted "form of communication" (Altheide, 2013, p. 225).

However, various authors have objected to the universalising the term "media logic" in the singular implies, as if society was subject to a single, all-encompassing media logic, irrespective of media genres, affordances, and historical times. Couldry, for instance, acknowledges that the term is useful for conceptualising media logic as "a structuring force" (2014b, p. 65). But he also insists that one should talk about media logics to account for the role of both media types and media changes in logics across time in processes of mediatisation (see e.g., Couldry, 2008; see also Klinger and Svensson, 2018).

Thus, noting that "the concepts of 'media' and 'logic' are both underspecified", Asp (2014, p. 257) uses the notion "news media logic". Similarly, to conceptualise the rise and proliferation of digital and social media and their role in mediatisation, scholars have proposed various terms to capture their logics. Dahlgren (1996) discusses "cyberspace's media logic" to refer to the media logic of cyber-communication, such as cyberjournalism (p. 64); Klinger and Svensson (2018) refer to "network media logic"; and Van Dijck and Poell (2013) to "social media logic". Focusing on fashion blogs, Kristensen and Christensen (2017), for instance, have discussed the ways the logic of blogs, in contrast with that of print media, shapes fashion communication.

Being attentive to the specificity of the media involved in mediatisation allows for a differentiated account of this process, but so does attention to its articulation in specific social spaces. As Couldry observes: "mediatizaton research must be alive to multiple explanatory models of how the meta-process of mediatization is worked through in specific domains and fields" (2014a, p. 243).

It is with this aim in mind that, in previous work (Rocamora, 2017, 2018), I have started interrogating the way mediatisation is articulated in the field of fashion, also focusing on digital media in order better to attend to calls to approach mediatisation as a differentiated process. From designers and brands designing products so that they photograph well for social media, to consumers fashioning themselves for social media, I have discussed the ways, in the field fashion, "practices of production, consumption, distribution and diffusion – are articulated through the media, and, more crucially, are dependent on the media for their articulation" (Rocamora, 2017, p. 509). There are still too few studies of everyday, ordinary processes of mediatisation, and even less with regards to social and digital media. In being inherently embedded in everyday life and in both practices of production and consumption, the field of fashion lends itself to such studies.

Fashion shows, for instance, once the privilege of a small elite, and closed to the media, are now designed "with social media in mind" and always feature "made-for-instagram moments" (Business of Fashion, cited in Rocamora, 2017, p. 510; see also Halliday, 2022). Fashion e-commerce has become mediatised too, with the distinction between the editorial and the commercial increasingly fuzzy, and brands and e-tailers media content providers too (Rocamora, 2017). In April 2021 *Voguebusiness*, for instance, reported on brands from the field of fashion and beauty that are investing in in-house film studios to create online long-format videos (Chitrakorn, 2021).

II Field theory and mediatisation theory

In the above I refer to fashion in terms of "field", a notion I borrow from the work of Pierre Bourdieu. A field is a social space of positions, position taking and relations (see, for instance, Bourdieu, 2015a). It is a hierarchical space made up of established players and institutions, as well as new entrants, which all have the power to "produce effects" in the field (Bourdieu, 2015b, p. 240). Fields are also spaces of struggles for its transformation or preservation, for the definition of its boundaries, values and rules, and for the power to decide who belongs and who does not (Bourdieu, 2015a, pp. 483–487).

Four main genres of capital operate in all fields. They are economic (financial resources), symbolic (consecration and prestige), social (network and connections) and cultural capital (knowledge, possession of cultural goods and educational titles), and all are at once the "social energy" that fuels a field, a stake in it, and a product of it (Bourdieu, 1986, p. 47; 2015a, pp. 519–520).

Fashion can be defined as a field, and indeed, Bourdieu, along with Yvette Delsaut, deployed field theory to discuss the 1970s French field of haute couture, looking at designers' position as dominant or dominated players, and the concurrent aesthetic values they upheld (Bourdieu and Delsaut,1975). Arguably, the field of fashion emerged in the nineteenth century with the "invention", in Paris, of the figure of the designer by Charles Frederick Worth. Worth set in place a series of rules and institutions that still exist to this day, though in altered guises, and have been crucial to shaping the practices and values currently at play in today's field of fashion (Rocamora, 2009; Steele, 2017).

All fields have agents of consecration and legitimation, which all participate in the definition of its boundaries, values and rules. Worth, for instance, was instrumental to the invention of the fashion show (Evans, 2013), an event central to the temporal and representational logic of fashion. He founded the Chambre Syndicale de la Confection et de la Couture pour Dames (now the Fédération de la Haute Couture et de la Mode), which regulates the fashion calendar, itself a tool of regulation of the temporal dynamic of fashion and its seasons. In the nineteenth century other instances of legitimation consolidated or emerged such as fashion magazines and department stores, which all participated in the formation of the field of fashion, whose geographical centre became Paris (Rocamora, 2009; Steele, 2017). Agents of consecration also include educational institutions and regulatory bodies, such as, in the United Kingdom, the British Fashion Council. In arguing that the field of fashion is a mediatised field, what are the implications for field theory? If mediatisation encompasses all social spheres, this has ramifications for social theory, including, as Couldry (2012) notes, Bourdieuian field theory, and one should look at the ways mediatisation theory can be brought into dialogue with field theory.

To create a "bridge" between the two theories, Couldry (2014b, p. 59) builds on Bourdieu's notion of meta-capital. The state, following Bourdieu, is a space of power that exercises forces on all fields and influences the conversion rate between capitals within fields (Couldry 2012; 2014a; 2014b). Bourdieu captures this influence with the term "meta-capital", a form of capital, then, that works across fields and has power over the other forms of capital (ibid.; see Bourdieu and Wacquant, 1992). In a similar vein, and to capture the idea of mediatisation as a meta-process, Couldry (2014b) proposes the term "meta media-capital", also building both on Krotz's (2007) notion of meta-process and Champagne's (1990) notion of media-capital (but see also Bolin, 2016 for a discussion of the limits of the concept of meta media-capital; and Couldry, 2019 for a response to this).

Jansson (2015) too has made a conceptual link between field theory and mediatisation theory; through the Bourdieuian notion of doxa – the uncontested norms and beliefs at play in a field (see e.g., Bourdieu and Wacquant, 1992, p. 73). Jansson (2015, p. 57) talks of "communicational doxa" to refer to that which "prescribes the ways in which social agents should communicate with one another, within and across fields, and with what media". This allows him to propose "a Bourdieusian understanding of mediatization", whereby mediatisation is a meta-process referring to the integration of media in a field's doxa (p. 58). Barnard (2018) also brings mediatisation theory into dialogue with Bourdieuian field theory to look at the mediatisation of the field of journalism, focusing on the ways Twitter shapes journalistic practices. He talks about "mediatized superstructure" to draw attention to the "new dynamics" that inform social spaces "in increasingly mediatized field contexts" (p. 49). Like Jansson, he mobilises the Bourdieuian notion of doxa to argue that Twitter has been incorporated into the orthodoxy of journalism.

To create another bridge between mediatisation theory and field theory, I turn to the notion of logic, for not only is it at the heart of mediatisation theory, as captured in the expression "media logic", but it is also a significant term in Bourdieu's writing. Couldry (2012, p. 137) evokes, but does not pursue this line of thought, a possible bridging of field theory and mediatisation theory via the notion of logic, when he notes: "mediatization as a term is perfectly compatible with field theory which insists upon paying attention to the 'logics' or working of specific field". Similarly, although he does not elaborate on Bourdieu's notion of logic nor on that of media logic, Jansson's (2015, p. 18) writing draws attention to the possible conceptual linking between field logic and media logic when he writes: "the problem [of specification in mediatisation research] lies in the difficulties of unpacking the relationships between media and other social forces, which together mould the logic of practice with different social forces" (p. 14). To talk about the mediatisation of a field, then, is to say that media logic has become a significant logic at play in this field.

"Logic" is a recurring term in Bourdieu's writing. Not only does it form the basis of a book title, *The Logic of Practice*, but it is also a key notion in his articulation of field theory, such as when he writes, for instance, "Fields are spaces. Their logics have invariants but can be defined as much by their variations, their singularities, their specificities as by their invariants" (Bourdieu, 2015b, p. 32). Fields are informed by universal as well as field-specific logics, which are the mechanisms and principles that inform a field's dynamic and the practices at play there (see e.g., Bourdieu, 2015a, p. 474; 1991). In that respect, when thinking about fashion in terms of field we can talk about the logic of fashion.

The field of fashion is informed by logics that are shared across all fields of cultural production, such as the logic of struggle between players, the quest for the dominant definition of the field and attendant values, or the tensions between commerce and art. Yet, certain logics are more salient in, or even particular to, this field. The logic of commerce, for instance, is central to it: fashion goods are largely produced to be sold on a market.

The logic of distinction is another key logic of the field of fashion, as authors such as Simmel (1957), Veblen (1994), and indeed Bourdieu (1996a) have argued. Whilst Veblen and Bourdieu focused on class distinction, more recently, fashion studies scholars have also looked at the role of gender, race, or ethnicity in the articulation of distinct individual and group identities through dress (see e.g., Barnard, 2020).

Speed has become a significant logic of the field of fashion too. Fashion is the orchestrated renewal of style, increasingly so at an accelerated speed: witness the birth, in the 1970s, of the fast fashion system, as well as the multiplication of fashion seasons. Where the fashion calendar once featured only the Spring/Summer and Autumn/Winter collections only, it is now also rhythmed by Resort and Pre-Fall collections, with the temporal flow of fashion also punctuated by one-off "drops" which consumers have access to for a very short period of time. Digital fashion media have also played an important role in the acceleration of fashion time, by promoting, for instance, a "now" time informed by the values of speed and transience (Rocamora, 2013).

Both in the work of Bourdieu and in mediatisation theory, the notion of logic helps us grasp the idea of formative foundational forces and patterns at play in a social space. The media exercise such a "social force" (Altheide and Snow, 1979, p. 9), as an interrogation of the mediatisation of the field of fashion indicates. To say that the field of fashion has become mediatised is to say that one of the key logics at play there is a media logic, and to investigate the mediatisation of the field of fashion involves identifying the media logics, and concurrent effects, that shape this field. As mentioned earlier, mediatisation has to be thought through as a differentiated process, which implies acknowledging that there is not a single overarching media logic but various media logics.

Recent developments in mediatisation theory are useful for interrogating a specific media logic at play in the field of fashion: datafication. In being digitised, media are not just means of communication but means of generating data too (Couldry and Hepp, 2018; Breiter and Hepp, 2018). With the deepening of our engagement with increasingly digitised media we have entered a new stage of mediatisation whereby our practices are being constructed through data (Couldry and Hepp, 2018; Hepp, 2020). Hepp calls this new stage "deep mediatization" (Hepp, 2016, p. 91). At this stage "all elements of our social world are intricately related to digital media and their underlying infrastructures"; data becomes entangled with our everyday experiences (Hepp, 2020, p. 5). Converted into digital information and computerised data sets, our practices have become datafied (Couldry and Yu, 2018, p. 4473). That is, deep mediatisation is a stage of "datafication"; a term Mayer-Schönberger and Cukier (2013, p. 78) coined to refer to the putting of a phenomenon into "a quantified format so it can be tabulated and analyzed". It is the process whereby large amounts of data are produced, collected, stored, and translated into quantifiable measures used to identify patterns and inform decisions and behaviours, thereby contributing to an increased quantification of the social (p. 78)

Outside of discussions of deep mediatisation, datafication is at the heart of much critical data studies, where, as with mediatisation theory, its sociocultural implications are problematised (see e.g., Beer, 2017; Gillespie, 2016; Kitchin, 2014; Lupton, 2016; Van Dijck et al., 2018). For Van Dijck and Poell (2013), who draw on Altheide and Snow, datafication is a defining logic of social media. They note that "in processing data, a platform does not merely 'measure' certain expressions or opinions, but also helps mould them" (p. 10). Although they do not refer to the term "mediatisation", their use of the word "mould" brings it to mind – Hepp (2013), for instance, regularly refers to the moulding power of the media in his writing on mediatisation – which points to the idea of datafication as a logic of deep mediatisation. Van Dijck and Poell restrict their analysis to social media but their linking of the notion of logic to that of datafication, together with their insistence on the moulding power of platforms through data, is useful for framing datafication more generally as a media logic at the stage of deep mediatisation. Andersen (2018, p. 1447) suggests as much, though without elaborating on it, when he writes:

The changes brought about by deep mediatization are, besides social and cultural, also epistemological changes to the extent they make us act, understand, and get to know about things according to the "logic" of data and algorithmic processing, archiving, or ordering.

In other words, and using Bourdieuian terminology, deep mediatisation is a stage at which datafication has become a key field logic. In the next section, I discuss some of its manifestations in the particular field of fashion by bringing into dialogue field theory, theories of mediatisation, and theories of datafication. Except maybe for the work of Couldry and Hepp, mediatisation scholars have not fully engaged with critical data studies to look at digital mediatisation. Conversely critical data studies scholars have tended to ignore the literature on mediatisation. I am advocating for a more systematic encounter between mediatisation theory and critical data studies, and in the remainder of this chapter I show that the two can usefully be brought into dialogue with each other to look at processes of digital mediatisation.

III Deep mediatisation of the field of fashion

In *The Aisles Have Eyes*, Turow (2017) discusses the datafication of the retail sector, often referring to the fashion industry. He gives the example of fashion brick and mortar stores that, upon a customer's entrance to the premises, send buying recommendations to their mobile, thanks to data accumulated through visits to the store's website and past purchases (p. 10; see also Lupton, 2016, p. 30).

The tracking and tracing of customer purchases is not a new thing – it developed throughout the twentieth century – but with the invention of digital technologies, faster computerisation and new communication tools such as mobile phones, it has intensified in recent years (Turow, 2017, p. 10). "Quantifying the world" is not new either and has existed for centuries (Mayer-Schönberger and Cukier, 2013, p. 79). However, in the past 50 years, and in particular since the beginning of the new millennium, it has significantly increased with the collection of large data sets (also known as Big Data) thanks to the wide reach of digital technologies and digitisation (Kitchin and Lauriault, 2018; Van Dijck et al., 2018).

In the field of fashion, in recent years algorithm-led fashion platforms have proliferated, which is part of a wider intensification of the datafication of fashion. Shopify, Farfetch, Depop, Lyst, Trouva, Stitch Fix, and Unmade are a few examples only. On such platforms data is collected to inform buying and selling decisions and recommendations, as well as the production of commodities that are predicted to be successful with customers. Fashion search platform Lyst (2020) put it thus: "[… we] track more than 10 million global searches a month, crunching queries, page views and sales statistics every minute, and we use this data to tell the stories of what the world wants to wear".

Fashion shopping means browsing in brick-and-mortar stores, but it also means online searching, now a common way of engaging with fashion that draws attention to its deep mediatisation. For digital search is one of its key features, and "a significant part of our current system of media" enabled by the processing of large data sets by search engines (Andersen, 2018, p. 1142). Andersen talks about a "culture of search", whereby online search has become a normalised everyday cultural activity and searching "a form of communicative action" at the heart of deep mediatisation (p. 1141).

Through their online searching fashion consumers leave traces that companies can track to gather data that feeds back into their business strategy. Digital traces are the basis of datafication and of deep mediatisation (Breiter and Hepp, 2018, p. 387). Adidas, for instance, can track the clickstream data of consumers who have watched their ads on YouTube to collect information about them (Amoore and Piotukh, 2016, p. 9). Digital tracking is also used in the field of fashion media, such as to inform media content. *Vogue International*, for instance, can track the content readers engage with throughout the day to identify reading patterns. Also monitoring social engagement and keyword searches, this enables them "to act on those behaviors and reach record readership" (Barber, 2020). The trend mentioned in the first part of this chapter for fashion and beauty companies to invest in film studios, is also an opportunity for the sector to collect customer data (Chitrakorn, 2021).

Thus, data analyst positions are now regularly advertised in the field of fashion to support "data-inspired decision making", as Burberry (2021) put it in a job advertisement for a "Business Analyst – Analytics". Fashion business site FashionUnitedUK writes of the "fashion data analyst":

> The world of fashion has changed tremendously in the last decade, paving the way for new jobs in fashion. [...] The responsibility of a data analyst working in fashion is to utilize all digital information collected to help retail and fashion companies become more profitable by predicting trends and consumer behaviour.
>
> (Yu, 2019)

2006 saw the creation of Launchmetrics, a marketing platform specialising in data analytics in the field of fashion, "that believes in the evolution of an industry where digital has changed the speed, expectations, and inspirations of the market", as they state on their website. Large data sets, thanks to the speed and power of digital technologies and computers, can be collected and analysed very quickly (Holmes, 2017). In the field of fashion, where speed is a key logic, being fast becomes an asset, which the fast collection of data is promoted as enabling.

Data has also become central to the discourse and practice of that new form of marketing born out of the rise of bloggers and Instagrammers: influencer marketing. Various start-ups have been created in recent years that place data at the heart of their services and self-representation. With titles such as influencer platform or influencer marketing data platform, companies such as Klear.com, Track, and socialbakers.com promote software and data as key players in the business of influence, now a significant global fashion business too. Klear.com, who, in their own words, "are data geeks", state: "Modern marketers need data-driven solutions to have a competitive edge and make the best decisions. Klear's sophisticated technology supports some of the world's largest organizations and empowers influencers around the world" (Klear, 2020). Such companies tap into what Van Dijck (2014, p. 198) calls dataism, that is, "the belief in Big Data", in quantification and in the tracking of human behaviour through online media technologies.

The term "belief" brings to mind the work of Bourdieu, for whom central to the functioning of a field is a belief in the values that inform it. Belief is a universal field logic; "an inherent part of belonging to a field" which exerts its forces on it (Bourdieu, 1997, p. 67). With deep mediatisation the belief in quantified data has become a dominant belief of social fields. As Mau (2019, p. 13) notes, "All numbers deployed in public discourse require a leap of faith – they have to be accepted as correct in order to exert their cold charisma. Numbers that no-one believes in have no value in social communication."

In the field of fashion, the belief in quantified data intensified during the Covid-19 pandemic, with the further digitisation of this field. Showrooms and trade shows, for instance, moved online, and a host of fashion brands adopted new digital features to support their e-commerce, "including live streams, 360-degree imagery, more data science and virtual reality" (McDowell, 2021, n.p.). In-person fashion shows were replaced by online events, further contributing to the mediatisation of fashion and its embrace of a logic of entertainment (see Rocamora, 2017), whilst the fashion retail sector moved further away from the high street and towards e-commerce (Collins, 2021). Fashion brands, already active on Instagram, started engaging with TikTok, a move indicative of a wider platformisation of fashion whereby brands are increasingly turning into content creators and media platforms (Rocamora, 2018).

This intensified digitisation of fashion has been celebrated and called for by many business advocates. At the core of their discourse is the idea that data is an answer to the current crisis. A McKinsey (2020) report puts it thus: "Some apparel, fashion, and luxury companies won't survive the current crisis; others will emerge better positioned for the future. Much will depend on their digital and analytics capabilities." "Digital and analytics", the report also claims, "will play a critical role in helping companies emerge stronger from the crisis".

The statements draw attention to the "trust in numbers" (Porter, 1995) that underpins the logic of datafication, but it also brings to light its commercial dimension. Indeed, datafication is a process deeply intertwined with commodification (Couldry, 2018; Morozov, 2015), a logic at the heart of the field of fashion too. Launchmetrics make this clear when they state that: "Data and technology bring a sharp focus to profitability, accountability, and efficiency while enabling the type of quick decision making required for agility." That is, data are to be capitalised on. In Bourdieuian terms, it is a form of capital. Thus Mau (2019, p. 8) draws on Bourdieu to propose the notion of "digital status data", a type of data that by virtue of being a sign of distinction and reputation "is a form of symbolic capital which can be used to one's own advantage and converted to other social currencies" (see also Sadowski (2019) on "data capital"). As Christin (2020, p. 4) has shown of journalists, for instance, metrics are "symbolic resources" they can mobilise in various institutional contexts.

Metrics are key resources for fashion influencers too (see also Rocamora 2022). Their number of social media "likes" and "followers", and the correlated engagement rate, are elements of their symbolic capital. Likes and followers metrics allow influencers to distinguish themselves by signalling their reputation and capitalising on it. Collected and stored, not only are they informed by the logic of datafication, but they are a currency influencers trade against money when selling their service in the "economy of 'likes'" (Lindell, 2017, p. 3; Hearn, 2010). Influencers are also an instance of what Hepp (2016) calls "media-related pioneer communities", and whose activities are central to deep mediatisation. By mediating fashion across digital platforms and attracting large audiences they have participated in further anchoring the field of fashion to the digital and datafication.

Deep mediatisation also means the transformation into digital media of objects not normally seen as media (Hepp and Hasebrink, 2018). An example is dress, as the case of wearables illustrates. Wearables are digitally connected devices worn on the body. Throughout the 1990s various designers started experimenting with the technology, developing jewellery and other accessories such as glasses. Wearables can be used to track users' emotions and bodily sensations. They are also "technologies of the self": wearers can use the data they provide to monitor themselves and shape their everyday activities, as the quantified-self movement indicates (see Lupton, 2016, after Foucault). The datafied self of wearables is a mediatised self.

At the heart of datafication are algorithms, a procedure for the rapid automatic processing of data based on pre-determined calculations and resulting in the creation of new informational outputs (Amoore and Piotukh, 2016; Bucher, 2018; Gillespie, 2014). Fashionunited, for instance, informs potential fashion data analysts that "using math skills and formulas, a data analyst will help create algorithms to optimize the brand's performance, sales and engagement online" (Yu 2019). In a context in which computational tools have become a pervasive medium of expression, algorithms are now "a key logic governing the flows of information on which we depend", the meaningfulness attributed to it, and the way it is perceived (Gillespie, 2014, p. 167). The power given algorithms is premised on a new "knowledge logic" whereby they are given a role once attributed to "credential experts, the scientific method, common sense, or the word of God" only (p. 168).

Algorithms, however, are not just technological, they are cultural and social too (Beer, 2017; Bucher, 2018; Cotter, 2018). They have a veneer of objectivity, but they are human made entities, and do not exist outside of the social (Gillespie, 2014; 2016). As Hepp (2020, p. 75) notes, noting the role of algorithms in the process of deep mediatisation:

> in specifying the possible molding power of algorithms it is important to keep in mind that the organizations – companies, state agencies, administrations – that commission the coding of software have certain purposes and interests as well as explicit and implicit models of the social which become inscribed in the algorithms they produce.

In their ability to filter, search, prioritise, and recommend, algorithms have the power to exclude, and are therefore tools "in the deployment or expression of power"; they can "create, maintain or cement norms" as well as "decide what matters" (Beer, 2017, pp. 3, 6). Hepp talks about the "moulding power of algorithms", insisting on their roles in the process of deep mediatisation. Looking at this process then entails looking at the role of algorithms and the way they select, include or exclude information in particular fields.

In the field of fashion algorithms have become key players. The head-line of a 2018 *Racked* article, for instance, reads "Style is an algorithm". It reports on Amazon and eBay's Echo Look application which, upon the user's uploading a selfie, selects a range of articles and tells them "which set of clothes looks better, processed by style-analyzing algorithms and some assistance from humans". Algorithms have taken on a central role in the circulation of fashion images too. Intrinsic to the working of Instagram, for instance, which is now a key space of "fashion media discourse" (Rocamora, 2009), algorithms have become significant players in the field of fashion media. By regulating the blending of posts edited by fashion influencers with those of brands and private individuals into a continuous flow of images on a user's feed, they have taken over human editors by becoming a sort of meta-editor, as in the metrics journalism that Christin (2020) discusses (see also Cardon, 2016). There, the algorithmic has become "a competing logic" to the editorial (Gillespie, 2014, p. 192). Algorithms operate "regimes of visibility" whereby decisions are made as to what content gets shown to whom, what information is included or excluded, who is seen and heard and who is not (Bucher, 2018, p. 82). At a time when being visible is often a path to success, algorithms grant the capital of visibility – a symbolic capital – necessary for success in a field (Lundahl, 2020). This is why they must be seen as a "powerful gatekeeper" (Bucher, 2018, p. 7); "the new 'gatekeepers' of public digital space", as Cardon (2016, p. 95) also puts it.

Bourdieu has insisted on the importance of gatekeeping in regulating membership of a field (see e.g., Bourdieu, 1996b). In the field of fashion, gatekeepers include established journalists, for instance, but they now also include algorithms. In this field, where the logic of visibility is central to one's membership (Entwistle and Rocamora, 2006) algorithms's power to decide who is seen and who is not is also a power to decide who belongs and who does not. This begs the question, what is the visual fashion media landscape as shaped by algorithms? This is an issue I addressed when looking at the role of search engines and Instagram in representation of "*la parisienne*", a trope of the discourse on fashionable style. A normative vision of fashionable Parisian femininity is promoted on Google and Instagram that privileges white, thin, young, non-disabled bodies at the expense of diversity and inclusion (Rocamora, 2019). Further studies are needed, in the field of mediatisation studies, to understand the role of algorithms in the moulding of discourses and representations at play in a particular field.

In representing information in particular ways, algorithms, Wade Morris (2015, p. 452) argues, are "like intermediaries" that exercise power over the way knowledge is constructed. He builds on Bourdieu's (1996a) notion of cultural intermediaries – taste makers situated between producers and consumers – to conceptualise algorithms' role in intermediation mechanisms, and their status as entities able to collect and process data to make taste recommendations. Like cultural intermediaries, algorithms shape the representation of culture. To capture this idea Wade Morris (2015, p. 459) defines algorithms as "infomediaries", also arguing that they deserve as much attention as other cultural intermediaries in studies of the mediation of culture or, following the terminology used in mediatisation theory, the deep mediatisation of culture.

Like Wade Morris, critical data theorists Gillespie (2014) and Bucher (2018) do not use the concept of mediatisation, but their writing often brings it to mind in drawing attention to the power algorithms have in moulding the social. Gillespie (2014, p. 187), for instance, notes that "the working logics of these algorithms not only shape user practices, but also lead users to internalize their norms and priorities". Likewise, Bucher (2018) writes that at the heart of her book is "the basic question of how software is shaping the conditions of everyday life", and she argues that moments of sociality "are mediated, augmented, produced, and governed by networked systems powered by software and algorithms" (p. 2). Woven into people's everyday life, algorithms have an "agential force" that has the power to produce new practices, experiences, and realities (p. 50). They "do something" to various social domains (p. 50).

This doing is instrumental to processes of deep mediatisation, such as in the field of culture. As Nieborg and Poell (2018, p. 6) note, "algorithmic logic" has become central to cultural production, since the creation and circulation of cultural goods is increasingly shaped by the recommendations and rankings of algorithms. Cultural production, they argue, has become contingent in two ways: contingent in that it is dependent on a group of powerful platforms, namely, in the West: Google, Amazon, Meta, Apple, and Microsoft; and contingent in that media products and services by being informed by data (such as datafied user feedback) are constantly open to revision and recirculation (Nieborg and Poell, 2019; 2018, p. 6). This results in what they call the "contingent commodity"; it has a "modular design" and is "continuously reworked and repackaged, informed by datafied user feedback" (Nieborg and Poell, 2018, p. 1). Similarly, Bucher (2018, p. 2) invites us to think about the ways dependence on data and algorithms "might funnel cultural production in particular directions". This raises the question: What is the contingent fashion commodity? More generally: How do algorithms and data shape the production, consumption, and representation of fashion? That is, what are the implications of deep mediatisation on practices, commodities, and players in the field of fashion?

In this chapter, I have started addressing those questions. Fully answering them is beyond its scope and necessitates empirical investigation. However, the ideas presented here will hopefully form a springboard researchers can appropriate to empirically research the deep mediatisation of fashion. In focusing on this field, I am not making any claims as to the extent and manifestation of mediatisation across all fields. Rather, by focusing on one particular field, in a particular historical time, the present chapter calls for, and supports, discussions of the differentiated nature and manifestations of mediatisation, and the idea that mediatisation varies across time and space. Furthermore, empirical research of processes of mediatisation, and in particular deep mediatisation are still too rare. Empirically grounded field-specific analyses should be conducted to fully interrogate the ways individual and institutional agents' practices and experiences are moulded by the media, as well as by data. Finally, whilst there is a growing body of empirical studies of the ways datafication shapes practices, most significantly perhaps in discussions of the quantified self (Lupton, 2016), those are too often split from discussions of mediatisation, a concept which precisely helps approach the idea of the structuring force of digital data in everyday life. By bringing mediatisation theory more systematically into dialogue with critical data studies, the complexities and interrelatedness of both processes – mediatisation and datafication – can be better understood.

Conclusion

The chapter offers a reflection on Bourdieuian field theory in light of theories of mediatisation, and in particular deep mediatisation. It answers Couldry's call for more attention to be given to the way mediatisation theory can contribute to social theory, including Bourdieuian theory. Focusing on the notions of logic and datafication, it has discussed the ways deep mediatisation is articulated in the field of fashion, also bringing into dialogue the wider scholarship on datafication with that on mediatisation. In doing so, the chapter also shows the relevance of Bourdieuian field theory and attendant concepts for understanding social and digital media. Finally, it provides a conceptual framework with which to investigate contemporary changes in the field of fashion. The chapter also offers scholars of mediatisation a possible point of comparison from which to assess the extent to which mediatisation may be context-dependent and a process differentiated across social spaces and media types. Further field-specific studies, and dialogue between studies of different fields, it is hoped, will allow one to grasp the complex and heterogeneous nature of mediatisation.

References

Altheide, D.L. (2004). Media Logic and Political Communication. *Political Communication*, 21 (3), 293–296.
Altheide, D.L. (2013). Media Logic, Social Control, and Fear. *Communication Theory* 23, 223–238.
Altheide, D.L. (2014). *Media Edge*. New York: Peter Lang.
Altheide, D.L. and Snow, P. (1979). *Media Logic*. London: Sage.
Amoore, L. and Piotukh, V. (2016). Introduction. In L. Amoore and V. Piotukh (eds) *Algorithmic life* (pp 1–18). London: Routledge.
Andersen, Jack (2018). Archiving, Ordering, and Searching. *Media, Culture and Society*, 40 (8), 1135–1150.
Asp, K. (2014). News Media Logic in a New Institutional Perspective. *Journalism Studies*, 15 (3), 256–270.
Barber, K. (2020). How Vogue's International approach to audience data helped it reach record readers. Digiday. https://digiday.com/media/how-vogues-internatio nal-approach-to-audience-data-helped-it-reach-record-readers/.
Barnard, S.R. (2018). Tweeting #Ferguson. *New Media and Society*, 20 (7), 2252–2271.
Barnard, M. (ed.) (2020). *Fashion Theory: A Reader*. London: Routledge.
Beer, D. (2017). The Social Power of Algorithms. *Information, Communication & Society*, 20 (1), 1–13.
Bolin, G. (2016). *Value and the Media*. London: Routledge.
Bourdieu, P. (1986). The Forms of Capital. In J.E. Richardson (ed.) *Handbook of Theory of Research for the Sociology of Education* (pp. 241–58). Greenwood Press.
Bourdieu, P. (1991). Le champ littéraire. *Actes de la Recherche en Sciences Sociales*, 89, September, 3–46.
Bourdieu, P. (1996a). *Distinction*. London: Routledge.
Bourdieu, P. (1996b). *The Rules of Art*. Cambridge: Polity.
Bourdieu, P. (1997). *The Logic of Practice*. Cambridge: Polity.
Bourdieu, P. (2015a). *Sociologie Générale I*. Paris: Seuil.
Bourdieu, P. (2015b). *Sociologie Générale II*. Paris: Seuil.
Bourdieu, P. and Delsaut, Y. (1975). Le couturier et sa griffe. *Actes de la Recherche en Sciences Sociales*, 1, 7–36.
Bourdieu, P. and Wacquant, L. (1992). *An Invitation to Reflexive Sociology*. Cambridge: Polity.

Breiter, A. and Hepp, A. (2018). The Complexity of Datafication. In A. Hepp, A. Breiter and U. Hasebrik (eds) *Communicative Figurations* (pp 387–404). Basingstoke: Palgrave.

Bucher, T. (2018). *If…Then*. Oxford: Oxford University Press.

Burberry (2021). Burberry. https://burberrycareers.com/job/London-Senior-Busin ess-Analyst-Not/715461200/?jobPipeline=Indeed

Cardon, D. (2016). Deconstructing the Algorithm. In R. Seyfert and J. Roberge (eds) *Algorithmic Cultures* (pp. 95–110). London: Routledge.

Champagne, P. (1990). *Faire l'opinion*. Paris: Minuit.

Chitrakorn, K. (2021). Entertaiment Studios. *Vogue Business*. https://www.vogueb usiness.com/beauty/entertainment-studios-should-beauty-brands-invest?utm_ source=Vogue+Business&utm_campaign=37560931dd-EMAIL_CAMPAIGN_2 021_04_21_05_39&utm_medium=email&utm_term=0_5d1e7914df-3756093 1dd-58931108

Christin, A. (2020). *Metrics at Work*. Princeton University Press.

Collins, S. (2021). The Landscape of Fashion Is Changing but It's Still All about the Brand. The Fashion Law. https://www.thefashionlaw.com/the-landscape-of-fash ion-retail-is-changing-but-its-still-all-about-the-brand/

Cotter, K. (2018). Playing the Visibility Game. *New Media & Society*, 21, 1–19.

Couldry, N. (2008). Mediatization of Mediation? *New Media & Society*, 10, 373–391.

Couldry, N. (2012). *Media Society World*. Cambridge: Polity.

Couldry, N. (2014a). Mediatization and the Future of Field Theory. In K. Lundby (ed.) *Mediatization of Communication* (pp. 227–248). Berlin: de Gruyter.

Couldry, N. (2014b). When Mediatization Hits the Ground (pp. 54–71). In A. Hepp and F. Krotz (eds) *Mediatized Worlds: Culture and Society in a Media Age*. New York: Macmillan.

Couldry, N. (2018). Tracing Capitalism's Turn to Data. *International Journal of Communication*, 12, 701–705.

Couldry, N. (2019) Is the "Field of Power" Really a Field? In F. Till and G. Bolin (eds) *Fritt Fran Fältet*, Södertörns Högskola.

Couldry, N. and Hepp, A. (2013). Conceptualizing Mediatization. *Communication Theory*, 23, 191–202.

Couldry, N. and Hepp, A. (2018). The Continuing Lure of Mediated Centre in Time of Deep Mediatization. *Media, Culture & Society*, 40 (1), 114–117.

Couldry N. and Yu, J. (2018). Deconstructing Datafication's Brave New World. *New Media & Society*, 20 (12), 4473–4491.

Dahlgren, P. (1996). Media Logic in Cyberspace. *Javnost – The Public*, 3 (3), 59–72.

Deacon, D. and Stanyer, J. (2014). Mediatization: Key Concept of Conceptual Bandwagon. *Media, Culture and Society*, 36 (7), 1–13. DOI: 10.1177/ 0163443714542218

Entwistle, J. and Rocamora, A. (2006). The Field of Fashion Materialized. *Sociology*, 40 (4), 735–751.

Evans, C. (2013). *The Mechanical Smile*. New Haven, CT: Yale University Press.

Gillespie, T. (2014). The Relevance of Algorithms. In T. Gillespie, P.J. Boczkowski and K.A. Foot (eds) (pp. 167–193). *Media Technologies*. Cambridge, MA: MIT Press.

Gillespie, T. (2016). Algorithms. In Peters, B. (ed.) *Key Words: a vocabulary of information society and culture*.

Halliday, R. (2022). *The Fashion Show Goes Live*. London: Bloomsbury.

Hearn, A. (2010). Structuring Feeling. *Ephemera*, 10 (3/4), 421–438.

Hepp, A. (2013/2011). *Cultures of Mediatization*. Cambridge: Polity.

Hepp, A. (2016). Pioneer Communities. *Media, Culture and Society*, 38 (6), 918–933.

Hepp, A. (2020). *Deep Mediatization*. Abingdon: Routledge.

Hepp, A. and Hasebrink, U. (2018). Researching Transforming Communications in Times of Deep Mediatization. In A. Hepp, A. Breiter and U. Hasebrink (eds) *Communicative Figurations* (pp. 387–404). Basingstoke: Palgrave.

Hjarvard, S. (2009). Soft Individualism. In K. Lundby (ed.) *Mediatization*. New York: Peter Lang, 159–177.

Holmes, D.E. (2017). *Big Data*. Oxford: Oxford University Press.

Jansson, A. (2015). Using Bourdieu in Critical Mediazation Research. *MedieKultur*, 58, 13–29.

Kitchin, R. (2014). *The Data Revolution*. Sage.

Kitchin, R. and Lauriault, T.P (2018). Toward Critical Data Studies. In J. Thatcher, A. Shears and J. Eckert (eds) *Thinking Big Data in Geography* (pp. 3–20). University of Nebraska Press.

Klear (2020). The Klear Influence Score. https://klear.com/what-is-influence

Klinger, U. and Svensson, J. (2018). The End of Media Logics? *New Media and Society*, 20 (12), 4653–4670.

Kristensen, Nete N. and Christensen, Christa L. (2017). The Mediatization of Fashion. In O. Driessens, G. Bolin, A. Hepp and S. Hjarvards (eds) *Dynamics of Mediatization* (pp. 225–245). London: Palgrave Macmillan.

Krotz, F. (2007). The Meta-Process of "Mediatization" as a Conceptual Frame. *Global Media and Communication*, 3 (3), 256–260.

Landerer, N. (2013). Rethinking the Logics. *Communication Theory*, 23, 239–258.

Lindell, J. (2017). Bringing Field Theory to Social Media. *Social Media + Society*, Oct.–Dec., 1–11.

Lundahl, O. (2020). Algorithmic Meta-Capital, *Information, Communication and Society*, 1–16. https://doi.org/10.1080/1369118X.2020.1864006

Lupton, D. (2016). *The Quantified Self*. Cambridge: Polity.

Lyst (2020). About. https://www.lyst.co.uk/about/

Mau, S. (2019/2017). *The Metric Society*. Cambridge: Polity.

Mayer-Schönberger, V. and Cukier, K. (2013). *Big Data*. London: John Murray.

McDowell, M. (2021). Digital Wholesaling Invites New Perks, New Complications. https://www.voguebusiness.com/technology/digital-wholesaling-invites-new-perks-new-complications (accessed 24-02-21).

McKinsey (2020). https://www.mckinsey.com/~/media/mckinsey/business%20functions/organization/our%20insights/to%20emerge%20stronger%20from%20the%20covid%2019%20crisis%20companies%20should%20start%20reskilling%20their%20workforces%20now/to-emerge-stronger-from-the-covid-19-crisis.pdf

Morozov (2015). Digital Technologies and the Future of Data Capitalism. Socialeurope. https://www.socialeurope.eu/digital-technologies-and-the-future-of-data-capitalism

Nieborg, D.B. and Poell, T. (2018). The Platformization of Cultural Production. *New Media & Society*, 20 (11), 1–18.

Nieborg, D.B. and Poell, T. (2019). The Platformization of Making Media. In M. Deuze and M. Pringer (eds) *Making Media* (pp. 85–96). Amsterdam: Amsterdam University Press.

Porter, T.M. (1995). *Trust in Numbers*. Princeton University Press.

Rocamora, A. (2009). *Fashioning the City*. London: I.B. Tauris.

Rocamora, A. (2013). New Fashion Times. In S. Black, A. de la Haye, J. Entwistle, A. Rocamora, R. Root and H. Thomas (eds) *The Handbook of Fashion Studies* (pp. 61–77). Oxford: Berg.

Rocamora, A. (2017). Mediatization and Digitization in the Field of Fashion. *Fashion Theory*, 21 (5), 505–522.

Rocamora, A. (2018). Mediatization and Digital Retail. In A. Geczy and V. Karaminas (eds) *The End of Fashion* (pp. 99–112). London: Bloomsbury.

Rocamora, A. (2019). #parisienne. In V. Steele (ed.) *Paris, Capital of Fashion* (pp. 164–181). London: Bloomsbury.

Rocamora, A. (2022). Datafication and the Quantification of Fashion: The Case of Fashion Influencers. *Fashion Theory*. https://doi.org/10.1080/13627 04X.2022.2048527

Sadowski, J. (2019). When Data Is Capital. *Big Data and Society*, 19 (Jan.– June), 1–12.

Simmel, G. (1957). Fashion. *The American Journal of Sociology*, 62 (6), 541–558.

Steele, V. (2017). *Paris Fashion*. London: Bloomsbury.

Strömbäck, J. (2008). Four Phases of Mediatization. *International Journal of Press/ Politics*, 13 (3), 228–46.

Strömbäck, J. and Dimitrova, D. (2014). Mediatization and Media Interventionism. *International Journal of Press/Politics*, 16 (1), 30–49.

Turow, J. (2017). *The Aisles Have Eyes*. New Haven, CT: Yale University Press.

Van Dijck, J. (2014). Datafication, Dataism and Dataveillance. *Surveillance & Society* 12 (2), 197–208.

Van Dijck, J. and Poell, T. (2013). Understanding Social Media Logic. *Media and Communication*, 1 (1), 2–14.

Van Dijck, J., Poell, T. and de Waal, M. (2018). *The Platform Society*. Oxford University Press.

Veblen, T. (1994/1899). *The Theory of the Leisure Class*. New York: Dover.

Wade Morris, J. (2015). Curation by Code. *European Journal of Cultural Studies*, 18 (4–5), 446–463.

Yu, A. (2019). Fashion Careers: What Does a Fashion Data Analyst Do? https:// fashionunited.uk/news/fashion/fashion-careers-what-does-a-fashion-data-anal yst-do/2019041942753

5 Mediatisation and Climate Change
Identifying and Facing Challenges

Sigrid Kannengießer and Patrick McCurdy

Mediatisation research has increased in quantity and complexity during the last decade. A growing number of publications, including this edited volume, show the research field's diversity and its importance. Mediatisation, as we define it in this chapter, is a meta-process through which media gain importance in all societal areas and through which media surroundings of individual users become more and more complex (Krotz, 2007a). In tandem with the increasing importance of media, and especially digital media technologies, are the immense material socio-ecological effects of mediatisation, harming human beings and the environment. We have argued elsewhere (Kannengießer & McCurdy, 2020) that mediatisation scholarship has largely ignored the socio-ecological effects, environmental issues, and impacts intertwined with mediatisation processes. Pointing to the resources and energy needed for mediatisation and the e-waste it produces, we showed that mediatisation implies a complex material dimension that mediatisation research must acknowledge – not only to understand these processes holistically but to confront their socio-ecological challenges. Restated, the digital media technologies which sustain our current state of "deep mediatization" (Hepp, 2020) consist of a vast number and array of digital media devices. These devices are often produced under severe working conditions with resources that have been extracted via destructive and polluting extraction processes and are frequently disposed after only a short while in use in likewise polluting and dangerous processes – in places like Agbogloshi in Ghana, the location of one of the world's largest e-waste dumps. Intertwined with digital devices is the multiplicity of online communication processes they facilitate and maintain. Not only are these processes a prominent component of mediatisation, but they require an ever-increasing amount of energy whose dominant mode of production still comes via fossil fuels (Kannengießer & McCurdy, 2020).

In this chapter we integrate parts of our previous argumentation (Kannengießer & McCurdy, 2020), extending our reasoning by focussing on the interplay between mediatisation and climate change. Here, we argue that mediatisation research must acknowledge mediatisation's link to climate change to better understand and make visible mediatisation's

DOI: 10.4324/9781003324591-8

socio-ecological effects on the climate. Within mediatisation research, climate change has mainly been dealt with as an issue of mediated discourse (Kunelius, 2014) and thereby relevant as media content. While we acknowledge and support Kunelius' focus on discourse, mediatisation scholars must also view mediatisation as a *material* process that *contributes* to climate change. In doing so, we argue that taking a material perspective on mediatisation and climate change must include a focus on energy and how the emission of carbon dioxide (produced through using fossil energy in the production, appropriation, and disposal of digital media technologies) promotes climate change. In recognising climate change as the most dangerous threat to humankind, it is also the responsibility of mediatisation research to consider how the immense effect of mediatisation on the climate can be reduced.

To make this argument, our chapter is structured as follows: first, we describe the field of mediatisation and the research gap in the interrelation between mediatisation and climate change. Here, we argue that mediatisation scholarship must grapple with the question of energy to acknowledge the effects of mediatisation on climate change. Second, research within media and communications on (i) *climate change* and (ii) *energy* are presented with an interest in links and gaps related to mediatisation. We conclude our chapter by arguing that mediatisation scholarship must recognise the interplay of digital media and climate change to make visible how mediatisation causes climate change and help develop solutions to address it and present some examples of how to research the interplay of mediatisation and climate change.

Mediatisation Research

Mediatisation, as we define it here, is a meta-process through which media gain in importance in all societal areas and by which the media surroundings of people become more and more complex (Krotz, 2007a; Livingstone & Lunt, 2014). A meta-process is a concept that can describe and explain theoretically specific economic, social, and cultural dimensions and levels of the actual change (Krotz, 2007a, p. 27). Mediatisation is thus a meta-process in tandem with other meta-processes such as globalisation, individualisation, and commercialisation. Related, Krotz (2017b) makes the point that other meta-processes may ultimately influence mediatisation and thus, there is not a singular mediatisation but different mediatisation paths. Indeed, research underwritten by a mediatisation perspective continues to be a popular approach for communication scholarship (e.g. Hepp, 2020; Skey et al., 2018; Driessens et al., 2017; Bolin, 2016; Couldry & Hepp, 2016; Hepp & Krotz, 2014; Hepp, 2013; Krotz, 2007a; 2007b; Lundby, 2008; 2014a, Hjavard, 2013; 2012; 2008).

Lundby (2014b) suggests three broad theoretical approaches to mediatisation theory: *institutional*, *cultural*, and *materialist* (2014b, p. 5;

also Hepp, Hjavard & Lundby, 2015, p. 4; for a more detailed description of the three different approaches, see Kannengießer & McCurdy, 2020, pp. 4–8). Although each orientation differs in focus, they all ask questions about the transformation of society through changes in media communication (for an overview of the historical development of the mediatisation discourse in media and communication studies, see Couldry & Hepp, 2013). According to Hjarvard (2013, p. 4), an institutionalist perspective takes a meso-level approach, thus allowing scholars to "make generalisations across individual micro-social encounters within a particular domain of culture and society" but not "totalizing accounts of universal media influence at the macro level". An institutional perspective examines how media has changed and influenced social domains and institutions such as science, religion, politics, and the arts (Lundby, 2014b).

The social-constructivist perspective (called "cultural" by Lundby, 2014b, p. 10) aims "to investigate the interrelation between the change of media communication and sociocultural change as part of everyday communication practices" (Hepp in Hepp, Hjavard & Lundby, 2015, p. 4). This approach analyses the construction of reality in media and communication processes and views a multiplicity of media processes, practices, and uses at play (Lundby, 2014b, p. 10). Facing current datafication processes, Hepp and Couldry stress the relevance of digitalisation by introducing the notion of "deep mediatization" observing the way *digital* media change society (Couldry & Hepp, 2016; Hepp, 2020).

Within mediatisation scholarship, the materialist perspective is the smallest research area. This perspective examines how media's form, composition, and configuration shape society (Lundby, 2014b, p. 28). However, within this body of research, only a handful of studies have analysed the material dimension of media technologies (e.g. Miller's 2017 analysis of the mediatisation of the automobile).

This approach to mediatisation fits into media and communication studies dealing with the visibility and invisibility of media technologies (Jansson, 2014 explicitly on mediatisation and the (in)visibility of media technologies; for a broader discourse within media and communication studies, see e.g. Lievrouw, 2014 or Gillespie, Boczkowski & Foot 2014). Bolin (2014) terms this mediatisation research strand "media as world", stressing the "roles of the hardware and software of communication in society" (Bolin, 2014, p. 188), looking at the way media technologies mould society. Although Bolin does not refer to the socio-ecological effects of mediatisation, perceiving "media as world" is a fruitful perspective for addressing scholarship's current failure to consider the effects of mediatisation on climate change. Thus our view of "media as world" must incorporate mediatisation's material dimension and, by extension, elaborate on the socio-ecological effects of the increasing importance of digital media technologies. However, before unpacking our argument in more detail, we will first sketch out the area of media and communication research that analyses climate change to show how much of this research field lacks the acknowledgement of materiality.

Climate Change in Media and Communication Research

The wicked problem of climate change has been studied from a number of perspectives within media and communications. O'Neill and Smith (2014) propose using Stuart Hall's 1973 encoding/decoding model as means to segment and review scholarship on what they term "climate visual mediated interactions". While O'Neill and Smith's focus is limited to the visual discourse of climate change, their innovative use of Hall's model offers a helpful framework for capturing climate change focussed scholarship within media and communication research. Thus drawing on both Hall (1973) and O'Neill and Smith (2014, p. 75), media and climate change scholarship may be viewed across three interrelated moments of the communication process: (1) *the moment of production*, which captures research on "the conditions and practices" surrounding the making of climate-change related texts and the production of (digital) media technologies themselves; (2) *the moment of the text*, which covers scholarship analysing the form and content of specific climate-change related texts; and (3) *the moment of consumption*, encompassing research on social actors (e.g. individuals, groups, organisations) making sense of and reacting to climate-change related texts and using (digital) media technologies. Below, we outline each of these moments in order to provide a sense as to the range and type of scholarship being conducted, and conclude this section by recognising some gaps in these approaches.

The Moment of Production

Research in this domain has studied the producers of climate communication such as journalists (e.g. Kunelius & Eide, 2012; Engesser & Brüggemann, 2016; Berglez, 2011; Schäfer & Painter, 2021), non-governmental organisations (e.g. Lück, Woznial & Wessler, 2016), celebrities (e.g. Anderson, 2011), as well as social movements (e.g. Wahlström et al., 2019). Such studies have analysed the working conditions of climate journalists, which worsened (Brüggemann & Engesser, 2013), attitudes of climate journalists (dominantly believing in climate change and not denying it, Brüggemann & Engesser, 2017), and describing climate journalists as mediators communicating scientific knowledge about climate change (Engesser & Brüggemann, 2017). This scholarship has disproportionately focussed on the global North (Schäfer & Painter, 2021). Studies have also integrated different actors, e.g. analysing the networks between journalists and agents of public relations at climate conferences organised by the United Nations (e.g. Adolphsen & Lück, 2012; Lück, Woznial & Wessler, 2016). In addition to journalists and non-governmental organisations, social movements such as Fridays for Future have come to occupy an important role in public climate change discourse on climate communication, warning about climate change and demanding action, mainly by politicians (e.g. Savolainen & Ylä-Anttila, 2021; Wahlström et al., 2019; Haunss & Sommer, 2020). Indeed a wide-ranging body of scholarship has examined how climate-change focussed social movements use the affordances of digital media to coordinate and produce their messages and politics (e.g. Askanius & Uldam, 2011; Della Porta & Parks, 2014). Our broad and brief sketch of this research field shows that media and communication research has mainly understood production as the production of texts – focussing on the actors producing media content representing climate change. But what is also highly important is the analysis of the production of media technologies themselves and their relation to climate change (see below).

The Moment of the Text

From television to film; from novels to news; a wide range of scholarship has examined how climate change has been represented across a variety of media and texts (e.g. Boyce & Lewis, 2009; Doyle, 2011; Eide, Kunelius & Kumpu, 2010; Sampei & Aoyagi-Usui, 2009; Shehata & Hopmann, 2012; Pearce et al., 2014; Wessler et al., 2016). Schäfer and Schlichting (2014) argue on the basis of a meta-analysis that print coverage of climate change has increased since the 1960s and finds its peak around political summits such as the World Summit on Sustainable Development. Indeed much academic scholarship has examined how news – across print, television, and online – has covered climate change (e.g. see above and Lester & Cottle, 2009). Topics covered include but are not limited to the politicisation and polarisation of climate change news (Chinn, Hart & Soroka, 2020), the framing of climate change news over time (Boykoff, 2007; Stecula and Merkley, 2019; Trumbo, 1996), during the COVID-19 pandemic (Stoddart, Ramos, Foster & Yla-Anttila, 2021) and news visuals (León and Erviti, 2015; O'Neil, 2013). Beyond news, scholarship has analysed popular cultural texts such as science fiction films (Svoboda, 2016; Podeschi, 2014), animated films (Starosielski, 2014), television series such as *The Simpsons* (Todd, 2009) and the growing literary genre of climate fiction (Milkoreit, 2016). Scholars have also studied the representations of climate issues and climate change in the media discourses of social movements such as, recently, *Fridays for Future* (e.g. Zabern & Tulloch, 2021) as well as the social media posts of climate-change social movements and non-governmental organisations (e.g. Blomberg et al., 2021). The studies given here are only examples from the research area dealing with media texts and climate change, which continues to be a vast and growing area of scholarship as climate change becomes an ever more threatening and tangible process.

The Moment of Reception

The effects on and reception of media users in respect to media content dealing with climate and climate change is a third area within the research field of climate communication (e.g. Boykoff, 2007; Olausson, 2011; Neverla & Taddicken, 2012; Schäfer, 2012; Taddicken & Reif, 2016; Walter, Brüggemann & Engesser, 2018; Wozniak, 2021; for an overview: Kannengießer, 2021). Schäfer and Bonfadelli (2016, pp. 331ff) summarise four recurring results in studies analysing media reception within climate communication: (1) mass media are an important and reliable source for information about climate change; (2) there is an agenda-setting effect, meaning that the relevance of climate change for recipients depends on the extent of reporting on climate change; (3) media use increases knowledge about climate change; and (4) media effects on the behaviour of recipients are still unclear. Taking a practice perspective, scholars have also considered how different actors use media – media as content and technologies – to contribute to sustainability, such as the repairing of media technologies or the fair production of media technologies (e.g. Kannengießer, 2020a; 2020b; 2019).

While climate communication scholarship has grown in scope and complexity, it still has not sufficiently grappled with how the increase in media's societal importance (call it "*mediatisation*") and digital media in particular (call it "*deep mediatisation*", see above) relates to the processes and consequences of climate change. Conscious of this oversight, we argue that it is within the responsibility of media and communication research in general and mediatisation research, in particular, to make visible and analyse the interplay between mediatisation and climate change, and to also think about solutions to reduce mediatisation's impact on the climate that can be identified when focussing on mediatisation's material dimension. Specifically, we view energy consumption within the production and appropriation of digital media as one of the core issues in mediatisation's contribution to climate change. Consequently, in the next section of this chapter, we sketch the interrelations between mediatisation and energy.

Mediatisation and Energy

Energy makes mediatisation possible.[1] Energy produces the devices and networks which create and enable our mediated worlds and energy powers them. While the production, distribution, and delivery of energy requires real-world systems and practices and has material outputs and consequences, the vital role of energy remains all but unacknowledged within mediatisation scholarship. Instead, energy's presence is assumed, taken for granted and too often folded in with the supposed immaterial nature of mediatisation processes. For example, Hjarvard's (2004) essay on the mediatisation of the global toy industry opens with the premise that "today, toys are increasing[ly] of an immaterial nature" (2004, p. 43). Hjarvard argues that toys were once solid tactile objects that children engaged with directly but now require media as a go-between. Video games, for example, are "immaterial" as they take place on screens and thus are not manipulated directly but instead by joysticks. For Hjarvard the shift from "bricks to bytes" – the shift to the immaterial – reflects the embedded nature of mediated information in contemporary culture. While Hjarvard astutely captures larger social trends, his use of "immaterial" overlooks and, indeed, masks the fact that systems and processes of mediatisation are reliant upon and intimately interwoven with systems of energy and energy production. Ecomaterialist scholar Gabrys (2015) has rightly and eloquently challenged claims concerning the immateriality of digital media and has called upon academics to recognise the "processes of materialization that digital media are entangled with" which includes energy as well as the other material aspects discussed in this section (p. 6).

The "material turn" (Bennett & Joyce, 2010) also called for by Gabrys (2015) seeks to make visible the taken for granted aspects of energy during the production, use, and disposal of media technologies (2015). This call is significant given the sheer breadth and scale of devices used to access and maintain our mediatised world. A world that is not only media hungry and data-hungry but simultaneously power-hungry. Evidence of this rests in the fact that ICTs – consumer devices, communication networks, and data centres – account for 2 per cent of the world's carbon emissions. This figure is on par with the aviation industry's carbon emissions from fuel (Jones, 2018). Moreover, electricity use by ICTs is expected to grow by 2030 to between 8 and 21 per cent of electricity demand (Andrae, 2017). Indeed, for over a decade, the increasing energy consumption and carbon emissions of ICTs have been the subject of a significant amount of academic research, policy initiatives, and professional, industry, government, and intergovernmental responses, including from the European Commission, OECD, Institute of Electrical and Electronics Engineers (IEEE), and International Telecommunications Union (ITU) among others. During this time, data-heavy companies such as Google, Facebook, and Apple have sought to "green" their energy mix by a shift towards renewable energy sources and refining data centre practices (e.g. see Hogan, 2015b); meanwhile, consortiums such as GreenTouch have formed that seek to drastically improve ICT energy efficiency (see Ahmed, Naeem & Iqbal, 2017; Cubitt, Hassan & Vollmer, 2011; Hogan, 2018).

Current attention has often focussed on the massive amounts of energy used by blockchain-based cryptocurrencies such as Bitcoin, Ethereum and Litecoin, and are frequently cited as an example of digital objects having material environmental and planetary impacts. Krause and Tolaymat (2018) conducted a comparative analysis of energy consumption between an assemblage of five cryptocurrencies (Bitcoin, Ethereum, Litecoin, and Monero) and conventional mining (aluminium, copper, gold, platinum, and rare earth oxides). The authors concluded that, except for aluminium, "cryptomining consumed more energy than mineral mining to produce an equivalent market value" and anticipate that energy use will rise further (ibid.). Stoll, Klaaßen and Gallersdörfer (2018) estimate that Bitcoin has a total annual electricity consumption of approximately 48.2 TWh, which is slightly more than the annual electricity consumption of Singapore. Meanwhile, a recent paper in *Nature Climate Change* warned that "Bitcoin usage, should it follow the rate of adoption of other broadly adopted technologies, could alone produce enough CO_2 emissions to push warming above 2°C within less than three decades" (Mora et al., 2018, p. 931). While the underlying models, assumptions, and projections that underwrite claims about the energy demands and environmental impact of cryptocurrencies should no doubt be subject to ongoing peer-reviewed critique (see Dittmar and Praktiknjo, 2019), that there are human and environmental impacts and externalities due to cryptomining is undeniable (Goodkind, Jones & Berrens, 2020).

Beyond cryptocurrencies, data centres comprise a significant portion of ICT energy use and are expected to account for 25 per cent of ICT energy use by 2025 (ibid.). Thus while accessing documents from the cloud, streaming 4k media content to a mobile device, or merely conducting an internet search may all have an air of lightness or even "immateriality" about them, these acts are connected to energy-hungry data centres in the material world. As Maxwell and Miller (2012b) note, the impact or even existence of data centres is rarely thought about: "a data centre's physical existence and impact might as well result from invisible magic for all we notice of them in the cluster of services known today as cloud computing". While the authors lament the lack of attention to the invisible yet material energy of data, they have simultaneously blazed a trail for critical scholarship into the relationship between media, energy, and the environment (Hogan, 2015a; 2015b; 2018; Rauch, 2018; Pötzsch, 2017; Velkova, 2016). Data centres and their components play a crucial role in the energy infrastructure of digitization (Cooper, 2021; Velkkova, 2021; Brodie & Velkova, 2021) and thereby the material dimension of mediatisation. Hogan (2015b) offers a particularly jarring exploration of the material "underbelly" of Facebook's digital archive by connecting the social media platform to the social-ecological impact of its physical data storage centres and vast network of machines.

Of course, the focus on energy extends beyond the energy of data to include the energy used to power or charge devices. As our number of networked devices increases, as the number of things connected to the "internet of things" expands, as mining for cryptocurrencies swells and becomes more intensive, as more and more artificial intelligence applications come online, all of these processes demand energy. While mediatisation scholars may have critically reflected on many of the above phenomena, they have generally failed to consider, or at least acknowledge, the social-ecological implications and effects of such mediatisation processes. Mediatisation, the production and appropriation of digital media, takes energy, and the sources of energy and its use have material social, political-economic and environmental consequences. However, mediatisation scholarship has largely failed to render these visible or make direct connections between mediatisation and energy in general and its impacts on climate and climate change in particular.

Mediatisation and Climate Change

This chapter's objective has been to stress the need for scholars to acknowledge and analyse the interplay between mediatisation and climate change and to specifically extend and connect mediatisation's discursive aspects with its material dimensions. Doing so, we argue, makes visible the material connection between mediatisation processes and climate change. In tandem with the multiplicity of climate change texts and discourses are the myriad screens on which these texts appear and are consumed: the mobile phones, tablets, laptops, and desktops. The tangled global network of wires, towers, routers, servers, switches, and computers whose assemblage makes the wired and wireless internet possible; that makes searching, streaming, and storing objects on the cloud or on the blockchain possible. We also must not overlook the architectural array of data warehouses, server farms, and crypto mines and other buildings, together, of course, with the politics, policies, laws, and bylaws that govern their use and disposal. These objects are also tied to mediatisation and, of course, what ties them all together is a need for energy. Thus, our argument rests upon seeing mediatisation as a meta-process whereby media have become increasingly important across all facets of society and their presence, volume, and utility only continue to grow. Yet, as this process unfolds and expands on a global scale, the material resources and energy needed for the production and use of digital media technologies – often obtained through the extraction and burning of fossil fuels – also continues to grow. Consequently, the issue of energy – its source, emissions, intensity – is a crucial component of mediatisation. Not only does energy make mediatisation possible but, given our current reliance on fossil fuels, contributes to climate change as the energy used for running various devices, systems, and processes thereby emits massive amounts of carbon dioxide which then drives climate change. However, this material connection and the direct planetary consequences remains overlooked in the literature.

The current changes we perceive and are experiencing in the Earth's climate are the direct result of anthropogenic climate change caused by the deliberate emission of carbon dioxide and other greenhouse gases into the atmosphere through the burning of fossil fuels. Mediatisation, as a process, is reliant upon fossil fuels particularly for the production and appropriation of digital media and related infrastructures. So far, we have shown that a small but important research field is analysing the relevance of energy consumption in the production and appropriation of digital media – energy that mainly comes from fossil fuel resources. By sketching the research field on mediatisation, we have also shown that this consumption of fossil energy is almost ignored in mediatisation studies, and consequently so too is mediatisation's impact on global warming and thus its contribution to climate change. Therefore, we argue that mediatisation research has to broaden its research perspective on the material dimension of mediatisation, on the one hand by pointing to and analysing the socio-ecological effects of the increase of digital media technologies in society, and on the other hand by stressing and examining initiatives which try to face these challenges and shape mediatisation in a more sustainable way. Taking a practical approach to the material dimension of mediatisation is one possibile way to analyse and take an active part in the socio-ecological transformation which is needed to face climate change (e.g. Kannengießer, 2020a).

In conclusion, and following Maxwell and Miller's argumentation for *Greening the Media* (2012a) and "Greening media studies" (Maxwell & Miller, 2015), we argue here that mediatisation research must make visible mediatisation's connection to and effects on the climate. Mediatisation scholars could benefit from the growing field of "elemental media" championed by materialist scholar Nicole Starosielski (2014; 2019) and others to connect mediatisation with its material entanglement and impact. To be clear, we are not calling on mediatisation scholars to focus exclusively on climate change, but are imploring them to recognise this connection. Moreover, there remains an urgent need for more research that works towards solutions that will reduce mediatisation's contribution to climate change, ranging from using renewable energy in the production and appropriation of digital media (from smartphones to cryptocurrency) or making the server centres needed for digital communication more sustainable. Energy is one, although not the only issue that has to be addressed when making mediatisation more sustainable and directly tackling climate change, which remains the most dangerous threat to humankind.

Note

1 This section has been adopted from Kannengießer and McCurdy, 2020, pp. 11–13).

References

Adolphsen, M., & Lück, J. (2012). Non-routine interactions behind the scenes of a global media event: How journalists and political PR professionals co-produced the 2010 UN climate conference in Cancún. *Medien- & Kommunikationswissenschaft*, Special issue no. 2, 141–158.

Ahmed, F., Naeem, M., & Iqbal, M. (2017). ICT and renewable energy: A way forward to the next generation telecom base stations. *Telecommunication Systems*, 64(1), 43–56. doi.org/10.1007/s11235-016-0156-4

Anderson, A. (2011). Sources, media, and modes of climate change communication: The role of celebrities. *Wiley Interdisciplinary Reviews: Climate Change*, 2(4), 535–546.

Andrae, A. S. G. (2017). Total consumer power consumption forecast. *Nordic Digital Business Summit*. Helsinki, Finland, 5 October 2017. Retrieved at: https://www.researchgate.net/publication/320225452_Total_Consumer_Power_Consumption Forecast.

Askanius, T., & Uldam, J. (2011). Online social media for radical politics: Climate change activism on YouTube. *International Journal of Electronic Governance*, 4(1–2), 69–84.

Bennett, T., & Joyce, P. (eds) (2010). *Material powers: Cultural studies, history and the material turn*. London: Routledge.

Berglez, P. (2011). Inside, outside, and beyond media logic: Journalistic creativity in climate reporting. *Media, Culture & Society*, 33(3), 449–465.

Blomberg, M., Seo, H., Liu, Y., Shayesteh, F., Do, H. V., & Vu, H. T. (2021). Social media and environmental activism: Framing climate change on Facebook by global NGOs. *Science Communication*, 43(1), 91–115.

Bolin, G. (2016). The rhythm of ages: Analyzing mediatization through the lens of generations across cultures. *International Journal of Communication* 10, 5252–5269.

Bolin, G. (2014). Institution, technology, world: Relationships between the media, culture, and society. In K. Lundby (ed.) *Mediatization of communication*. Handbooks of Communication Science vol. 21 (pp. 175–198). Berlin: De Gruyter Mouton.

Boyce, T., & Lewis, J. (eds) (2009). *Climate change and the media*. Peter Lang.

Boykoff, M. T. (2007). Flogging a dead norm? Newspaper coverage of anthropogenic climate change in the United States and United Kingdom from 2003 to 2006. *Area*, 39(4), 470–481.

Brodie, P., & Velkova, J. (2021). Cloud ruins: Ericsson's Vaudreuil-Dorion data centre and infrastructural abandonment. *Information, Communication & Society*, DOI: 10.1080/1369118X.2021.1909099

Brüggemann, M., & Engesser, S. (2017). Beyond false balance: How interpretive journalism shapes media coverage of climate change. *Global Environmental Change*, 42, 58–67. doi:10.1016/j.gloenvcha.2016.11.004.

Brüggemann, M., & Engesser, S. (2014). Between consensus and denial: Climate journalists as interpretative community. *Science Communication*, 36(4), 399–427.

Brüggemann, M., & Engesser, S. (2013). Journalists as interpretative community: Identifying transnational framing of climate change. Working paper 59. Zürich: NCCR Democracy, University of Zürich.

Chinn, S., Hart, P. S., & Soroka, S. (2020). Politicization and polarization in climate change news content, 1985–2017. *Science Communication*, 42(1), 112–129.

Cooper, Z. G. T. (2021). Of dog kennels, magnets, and hard drives: Dealing with Big Data peripheries. Big Data & Society, 8(2). https://doi.org/10.1177/2053951721 1015430

Couldry, N., & Hepp, A. (2016). *The mediated construction of reality*. Cambridge: Polity Press.

Couldry, N., & Hepp, A. (2013). Conceptualizing mediatization: Contexts, traditions, arguments. *Communication Theory*, 23, 191–202. https://doi.org/10.1111/comt.12019

Cubitt, S., Hassan, R., & Vollmer, I. (2011). Does cloud computing have a silver lining? *Media, Culture and Society*, 33(1), 149–158. http://dx.doi.org/10.1177/0163443710382974

Della Porta, D., & Parks, L. (2014). Framing processes in the climate movement: From climate change to climate justice. *Routledge handbook of climate change movements*, 19–31.

Dittmar, L., & Praktiknjo, A. (2019). Could bitcoin emissions push global warming above 2°C? *Nature Climate Change*, 9, 656–657. DOI: 10.1038/s41558-019-0534-5

Doyle, J. (2011). *Mediating climate change*. London: Routledge.

Driessens, O., Bolin, G., Hepp, A., & Hjarvard, S. (eds) (2017). *Dynamics of mediatization: Institutional change and everyday transformations in a digital age.* Cham, Switzerland: Palgrave.

Eide, E., Kunelius, R., & Kumpu, V. (2010). *Global climate, local journalism: A transnational study of how media make sense of climate summits.* Bochum/Freiburg: Projekt.

Engesser, S., & Brüggemann, M. (2017). Mapping the minds of the mediators: The cognitive frames of climate journalists from five countries. *Public Understanding of Science*, 25(7), 825–841.

Gabrys, J. (2015). Powering the digital: From energy ecologies to electronic environmentalism. In R. Maxwell, J. Raundalen & N. Lager Vestberg (eds) *Media and the ecological crisis* (pp. 3–18). New York and London: Routledge. http://dx.doi.org/10.4324/9781315885650

Gillespie, T., Boczkowski, P. J., & Foot, K. A. (2014). Introduction. In T. Gillespie, P. J. Boczkowski & K. A. Foot (eds) *Media technologies: Essays on communication, materiality, and society* (pp. 1–19). Cambridge, MA: MIT: Press. http://dx.doi.org/10.7551/mitpress/9780262525374.001.0001

Goodkind, A., Jones, B., & Berrens, R. (2020). Cryptodamages: Monetary value estimates of the air pollution and human health impacts of cryptocurrency mining. *Energy Research & Social Science*, 59: 101281. http://dx.doi.org/10.1016/j.erss.2019.101281

Hall, S. (1973). Encoding and decoding in the television discourse. Discussion paper. University of Birmingham, 24 December 2021. Retrieved at: https://core.ac.uk/download/pdf/81670115.pdf

Haunss, S., & Sommer M. (eds) (2020). *Fridays for Future – Die Jugend gegen den Klimawandel. Konturen der weltweiten Protestbewegung* [Fridays for Future – Youth against climate change. Contours of a worldwide protest movement]. Bielefeld: transcript.

Hepp, A. (2020). *Deep mediatisation*. Cambridge: Polity Press.

Hepp, A. (2013). *Cultures of mediatization*. Cambridge: Polity Press.

Hepp, A. & Krotz, F. (2014). *Mediatized worlds. Culture and society in a media age.* London: Palgrave Macmillan. http://dx.doi.org/10.1057/9781137300355

Hepp, A., Hjavard, S., & Lundby, K. (2015). Mediatization: Theorizing the interplay between media, culture and society. *Media, Culture & Society*, 37(22), 314–324. http://dx.doi.org/10.1177/0163443715573835

Hjarvard, S. (2013). *The mediatization of culture and society*. London: Routledge. http://dx.doi.org/10.4324/9780203155363

Hjarvard, S. (2012). Doing the right thing: Media and communication studies in a mediatized world. *Nordicom Review*, 33(1), 27–34.

Hjarvard, S. (2008). The mediatization of society. A theory of the media as agents of social and cultural change. *Nordicom Review*, 29(2), 105–134. http://dx.doi.org/10.1515/nor-2017-0181

Hjarvard, S. (2004). From bricks to bytes: The mediatization of a global toy industry. In I. Bondebjerg & P. Golding (eds) *European Culture and the Media* (pp. 43–63). Bristol: Intellect.

Hogan, M. (2015a). Data flows and water woes: The Utah data center. *Big Data & Society*, 2(2). Epub ahead of print, 13 July 2015. DOI: https://doi.org/10.1177/2053951715592429

Hogan, M. (2015b). Facebook data storage centers as the archive's underbelly. *Television & New Media*, 16(1), 3–18. DOI: 10.1177/1527476413509415

Hogan, M. (2018). Big data ecologies. *Ephemera*, 18(3), 631–657.

Jansson, A. (2014). Indispensable things: On mediatization, materiality, and space. In K. Lundby (ed) *Mediatization of communication*. Handbooks of Communication Science vol. 21 (pp. 273–295). Berlin: De Gruyter Mouton. DOI: 10.1515/9783110272215.273

Jones, N, (2018). How to stop data centres from gobbling up the world's electricity. *Nature*, 561: 163–166. DOI: 10.1038/d41586-018-06610-y

Kannengießer, S. (2021). Media reception, media effects and media practices in sustainability communication. In M. Karmasin, L. Krainer & F. Weder (eds) *Handbook of sustainability communication* (pp. 323–338). Wiesbaden: Springer.

Kannengießer, S. (2020a): Acting on media for sustainability. In H. Stephansen & E. Treré (eds) *The turn to practice in media research: Implications for the study of citizen- and social movement media* (pp. 176–188). London and New York: Routledge.

Kannengießer, S. (2020b). Fair media technologies: Innovative media devices for social change. *Media Innovations*, 6(1). https://doi.org/10.5617/jomi.7832

Kannengießer, S. (2019). Engaging with and reflecting on the materiality of digital media technologies: Repair and fair production. *New Media & Society*, 22(1), 123–139.

Kannengießer, S., & McCurdy, P. (2020). Mediatization and the Absence of the Environment. *Communication Theory*. https://doi.org/10.1093/ct/qtaa009

Krause, M. J. & Tolaymat, T. (2018). Quantification of energy and carbon costs for mining cryptocurrencies. *Nature Sustainability*, 1(11), 711–718. DOI: 10.1038/s41893-018-0152-7

Krotz, F. (2007a). *Mediatisierung. Fallstudien zum Wandel von Kommunikation*. Wiesbaden: VS Verlag für Sozialwissenschaften. DOI: 10.1007/978-3-531-19021-1_45

Krotz, F. (2007b). The meta-process of mediatization as a conceptual frame. *Global Media and Communication*, 3(3), 256–260. DOI: 10.1177/1742766507003003010103

Krotz, F. (2017). Explaining the mediatisation approach. *Javnost – The Public*, 24(2), 103–118. DOI: 10.1080/13183222.2017.1298556

Kunelius, R. (2014). Climate change challenges: An agenda for de-centered mediatization research. In K. Lundby (ed.) *Mediatization of communication*. Handbooks of Communication Science vol. 21 (pp. 63–86). Berlin: De Gruyter Mouton.

Kunelius, R., & Eide, E. (2012). Moment of hope, mode of realism: On the dynamics of a transnational journalistic field during UN climate change summits. *International Journal of Communication*, 6(1), 266–285.

León, B., & Erviti, M. C. (2015). Science in pictures: Visual representation of climate change in Spain's television news. *Public Understanding of Science*, 24(2), 183–199.

Lester, L., & Cottle, S. (2009). Visualizing climate change: Television news and eco-logical citizenship. *International Journal of Communication*, 3(17), 920–936.

Lievrouw, L. (2014). Materiality and media in communication and technology studies. In T. Gillespie, P. J. Boczkowski and Foot, K. A. (eds) *Media technologies: Essays on communication, materiality, and society* (pp. 12–52). Cambridge, MA: MIT: Press. http://dx.doi.org/10.7551/mitpress/9780262525374.003.0002

Livingstone, S. & Lunt, P. (2014). Mediatization: An emerging paradigm for media and communication studies. In K. Lundby (ed.) *Mediatization of communication*. Handbooks of Communication Science vol. 21 (pp. 703–724), De Gruyter Mouton: Berlin.

Lück, J., Wozniak, A., & Wessler, H. (2016). Networks of coproduction. How journalists and environmental NGOs create common interpretations of the UN climate change conferences. *International Journal of Press/Politics*, 21(1), 25–47.

Lundby, K. (ed.) (2014a). *Mediatization of communication*. Handbooks of Communication Science vol. 21. Berlin: De Gruyter Mouton. http://dx.doi.org/10.1515/9783110272215.3

Lundby, K. (2014b). Mediatization of communication. In K. Lundby (ed.) *Mediatization of communication*. Handbooks of Communication Science vol. 21 (pp. 3–35). Berlin: De Gruyter Mouton. http://dx.doi.org/10.1515/9783110272215.3

Lundby, K. (2008). *Mediatized stories. Self-representation in new media*. New York: Peter Lang.

Maxwell, R., & Miller, T. (2020). *How green is your smartphone?* Cambridge: Polity.

Maxwell, R., & Miller, T. (2015). Greening media studies. In R. Maxwell, J. Raundalen & N. Lager Vestberg (eds) *Media and the ecological crisis* (pp. 87–98). New York and Abingdon: Routledge.

Maxwell, R., & Miller, T. (2012a). *Greening the media*. Oxford: Oxford University Press.

Maxwell, R., & Miller, T. (2012b). The great illusion of media and communications. *European Financial Review*, June 19, 2012. http://www.europeanfinancialreview.com/?p=1746

Maxwell, R., Raundalen J., & Lager Vestberg, N. (2015) Introduction. Media ecology recycled. In R. Maxwell, J. Raundalen & N. Lager Vestberg (eds) *Media and the ecological crisis*, (pp. xi–xxi). New York and Abingdon: Routledge.

Milkoreit, M. (2016). The promise of climate fiction: Imagination, storytelling, and the politics of the future. In *Reimagining climate change* (pp. 171–191). Abingdon: Routledge.

Miller, J. (2017). Mediatization of the automobile. In O. Driessens, G. Bolin, A. Hepp & S. Hjarvard (eds) *Dynamics of mediatization: institutional change and everyday transformations in a digital age* (pp. 203–224). Cham, Switzerland: Palgrave. http://dx.doi.org/10.1007/978-3-319-62983-4_10

Mora, C., Rollins, R. L., Taladay, K., Kantar, M. B., Chock, M. K., Shimada, M., & Franklin, E. C. (2018). Bitcoin emissions alone could push global warming above 2° C. *Nature Climate Change*, 8(11), pp. 931–933. DOI: 0.1038/s41558-018-0321-8.

Neverla, I., & Taddicken, M. (2012). Der Klimawandel aus Rezipientensicht: Relevanz und Forschungsstand. [Climate change in the view of recipients: Relevance and state of research] In I. Neverla & M.S. Schäfer (eds) *Das Medien-Klima. Fragen und Befunde der kommunikationswissenschaftlichen Klimaforschung* (pp. 215–232). Wiesbaden: Springer.

Olausson, U. (2011). "We're the ones to blame": Citizens' representations of climate change and the role of the media. *Environmental Communication*, 5(3), 281–299.

O'Neill, Saffron J. (2013). Image matters: Climate change imagery in US, UK and Australian newspapers. *Geoforum*, 49, 10–19.

O'Neill, S. J., & Smith, N. (2014). Climate change and visual imagery. *Wiley Interdisciplinary Reviews: Climate Change*, 5(1), 73–87.

Pearce, W., Holmberg, K., Hellsten, I., & Nerlich, B. (2014). Climate change on Twitter: Topics, communities and conversations about the 2013 IPCC Working Group 1 Report. *Plos One*, 9(4). https://doi.org/10.1371/journal.pone.0094785

Podeschi, C. W. (2014). The nature of future myths: Environmental discourse in science fiction film, 1950–1999. In A. Hansen(ed.) *Media and the environment: Critical concepts in the environment* (pp. 452–487). London: Routledge.

Pötzsch, H. (2017). Media matter. Triple C: Communication, capitalism & critique. *Journal for a Global Sustainable Information Society*, 15(1), 148–170. http://dx.doi.org/10.31269/triplec.v15i1.819

Rauch, J. (2018). *Slow media: Why "slow" is satisfying, sustainable, and smart*. Oxford: Oxford University Press.

Sampei, Y., & Aoyagi-Usui, M. (2009). Mass-media coverage, its influence on public awareness of climate-change issues, and implications for Japan's national campaign to reduce greenhouse gas emissions. *Global Environmental Change*, 19(2), 203–212.

Savolainen, S., & Ylä-Anttila, T. (2021). The climate change movement and political parties: Mechanisms of social media and interaction during the 2019 electoral period in Finland. *Nordic Journal of Media Studies*, 3(1), 2021, 40–60. https://doi.org/10.2478/njms-2021-0003

Schäfer, M. S. (2012). Online communication on climate change and climate politics: A literature review. *WIREs Climate Change*, 3(6), 527–543.

Schäfer, M. S., & Bonfadelli, H. (2016). Umwelt- und Klimawandelkommunikation. [Environmental and climate communication] In H. Bonfadelli, B. Fähnrich, C. Lüthje, J. Milde, M. Rhomberg & M. S. Schäfer (eds) *Forschungsfeld Wissenschaftskommunikation* [Research field of science communication] (pp. 315–338). Wiesbaden: Springer.

Schäfer, M. S., & Painter, J. (2021). Climate journalism in a changing media ecosystem: Assessing the production of climate change related news around the world. *Wiley Interdisciplinary Reviews: Climate Change*, 12(1), 675. https://wires.onlinelibrary.wiley.com/doi/epdf/10.1002/wcc.675

Schäfer M. S., & Schlichting, I. (2014). Media representations of climate change: A meta-analysis of the research field, *Environmental Communication*, 8(2), 142–160.

Shehata, A., & Hopmann, D. N. (2012). Framing climate change. A study of US and Swedish press coverage of global warming. *Journalism Studies*, 13(2), 175–192.

Skey, M., Stone, C., Jenzen, O., & Mangan, A. (2018). Mediatization and sport: A bottom-up perspective. *Communication & Sport*, 6(5), 588–604. https://doi.org/10.1177/2167479517734850

Starosielski, N. (2019). The elements of media studies. *Media+ Environment*, 1(1), https://doi.org/10.1525/001c.10780.

Starosielski, N. (2014). "Movements that are drawn": A history of environmental animation for The Lorax to FernGully to Avatar. In A. Hansen (ed.) *Media and the environment: Critical concepts in the environment* (pp. 506–526). London: Routledge.

Stecula, D.A., & Merkley, E. (2019). Framing climate change: Economics, ideology, and uncertainty in American news media content from 1988 to 2014. *Frontiers in Communication*, 4, 6. https://doi.org/10.3389/fcomm.2019.00006

Stoddart, M. C., Ramos, H., Foster, K., & Ylä-Anttila, T. (2021). Competing crises? Media coverage and framing of climate change during the COVID-19 pandemic. *Environmental Communication*, 1–17.

Stoll, C., Klaaßen, L. & Gallersdörfer, U. (2018). The carbon footprint of bitcoin. MIT CEEPR working paper 2018-018. Retrieved at: http://ceepr.mit.edu/files/pap ers/2018-018-Brief.pdf

Svoboda, M. (2016). Cli-fi on the screen(s): Patterns in the representations of climate change in fictional films. *Wiley Interdisciplinary Reviews: Climate Change*, 7(1), 43–64.

Taddicken, M. (2013). Climate change from the user's perspective: The impact of mass media and internet use and individual and moderating variables on knowledge and attitudes. *Journal of Media Psychology*, 25(1), 39–52.

Todd, A. M. (2009). Prime-time subversion: The environmental rhetoric of The Simpsons. In L. King and D. McCarthy (eds) *Environmental sociology* (pp. 230–246). Lanham, MD: Rowman & Littlefield.

Taddicken, M., & Reif, A. (2016). Who participates in the climate change online discourse? A typology of Germans' online engagement. *Communications*, 41(3), 315–337.

Trumbo, C. (1996). Constructing climate change: Claims and frames in US news coverage of an environmental issue. *Public Understanding of Science*, 5(3), 269.

Velkova, J. (2021). Thermopolitics of data: Cloud infrastructures and energy futures. *Cultural Studies*, 35(4–5), 663–683, DOI: 10.1080/09502386.2021.1895243

Velkova, J. (2016). Data that warms: Waste heat, infrastructural convergence and the computation traffic commodity. *Big Data & Society*, 3(2). Epub ahead of print, 1 December 2016. DOI: https://doi.org/10.1177/2053951716684144

Wahlström, M., Sommer, M., Kocyba, P., de Vydt, M. de Moor, J., Davies, S., Wouters, R., et al. (2019). Protest for a future: Composition, mobilization and motives of the participants in Fridays For Future climate protests on 15 March 2019 in 13 European cities. Stockholm a.o. https://protestinstitut.eu/wp-content/uploads/2019/07/20190709_Protest-for-a-future_GCS-Descriptive-Report.pdf

Walter, S., Brüggemann, M., & Engesser, S. (2018). Echo chambers of denial: Explaining user comments on climate change. *Environmental Communication*, 12(2), 204–217.

Wessler, H., Wozniak, A., Hofer, L., & Lück, J. (2016). Global multimodal news frames on climate change: A comparison of five democracies around the world. *International Journal of Press/Politics*, 21(4), 423–445.

Wozniak, A. (2021). Just "performance nonsense"?: How recipients process news photos of activists' symbolic actions about climate change politics. *Nordic Journal of Media Studies*, 3(1), 61–78. https://doi.org/10.2478/njms-2021-0004

Zabern, L. von, & Tulloch, C. D. (2021). Rebel with a cause: The framing of climate change and intergenerational justice in the German press treatment of the Fridays For Future protests. *Media, Culture and Society*, 43(1), 23–47.

6 Mediatisation, Economy, and Infrastructural Dynamics in the Digital Risk Society

Tilo Grenz

Introduction: Agentic Change and Infrastructural Dynamics

This contribution is motivated by the growing relevance of digital infrastructures for the mediatisation approach, which is driven especially by a rising awareness and study of economically motivated media environments, i.e., platforms. Digital infrastructures ultimately underlie the shape and rules of today's media and communicative action. They have become the very layer of the social. The desktop computer I have been using to write these lines (during the second half of 2021) is one of an estimated 46 billion devices that are connected worldwide – not only to the widely known internet at the surface. Digital infrastructures are becoming increasingly complex and opaque. But they are by no means static as their "classic" physical pendants like communication infrastructure, traffic infrastructure or power supply and the like imply. They are neither solely determined by economic (global) players, as most of the recent (critical) positions in sociology, media, and communication studies suggest. A number of indications point to the enormous relevance of infrastructural dynamics, that no longer remain within closed circles, such as computer science. Yet, infrastructural dynamics have been widely neglected so far. They open up a new and different level of inquiry that has not been unlocked in the mediatisation approach to date.

Its negligence or conceptual marginalisation is by no means unique to mediatisation research. It affects nearly all current sociological, communication, and media studies that deal with the digitalisation of culture and society. With an expanded view as it is presented in this chapter, questions about particular agents of change – be they economic, political, pioneers, everyday appropriating users or collectives or both – prove to be only one part of the game. At the same time, according to the argument made here, such an expanded view would allow the mediatisation approach to become a strong interdisciplinary authority in observing, researching, and paying attention to the Digital Risk Society. Nevertheless, in order to achieve that goal, discourses and references other than the previous ones must be brought into focus. This even means moving beyond the recently called for

DOI: 10.4324/9781003324591-9

and already conducted disciplinary expansion towards software studies, sociology of technology, science and technology studies (Hepp, 2020, p. 15). Rather, key studies are available in other disciplines and research fields, including information systems sciences, service and outlaw innovation, as well as cybersecurity studies. This chapter intends to offer a sensitising debut to these very discourses.

The following section briefly traces the path from the economy and economic actors within the mediatisation approach, via platforms as a key topic, to the growing awareness and importance of digital infrastructures within the mediatisation approach. However, this awareness is based on a more static conception of digital infrastructures as an economically built background skeleton. Consequently, the next section then draws on three selected strands of research that emphasise infrastructural dynamics: first, conceptual positions from information systems science are presented. Second, the chapter draws on platform contestation as it has been prominently tackled within service ecology and studies on (outlaw) innovation. Then, cybersecurity as an area that deals with the most urgent socio-technological instabilities will be introduced. The next section then promotes three paths that allow a connection between the dynamics of digital infrastructure and the mediatisation approach. Subsequently, the last section briefly discusses the challenges presented to the mediatisation approach in its relevance to the contemporary Digital Risk Society.

Economy and Mediatisation: a Selective History

Stating that mediatisation of contemporary cultures and societies refers to media appropriation and thus includes technology, politics, and economic developments has become almost a matter of course. Considering the more recent history of mediatisation research since its upswing about 15 years ago, the role that businesses and their media-related strategies play in mediatisation has long been somewhat shortened. Mediatisation has often been equated with either "medialisation", i.e., media logic's economy, or simply associated with success-oriented media use or media development. Within corporate communication, mediatisation even became another trend similar to the "platform metaphor" (Gillespie, 2017). Certainly, the marginalisation of the economy and economic actors is also related to scientific or disciplinary demarcations, according to which mediatisation has been defined as a "meta-process" alongside others like "commercialization" (Krotz, 2007, p. 256 ff).

However, with more and more advanced techno-economic means of media intruding even "deeper" into everyday life and culture (Grenz, 2017, p. 26 ff; Hepp, 2020, p. 19; Murdock, 2017; Wojtkowski, 2017), the recent mediatisation approach has been criticised for insufficiently including economics and economic actors. From that point, some mediatisation scholars have rather pushed these developments aside, referring to the already existing research on commercially driven media production. Thus, the long-lasting topic of the blurring boundaries between producers and consumers (Castells, 2010, p. 31), the role of contemporary active (digital) audiences (on digital media – Schäfer, 2009) and, of course, the new "participatory culture" (Jenkins, 2007; 2009) form part of more recent mediatisation's prehistory.

For about ten years now, mediatisation scholars have emphasised the role of (global) corporations and "their" media technologies as agentic drivers of mediatisation processes, i.e., as inherent, or even core elements of mediatisation's conception of change. Without any doubt, the growing platform debate that successively crossed the disciplines and areas played a crucial role here (Gillespie, 2010). Different studies from the field of economics have pointed to the significant spread of platforms and the so-called platform economy (Kirchner & Beyer, 2016; Srnicek, 2016). But the claim of mediatisation research and its role in connection with new platform economies has remained thoroughly ambivalent. Beyond disciplinary claims, this concerns the old question of the origins of social and cultural change and the role that technology and economics play in it. Subsequently, on the one hand, there are warnings against an "economic reductionism" (Hepp, 2020, p. 29), and on the other hand, there are critical positions that even argue for a replacement of "deep mediatisation" by "deep capitalism", i.e., "market fundamentalism" (Murdock, 2017).

However, this juxtaposition as it is made here is of course too simplistic. Rather, it is the interplay of economics and the latest media technologies – as it is theoretically and conceptually conceived in different ways – that brings about change. In this respect, two relevant positions can currently be found. First, there are concepts and corresponding empirical studies such as "platform biographies" (Bruns & Burgess, 2016 using Twitter as an example) or "platform vernaculars" (Gibbs et al., 2015 using Instagram as an example) which assume a more or less harmonious, mutual adaptation between platform operators, platforms, and users. Second, researchers increasingly stress the asymmetry of change and the unparalleled influence of economic change agents and "deep" technologies. Communicative action, thus, is based on or even intermeshed with technological resources (affordances) that are made possible by deep "material processes" (datafication) – which in turn are developed, managed, and adapted by global, profit-oriented corporations (Couldry & Hepp, 2017, p. 3). Although it is problematic to equate platforms with (digital) infrastructures (Plantin et al., 2018), it can be stated that the attention to digital infrastructures within sociology, media, and communication studies has merged with the discourses on the oligopolistic structures of the Western world.

Tracing the Dynamics of Digital Infrastructures

As mentioned in the introduction, the understanding of digital infrastructures that has emerged in recent years is quite peculiar. In some cases, "platforms" and "digital infrastructures" are used synonymously, or digital infrastructures are sometimes referred to merely as hardware ("communication infrastructure"). In addition, the potentials for construction and change are being identified in economic-technical innovation thrusts. Although highly topical and empirically urgent, infrastructural dynamics have been surprisingly neglected in the mediatisation approach. Infrastructural dynamics highlight that there are tensions and a typical uncontrollability inherent to today's digital infrastructures, demonstrating that other – contesting – actors than the "classical" ones are involved. It becomes apparent that digital infrastructures are permanently challenged beyond (economic) platforms and emerge in an opaque field of actors and technologies (as in the case of distributed cybersecurity).

Inherent Socio-technical Tensions

For about 15 years, information systems science has been drawing on the actual design and development of digital infrastructures as something beyond the mere realm of informatics. "Digital infrastructures (...) form a new stage in the evolution of IT, reflecting the fact, that IT has become deeply embedded socially" (Tilson et al., 2010). Likewise, the linking of complex, interdependent IT systems regarding internet governance was associated with the hope that uncoordinated complexity (and on the basis of an "open Internet") would let innovation prosper – initially in the field of IT and coding. Thus, one of the key concepts was "generativity" as "a technology's overall capacity to produce change driven by large, varied, and uncoordinated audiences" (Zittrain, 2006, p. 1980). However, scholars of information systems science emphasised the inherent dilemma in the structure of digital infrastructures, i.e., the "paradox of control" that arises with infrastructures that build on conceptions of generativity. It was also clear that overregulation of digital infrastructures makes creativity unlikely, which is why, paradoxically, flexibility is necessary at the same time. In this dialectical structure of stability and flexibility alone, digital infrastructures as a post-2000 phenomenon present themselves as highly risky for stakeholders. The issue was (and still is) that open IT systems offer enormous potential for innovation, but at the same time, centralised control of interfaces and protocols is sacrificed in favour of decentralised distribution (Tilson et al., 2010). Anyway, generativity in endless variants was successively expanded in economic and technical progress (see also O'Reilly, 2005). The control-paradox aspect particularly brings into consideration that digital infrastructures connect more and more components, software applications, and services (e.g., app stores, digital marketplaces, mapping services). Its complexity "arises from the continuing and evolving entanglement of the social (human agency), the symbolic (symbol-based computation in digital technologies), and the material (physical artifacts that house or interact with computing machines)" (Benbya et al., 2020, p. 3). Pointedly, the term "digital infrastructures" as coined there "captures the [risen, T.G.] notion of the emergence of increasingly complex assemblages of diverse actors and technologies" (Koutsikouri et al., 2017, p. 4716).

Respective work highlights the fact that digital infrastructures are "beyond rational managerial control" (Koutsikouri et al., 2017, p. 4717; Hanseth & Lyytinen, 2010; Tilson et al., 2010). This is probably also one reason why information systems scholars account for digital infrastructures as an "evolutionary process" (Edwards et al., 2009; Koutsikouri et al., 2017, p. 4716). Emphasising the increasing inter-connectedness of information systems, in a seminal study, Henfridsson and Bygstad (2013) further developed such evolutionary "logics". They state that all contemporary digital infrastructures are based on "generative mechanisms" (Henfridsson & Bygstad, 2013, p. 11). These mechanisms would be "self-reinforcing" because of the embedded technological "feedback loops [which move, T.G.] beyond single stakeholders' control". Thus, more recently, information systems scholars ask for new approaches to analyse and understand digital infrastructure's complexity. Given the most recent developments in digital infrastructures such as algorithmic decision making, the information systems sciences call for approaches to understand the "hyper-connections and mutual dependencies among human actors, technical artifacts, processes, organizations, and institutions" (Benbya et al., 2020, p. 1).

Platform Contestation and Beyond

Digital infrastructures, as discussed above, have spread massively through what has been described as an "infrastructural turn", caused by the growing importance of online platforms (Plantin & Punathambekar, 2019). Platforms have been described as a new kind of socio-economic "intermediaries" that significantly structure possible expressions and movements of users (Dolata, 2018, p. 6; Srnicek, 2016). However, drawing on an information science foundation, scholars from the digital service economy also referred to the paradoxical and uncontrollable "nature" of digital service ecologies. In a groundbreaking article dealing with the histories of Apple's and Google's app store platforms and respective incidents (e.g. the modifying of operating systems called "jailbreaking"), Eaton et al. (2011) have pointed to a conflictual relationship between what they call "protagonists" and "antagonists."

With regard to the emergence of computer game modelling, adware, spyware, and file sharing, research in the field of "outlaw innovation" has also drawn attention to the unintentional (concerning respective providers and official developers), i.e., non-official and at times illegal appropriation of digital systems. This practice shapes and creates new or unprecedented socio-technical rules and architectures (Flowers, 2008). Stephen Flowers argues that most of today's digital information and communication media cannot be traced back to research and development within firms. Therefore, he asserts, the idea of the solitary, visionary, and successful entrepreneur – as harmoniously framed co-development – is outdated. Rather, Flowers focuses on user activities that modify the features of a product in such a way that the intentions of the original designers are distorted, design flaws that are used in order to circumvent security systems, and the creation of software-based systems or services with dubious legality (Flowers, 2008, p. 178):

> These activities may violate intellectual property and pose a direct threat to established suppliers with the result that the work will often be underground in nature, operating either anonymously or with those involved seeking to obscure their links to such activities. Within this milieu, innovations will emerge from non-cooperative, non-consensual relationships in which the user may be unknown to the supplier and in which there is possibly no free flow of information between the two parties.

Within the framework of mediatisation, there have already been first studies that deal with these negotiations focusing on the recent history of the Apple app store (Grenz & Kirschner, 2018) and online poker platforms (Grenz & Eisewicht, 2017). The authors showed that the increasing economic and technical expansion of the respective platforms (e.g., the outsourcing of data processing to clients in the case of online poker), but also the intentionally limited opportunities for creative appropriation (the conception of Apple's first iOS versions as a closed system) led to non-intended contestation and appropriations of platform rules and technologies that gave these platforms their current "shapes". According to these studies, platform dynamics tend to be a never-ending, friction-filled process of challenges and responses (Grenz, 2013).

Taken together, platforms prove to be not only drivers of unrestrained mediation but also "sites" of negotiation of *material* meaning, which in turn affects the shape and orientation of the very platforms (Gibbs et al., 2015). Their "explosive" hyperconnectivity massively widened the domain of these frictional spaces of negotiation in recent years, first, in view of the massive quantitative increase of internet-connected devices. Second, this development, described as the "internet of things" (Ray, 2018) is complemented by "unsupervised" procedures such as "machine learning" or AI-driven developments (Bechmann & Bowker, 2019). Generativity, as mentioned above, and hyperconnectivity, pushed forward by the platform economy and an increasing number of connected devices, opened up digital infrastructures to a range and variety of unforeseen accesses, intrusions, and interventions. These even go beyond the more or less limited field of today's online platforms, as shown in the following section.

Infrastructuring Cybersecurity

Given the proliferation of digital infrastructures, their overall interconnectedness and inherent generative dynamics, cybersecurity events represent one of the most common drivers of socio-technical instabilities (World Economic Forum, 2018; 2019, p. 16). It has been argued that recent history mirrors a new quantity of cyberattacks and respective quality of impact, from closed and limited to largely coupled information systems (Craigen et al., 2014). In an explorative information systems study conducted in 2007, which focused on "brute force" hacking (a technique that uses "dictionary scripts" to randomly attack large numbers of connected computers), researchers recorded that on average, computers connected to the internet were subject to a cyberattack once every 39 seconds (Condon et al., 2008; Cukier, 2007). The aforementioned *Global Risks Report* by the World Economic Forum (2019, p. 16 ff) highlights two kinds of "cyberattack" in particular: "theft of data/money" and "disruption of operations and infrastructure". According to WEF experts in 2018 (World Economic Forum, 2018), cyberattacks are one of the top three risks to society ahead of natural disasters.

Insights gained in the field of cybersecurity studies reveal that cybersecurity nowadays is constituted by a peculiar technological and social indeterminacy. That means that cybersecurity and the respective emergence of rules and technologies is refraining from former role sets and causal attributions. In order to illustrate this, we can refer to the "Wannacry" worm attack in 2017 that used a leak within Microsoft Windows operating systems and affected 200,000 IT systems in 150 countries. Insightful views such as the stunning one published by Greenberg (2020) reveal a complex, unmanageable network of human and non-human actors and activities, unfolding in a pressure-temporal window. The mentioned inappropriateness of old assumptions does not only hold true for the "classic" concept of the (black hat or white hat) hacker (Stevens, 2015, 8). Governances, for instance, work together with actors in the private sector in order to close security vulnerabilities. At the same time, they store cyber vulnerabilities without informing private sectors in case they use it for their own "defending forward" strategies (Smith, 2017). From a cybersecurity perspective, the dynamics of digital infrastructures result from a "rapid offense-defence cycle" (Smeets, 2018, p. 12), a spiral-like dynamic of a digital arms race (Clinton, 1999 in Auerswald et al., 2003, p. 73; also cited by Smeets, 2018; Beck, 2014; Deibert, 2011).

The ceaselessness, speed, and variety of cyberattacks constantly challenge commercial and critical digital infrastructures and advance precautions, decisions, and permanent adjustments. Infrastructuring, understood here as the inter-related activities that give digital infrastructures their temporal governance, rules, and technical backbone, happens in a complex field of heterogeneous actors that has been described as an emerging "distributed" cybersecurity between private sector actors, civil society actors, and political actors (Deibert, 2016, p. 179). Yet, in a sense, "distribution" only serves as a proxy term. "[C]yberspace is entering into a period of intense contests and potential chaos, as a multitude of different actors (states, civil society, businesses, militants, and organized criminal groups) compete to shape the domain in their strategic interests" (Deibert, 2016, p. 172). Remarkably, perhaps for this very reason, a fascinating conception of cybersecurity issues has been established. Drawing on computer security, in cybersecurity studies a distinction is made between "cybersecurity events" and "cybersecurity incidents": While an event "attracts attention or appears abnormal", an incident represents an event "that has been verified as attributable to a secure failure (as opposed to a hardware failure or misinterpretation of data)" (Condon et al., 2008, p. 79). A number of lists and associated databases collect past events and thus, eventually, mediate the construction of digital risk incidents as a social fact. List entries, i.e., specifically coded cybersecurity incidents, form part of automatic security-check procedures within software development (cf. the "massive" CVE List, CVE, 2021).

(Re)Positioning Mediatisation?

So far, mediatisation research has played only a minor role in this chapter. Yet, the strands of research and insights listed above address several forms of today's (digital) infrastructural dynamics. Now it could be critically argued that security protocols, interface work, etc., have little to do with mediatisation – maybe because they somehow happen "below the surface" of everyday media use. However, according to the argumentation here, this would be to close one's eyes to the core dynamics of current mediatised societies. It might be worthwhile in several respects to connect the mediatisation approach with the dynamics and resources distinguished here – even if this entails challenges (which this volume and its contributions are, after all, addressing intentionally). For this reason, out of a whole series of possible links, three connections will be highlighted here.

Opening Arenas and the Scaling of Negotiation

The attractiveness of the mediatisation approach is, after all, also due to the fact that mediatisation is able to combine a broad spectrum of rather scattered theoretical and empirical works with a reference to the present (Grenz & Pfadenhauer, 2017, p. 5; Hepp, 2020, p. 15). Their lowest common denominator is the interest in change at different, not always clearly differentiated levels of analysis. At the centre, at least of the empirical or empirically oriented works, is the far-reaching concept of negotiation, which takes place in a sign-like, symbolic, and also technical-material way in diverse areas. Infrastructural dynamics offer a new kind of (previously closed) arena, while change has so far been attributed mainly to economic motives and external innovation pushes ("waves"). The presented literature and research strands focus on different scales and, thus, resources, effects, and visibilities of negotiation. While platform contestations tend to aim attention at limited spaces of negotiation (app stores, etc.), insights from cybersecurity studies also extend to the realm of global information systems – beyond economic distribution platforms and the like.

Types and Temporalities of Change

The insights presented suggest that the mediatisation approach should take into account different temporalities of change in respective fields of research. This aspect is disconnected from the figure of the *"panta rhei"*, namely that everything is always in flux anyway (a perspective closely related to current relationist perspectives in infrastructure research). But it also entails a move away from the view that there are always specific or determinable roles of change agents (such as economic, global actors) and their respective strategies (e.g., innovation strategies). What is meant here is – the seemingly rather naïve-realistic point – that certain contestations and subsequent phases of change take place in concrete periods of time. Change, thus, in turn, is conceptualised (or even modelled) in different ways, e.g., as a challenge–response sequence. Recent research in the field of cybersecurity studies, however, also points to the quality of uniqueness or singularity of conflicts responsible for infrastructural dynamics. If taken seriously, change in certain cases occurs in arenas whose actors and activities (human and non-human), technologies, and issues are always uniquely produced and connected in an unfolding process. This poses further methodological challenges – the construction of an event as a significant temporally unfolding process and the respective heterogeneous elements. However, methodological debates can be fruitfully brought together and applied to the infrastructural dynamics that are presented in this chapter (Grenz, 2020; Latour & Venturini, 2010; Sewell, 2005).

Connecting Metaprocesses

From its inception, the mediatisation approach is meant to allow a connection to the broader modernisation theory. This way, mediatisation has been described as a historical metaprocess alongside other metaprocesses (such as individualisation, economisation, globalisation) (Krotz, 2007, p. 257). The insights into the conflicts and underground dynamics to which this paper is intended to sensitise, bring the comprehensive approach of Reflexive Modernisation into view (Beck et al., 1994). Two central figures to which empirical research on mediatisation could also make a weighty contribution, are key: reflexivity and risk (Eid, 2004). Empirically grounded work on a theory of "Reflexive Mediatization" (Grenz, 2013; Grenz et al., 2014; Möll, 2018; Möll & Hitzler, 2017) has already drawn attention to reflexivity. Here, the focus lies on the aspect of risks or digital risks.

Over the past 20 years, several authors in sociology and social sciences have drawn attention to *digital* risks. Deeply influenced by the aftermath of

Edward Snowden's disclosure of the activities of the national security agency (NSA), Ulrich Beck (2014) famously referred to "digital risks" as a new form of risk. Beck emphasised a new kind of "digital freedom risk" (ibid.) that he attributed to the increasing digital surveillance infrastructure Snowden had made visible. Building on the significance of "digital surveillance", Lupton (2016, p. 301) points to the different "intersections between risk and digital technologies". Lupton distinguishes digital risks in terms of risky digital technology (surveillance), the use of digital technology (e.g., illegal internet activities) and new forms of digital social inequalities. Digital risks or "cyber risks" are highly dynamic, particularly because of a "vitality of digital data [...] their ceaseless movement and repurposing by a multitude of actors" (Amoore, 2011; Lash, 2007; Lupton, 2016, p. 302; Manovich, 2013). With regard to computer viruses, van Loon (2000, p. 169), and in a comparable manner Lupton (2016, p. 305), started to think about the above-mentioned technological dimension of this mediation.

In a revealing way, later on, van Loon (2014, p. 447) used the computer virus example in order to describe the particular self-reinforcing quality of digital artefacts like those viruses. Following van Loon, it is time to understand risk mediation not only in terms of "representation" (which means risk communication) but also performatively (ibid.). Scott Lash (2003, p. 54) also called for a revision of the theory of Risk Society in order to account for the technological condition nowadays, albeit in a theory-wise different way. According to Lash (ibid.), more and more institutions are getting "socio-technical" (e.g., protocols, standards, power relations inscribed in operating systems, etc.). Because of this entanglement, it becomes crucial to understand contemporary institutions' dynamics. However, those calls for a revision of the theory of the Digital Risk Society have been pursued surprisingly sparsely in the last 15 years.

A Promising Challenge

In this chapter, a hitherto underestimated or even neglected perspective on the ongoing transformation of digital infrastructures that underlie digital media and thus culture and society, was highlighted. As argued here, with digital mediatisation, the interventions in ever-more interconnected digital systems have become massively pluralised. And so have the actors, tactics, and strategies on the part of the businesses (but also other private and civil society actors) that try to come up with increasingly adaptive approaches. Resulting dynamics have progressed so far that it is no longer adequate to expect a confrontation of competing, more or less influential groups of actors (e.g., businesses and hackers, or contenders). Rather, socio-economically driven processes of mediatisation have undergone a deep and massive structural change. New and old – both human and non-human, self-reinforcing procedures (like viruses or worms, van Loon, 2014)) – agencies, plural interests and techno-material procedures merge into increasingly unstable, fast, and uncontrollable mediatisation processes. Thus, to account for these infrastructural dynamics turns out to be one of the greatest challenges of research on mediatisation – theoretically, methodologically, as well as empirically.

However, this challenge is also associated with a great gain. To date, the debate on the Digital Risk Society has not made any significant contributions to the technical mediation of digital risks (beyond the earlier works mentioned above). At the same time, digital risks play almost no role in the more recent mediatisation approach. Yet, reasonably practical aspects of risk assessment and risk mitigation, etc., are obligatory for the design of digital media and platforms. This text has only begun to demonstrate a potential alliance, a joint venture of mediatisation and Digital Risk Society, and there is still much work to be done. It is more than ever time to think about the "meta-" connections or interrelations of mediatisation and (Reflexive) Modernisation (Krotz, 2007; 2014), i.e., Risk Society. This attempt has perhaps been somewhat neglected in recent years in favour of small-scale analyses of most current phenomena, conjunctures of certain topics, or entrenched large-scale descriptions of mediatised societies.

Literature

Amoore, L. (2011). Data derivatives: On the emergence of a security risk calculus for our times. *Theory, Culture & Society, 28*(6), 24–43. https://doi.org/10.1177/0263276411417430

Auerswald, P., Duttweiler, C., & Garofano, J. (Eds.) (2003). *Clinton's Foreign Policy: A Documentary Record* (1st edition). Kluwer Law International.

Bechmann, A., & Bowker, G. C. (2019). Unsupervised by any other name: Hidden layers of knowledge production in artificial intelligence on social media. *Big Data & Society, 6*(1), 205395171881956. https://doi.org/10.1177/2053951718819569

Beck, U. (2014, April 8). Ulrich Beck: Digital risk in the modern society. *Social Europe.* https://www.socialeurope.eu/digital-risk

Beck, U., Giddens, A., & Lash, S. (1994). *Reflexive Modernization: Politics, Tradition and Aesthetics in the Modern Social Order.* Stanford, CA: Stanford University Press.

Benbya, H., Nan, N., Tanriverdi, H., & Yoo, Y. (2020). Complexity and information systems research in the emerging digital world. *Management Information Systems Quarterly, 44*(1), 1–17.

Bruns, A., & Burgess, J. (2016). Methodological innovation in precarious spaces: The case of Twitter. In H. Snee, C. Hine, Y. Morey, S. Roberts, & H. Watson (Eds.), *Digital Methods for Social Science: An Interdisciplinary Guide to Research Innovation* (pp. 17–33). Palgrave Macmillan UK. https://doi.org/10.1057/9781137453662_2

Castells, M. (2010). *The Rise of the Network Society* (2nd edition, with a new preface). Wiley-Blackwell. https://doi.org/10.1002/9781444319514

Condon, E., He, A., & Cukier, M. (2008). Analysis of computer security incident data using time series models. 19th International Symposium on Software Reliability Engineering (ISSRE), 77–86. https://doi.org/10.1109/ISSRE.2008.39

Couldry, N., & Hepp, A. (2017). *The Mediated Construction of Reality*. Polity.

Craigen, D., Diakun-Thibault, N., & Purse, R. (2014). Defining cybersecurity. *Technology Innovation Management Review*, 4(10), 13–21.

Cukier, M. (2007). Study: Hackers attack every 39 seconds. https://eng.umd.edu/news/story/study-hackers-attack-every-39-seconds

CVE (2021). Common vulnerabilities and exposures. https://cve.mitre.org/about/index.html

Deibert, R. (2011). Tracking the emerging arms race in cyberspace. *Bulletin of the Atomic Scientists*, 67(1), 1–8. https://doi.org/10.1177/0096340210393703

Deibert, R. (2016). *Cyber-Security*. Routledge Handbooks Online. https://doi.org/10.4324/9781315753393.ch16

Dolata, U. (2018). Privatisierung, Kuratierung, Kommodifizierung: Kommerzielle Plattformen im Internet (SOFI Working Paper Series). https://www.econstor.eu/handle/10419/179973

Eaton, B., Elaluf-Calderwood, S., Sorensen, C., & Yoo, Y. (2011, April). Dynamic structures of control and generativity in digital ecosystem service innovation: The cases of the Apple and Google mobile app stores (LSE Working Paper Series) [Monograph]. www.lse.ac.uk/management/research/academic-groups/information-systems-and-innovation/home.aspx

Edwards, P., Bowker, G., Jackson, S., & Williams, R. (2009). Introduction: An agenda for infrastructure studies. *Journal of the Association for Information Systems*, 10(5), 346–373.

Eid, M. (2004). Reflexive modernity and risk society. *International Journal of the Humanities: Annual Review*, 1(1), 0–0. https://doi.org/10.18848/1447-9508/CGP/v01/58162

Flowers, S. (2008). Harnessing the hackers: The emergence and exploitation of outlaw innovation. *Research Policy*, 37(2), 177–193.

Gibbs, M., Meese, J., Arnold, M., Nansen, B., & Carter, M. (2015). #Funeral and Instagram: Death, social media, and platform vernacular. *Information, Communication & Society*, 18(3), 255–268. https://doi.org/10.1080/1369118X.2014.987152

Gillespie, T. (2010). The politics of "platforms." *New Media and Society*, 12(3), 347–364. https://doi.org/10.1177/1461444809342738

Gillespie, T. (2017). The platform metaphor, revisited. *Culture Digitally*. http://culturedigitally.org/2017/08/platform-metaphor/

Greenberg, A. (2020). The confessions of the hacker who saved the internet. *Wired*. https://www.wired.com/story/confessions-marcus-hutchins-hacker-who-saved-the-internet/

Grenz, T. (2013). Reflexive mediatization: The frictional interplay between customers and providers. Department of Sociology, Karlsruhe Institute of Technology. https://www.researchgate.net/publication/340024047_Reflexive_Mediatization_The_frictional_interplay_between_Customers_and_Providers_KIT-WPS. (KIT-WPS).

Grenz, T. (2017). *Mediatisierung als Handlungsproblem: Eine wissenssoziologische Studie zum Wandel materialer Kultur*. Springer.

Grenz, T. (2020). Processualizing data: Variants of process-produced data. *Canadian Review of Sociology/Revue Canadienne de Sociologie*, 57(2), 247–264. https://doi.org/10.1111/cars.12280

Grenz, T., & Eisewicht, P. (2017). Variants of interplay as drivers of media change. *Media and Communication*, 5(3), 5–14. https://doi.org/10.17645/mac.v5i3.971

Grenz, T., & Kirschner, H. (2018). Unraveling the app store: Toward an interpretative perspective on tracing. *International Journal of Communication, 12,* 612–628.

Grenz, T., Möll, G., & Reichertz, J. (2014). Zur Strukturierung von Mediatisierungsprozessen. In F. Krotz, C. Despotović, & M.-M. Kruse (Eds.), *Die Mediatisierung sozialer Welten* (pp. 73–91). Springer VS. https://doi.org/10.1007/978-3-658-04077-2_4

Grenz, T., & Pfadenhauer, M. (2017). De-Mediatisierung: Diskontinuitäten, Non-Linearitäten und Ambivalenzen im Mediatisierungsprozess. In M. Pfadenhauer & T. Grenz (Eds.), *De-Mediatisierung* (pp. 3–23). Springer VS. https://doi.org/10.1007/978-3-658-14666-5_1

Hanseth, O., & Lyytinen, K. (2010). Design theory for dynamic complexity in information infrastructures: The case of building internet. *Journal of Information Technology, 25*(1), 1–19. https://doi.org/10.1057/jit.2009.19

Henfridsson, O., & Bygstad, B. (2013). The generative mechanisms of digital infrastructure evolution. *Management Information Systems Quarterly, 37*(3), 896–931.

Hepp, A. (2020). *Deep Mediatization: Key Ideas in Media & Cultural Studies.* Abingdon: Taylor and Francis. https://doi.org/10.4324/9781351064903

Jenkins, H. (2007). "Vernacular creativity": An interview with Jean Burgess (Part One). http://henryjenkins.org/blog/2007/10/vernacular_creativity_an_inter.html

Jenkins, H. (2009). *Confronting the Challenges of Participatory Culture.* Cambridge, MA: MIT Press.

Kirchner, S., & Beyer, J. (2016). Die Plattformlogik als digitale Marktordnung. *Zeitschrift Für Soziologie, 45*(5), 324–339. https://doi.org/10.1515/zfsoz-2015-1019

Koutsikouri, D., Lindgren, R., & Henfridsson, O. (2017, January 4). Building digital infrastructures: Towards an evolutionary theory of contextual triggers. Hawaii International Conference on System Sciences. https://doi.org/10.24251/HICSS.2017.575

Krotz, F. (2007). The meta-process of "mediatization" as a conceptual frame. *Global Media and Communication, 3*(3), 256–260. https://doi.org/10.1177/17427665070030030103

Krotz, F. (2014). 6. Mediatization as a mover in modernity: Social and cultural change in the context of media change. In *Mediatization of Communication* (pp. 131–162). De Gruyter Mouton. www.degruyter.com/document/doi/10.1515/9783110272215.131/html

Lash, S. (2003). Reflexivity as non-linearity. *Theory, Culture & Society, 20*(2), 49–57. https://doi.org/10.1177/0263276403020002003

Lash, S. (2007). Power after hegemony: Cultural studies in mutation? *Theory, Culture & Society, 24*(3), 55–78. https://doi.org/10.1177/0263276407075956

Latour, B., & Venturini, T. (2010). The social fabric: Digital traces and quali-quantitative methods. *Proceedings of Future En Seine 2009.* https://medialab.sciencespo.fr/en/productions

Lupton, D. (2016). Digital risk society. In A. Burgess, A. Alemanno, & J. Zinn (Eds.), *The Routledge Handbook of Risk Studies* (pp. 301–309). Abingdon and New York: Routledge.

Manovich, L. (2013). *Software Takes Command.* London: A&C Black.

Möll, G. (2018). Die Verdatung des Glücks. Varianten reflexiver Mediatisierung in den sozialen Welten des kommerziellen Glücksspiels. In T. Mämecke, J.-H. Passoth, & J. Wehner (Eds.), *Bedeutende Daten: Modelle, Verfahren und Praxis der Vermessung und Verdatung im Netz* (pp. 105–141). Springer Fachmedien. https://doi.org/10.1007/978-3-658-11781-8_7

Möll, G., & Hitzler, R. (2017). Zwischen spekulativen Strategien und strategischen Spekulationen. Zur reflexiven Mediatisierung riskanter Geldverausgabung. In F. Krotz, C. Despotović & M.-M. Kruse (Eds.), *Mediatisierung als Metaprozess: Transformationen, Formen der Entwicklung und die Generierung von Neuem* (pp. 211–232). Springer Fachmedien. https://doi.org/10.1007/978-3-658-16084-5_10

Murdock, G. (2017). Mediatisation and the transformation of capitalism: The elephant in the room. *Javnost – The Public*, 24(2), 119–135. https://doi.org/10.1080/13183222.2017.1290745

O'Reilly, T. (2005). *What Is Web 2.0*. https://oreilly.com [file].

Plantin, J.-C., Lagoze, C., Edwards, P. N., & Sandvig, C. (2018). Infrastructure studies meet platform studies in the age of Google and Facebook. *New Media & Society*, 20(1), 293–310. https://doi.org/10.1177/1461444816661553

Plantin, J.-C., & Punathambekar, A. (2019). Digital media infrastructures: Pipes, platforms, and politics. *Media, Culture & Society*, 41(2), 163–174. https://doi.org/10.1177/0163443718818376

Ray, P. P. (2018). A survey on Internet of Things architectures. *Journal of King Saud University – Computer and Information Sciences*, 30(3), 291–319. https://doi.org/10.1016/j.jksuci.2016.10.003

Schäfer, M. T. (2009). Participation inside. In J. Raessens, M. van den Boomen, S. Lammes, A.-S. Lehmann, & M. T. Schäfer (Eds.), *User Activities between Design and Appropriation: Vol. Digital Material: Tracing New Media in Everyday Life and Technology* (pp. 147–158). Amsterdam University Press.

Sewell, W. (2005). *Logics of History: Social Theory and Social Transformation*. Chicago: University of Chicago Press.

Smeets, M. (2018). A matter of time: On the transitory nature of cyberweapons. *Journal of Strategic Studies*, 41(1–2), 6–32. https://doi.org/10.1080/01402390.2017.1288107

Smith, B. (2017, May 14). The need for urgent collective action to keep people safe online: Lessons from last week's cyberattack. Microsoft On the Issues. https://blogs.microsoft.com/on-the-issues/2017/05/14/need-urgent-collective-action-keep-people-safe-online-lessons-last-weeks-cyberattack/

Srnicek, N. (2016). *Platform Capitalism*. Cambridge: Polity Press.

Stevens, T. (2015). *Cyber Security and the Politics of Time*. Cambridge University Press. https://doi.org/10.1017/CBO9781316271636

Tilson, D., Lyytinen, K., & Sørensen, C. (2010). Digital infrastructures: The missing IS research agenda. *Information Systems Research*, 21(4), 748–759.

van Loon, J. (2000). Virtual risks in an age of cybernetic reproduction. In J. van Loon & B. Adam (Eds.), *The Risk Society and Beyond: Critical Issues for Social Theory* (pp. 165–182). Sage. https://doi.org/10.4135/9781446219539

van Loon, J. (2014). Remediating risk as matter–energy–information flows of avian influenza and BSE. *Health, Risk & Society*, 16(5), 444–458. https://doi.org/10.1080/13698575.2014.936833

Wojtkowski, Ł. (2017). The present tense of mediatization studies. *Mediatization Studies*, 1(1), 9. https://doi.org/10.17951/ms.2017.1.9

World Economic Forum. (2018). *The Global Risks Report 2018*. World Economic
    Forum. https://www.weforum.org/reports/the-global-risks-report-2018/
World Economic Forum. (2019). *The Global Risks Report 2019*. World Economic
    Forum. https://www.weforum.org/reports/the-global-risks-report-2019/
Zittrain, J. L. (2006). The generative internet. *Harvard Law Review*, *119*, 1974–2040.

7 Mediatisation of War and the Military

Current State, Trends, and Challenges in the Field

Roman Horbyk

Introduction

Communication and information have always been an integral part of warfare. A range of concerns from communicating with the troops to propaganda and disinformation can be traced back to such foundational works as The Seven Military Classics of Ancient China or Thucydides' *History of the Peloponnesian War*, and even beyond that, into the realm of myth and legend. Was not the story of the Trojan horse a successful psychological operation planting a narrative among the enemy that subverted that enemy from within, in the spirit of what we would today call reflexive control?

Moreover, war itself is sometimes seen as a form of communication. In the words of a contemporary expert: "Almost any use of military force is, first and foremost, an act of communication" (Rid, 2016 [2010], p. 434). And in his classic work of military strategy, Carl von Clausewitz wrote of the nations that move from communication by diplomacy to communication by warfare: "Is war not just another expression of their thoughts, another form of speech or writing?" (Clausewitz, 2007 [1832], p. 252).

The problem of the interrelation of the military, war, and media is of a narrower scope and of more recent origin. It is clearly the product of a society where the military and the information apparatuses are self-contained institutions. Many authors date the media–military nexus to the Crimean War (1853–1856) as the first large-scale conflict extensively covered by the press using the era's cutting-edge technology (Badsey, 2016 [2010]). The devastating global conflicts of the first half of the twentieth century signified intensified control over the media (ibid.), which continued into the Cold War era, with remarkable examples of media influence such as the Vietnam War (Hallin, 1986). Thanks to extensive changes in technology and the advent of mediatisation theory, the traditional questions about the interrelation of media and the military are being reframed in terms of how warfare is affected by mediatisation. The consensus is that the boundaries between the media and the military have shattered, sometimes to the point where "the media indeed [function] increasingly as the fourth branch of

DOI: 10.4324/9781003324591-10

military operations" (Horten, 2011, p. 43), alongside the army, navy, and air force.

This chapter aims to map the research field of mediatisation of war and/ or mediatisation of the military by presenting a comprehensive analysis of studies dealing with this problem. It will propose a typology thereof, as well as identify key challenges to developing theoretical perspectives on mediatisation of war. The chapter is structured accordingly. The next section reviews the concept of "mediatisation of war" through analysing the theoretical discussion around it. The third section compares this conceptual development with the extant empirical, applied studies that claim to use "mediatisation of war/the military" as their framework. The fourth section will summarise and discuss key outcomes of the analysis, leading to a concise conclusion.

Mediatisation of the military: Theory on the offensive

In this section, I will analyse the core of the *theoretical* conversation on how the military is integrated with media (i.e., becomes mediatised).

What is mediatisation?

The post-Cold War transformations of military strategy and practice sparked speculations of new types of war, such as "Revolution in Military Affairs", "netwar", "media war" or "cyberwar" (Arquilla & Ronfeldt, 1996; Badsey, 2016 [2010]; Cavelty, 2016 [2010]; Whyte et al., 2021). These transformations take place against the background of the overall integration of media and communication technologies within all spheres of social life. The concept of mediatisation serves to capture and explain this integration, whereby various institutions and phenomena become dependent on mediation and technologies that enable it. It is a form of conceptualising media change and influence without simplistic constructs such as straightforward media effects.

Mediatisation is approached from two distinct traditions. The institutionalist tradition strives to trace how social institutions are increasingly adopting "media logic", which requires treating media as a separate institution to begin with. The social-constructivist tradition focuses on how people do things differently when new technologies with new forms of mediation come into use.

One could suggest that both approaches bring different benefits to the study of war and the military. The institutionalist approach is fitting when studying macro-level interactions of clearly delineated institutions of modern society, such as the military and the media. On the other hand, the blurring of institutional boundaries may complicate such clear-cut analysis. A turn towards practices and cultures, inherent in the social-constructivist approach, may be more productive, especially on the micro level, which makes the author of this chapter incline towards this perspective in empirical studies on the ongoing mediatisation of war.

Mediatisation of war: Origins

Even though war and communication are inherently linked, and some suggest that "[t]hroughout history, violent conflict has always been mediatized" (Kaempf, 2013, p. 586), it was not always studied as such. War and media is a field spanning decades of research but obviously not every study of war reportage can be associated with mediatisation theory. Most research focuses on (mediated) representation of war or the institutional tug-of-war between journalists and military leadership. While these approaches are interesting and important in themselves, they miss the characteristic marks of mediatisation: focus on media change, technology, and mutual integration of logics and practices.

A distant precursor of the mediatisation of war approach can be traced back to Marshall McLuhan, who also theorised media landscapes of modern war. "World War 3 is a guerrilla information war with no division between military and civilian participation", McLuhan (1968, p. 66) wrote in 1968 while US public support for intervention in Vietnam crumbled during the Tet offensive, Vietkong's military disaster and media success. In fact, one can easily view McLuhan as an early visionary of "new wars" and hybrid warfare.

For a while, the military's integration with the media found a conceptual home in (post)structuralist and semiotic tradition. Jean Baudrillard had been one of the first to use the term "mediatisation" since 1971, in the context of sign value dominating use value of exchange objects and information becoming a self-referential reflection of the media code rather than representation of reality (Bolin, 2014, pp. 179–185). He also famously proclaimed later that the Gulf War was a simulacrum (Baudrillard, 1995). Theoreticians with strong cultural studies or anthropological perspectives described "cybernetic wars of persuasion and dissuasion" (Virilio, 2002, p. ix) and pictured the "military-industrial-media-entertainment" complex that merges war and amusement (Der Derian, 2002). Lucrecia Escudero (1996) developed Eliseo Verón's theory of mediatisation as social meaning-making, and studied the 1982 Falklands War as as an example of "the change from a society with a representation regime founded on media that 'tell the truth' to a new regime where media produce the reality" (Scolari & Rodriguez-Amat, 2018, p. 143; see Escudero, 1996; 2014).

The new turn: The 2000s

The scholarly effort to trace the transformation of the military–media relationship from the perspective of mediatisation theory intensified around 2006–2008. It was stimulated both by the contemporary US-led wars in Iraq and Afghanistan (also the key source of cases) and by the earlier philosophical and anthropological explications of media war. This effort consolidated and achieved a certain theoretical autonomy as recently as the 2010s.

It is hard to disagree with Crosbie (2015, p. 102) – even years later – that "there has yet to emerge a shared understanding of what the mediatization of wars and militaries might look like or how it might best be studied". To date, it mostly focuses on how the military adapts to the "'mediatized' environment in which the policies of states are formulated, debated and presented to the public" (McQuail, 2006) and how the military increasingly uses the media to negotiate both with its political governors and the broad public (Maltby, 2012; Crosbie, 2015). Another approach tries to dissect different phases of mediatisation of the military to find how it co-opts participatory and web 2.0 content for its institutional purposes (Hoskins and O'Loughlin 2010b; 2015). Finally, mediatisation is invoked in the very different corpus of studies dealing with the coverage of war by new media (Karlin & Matthew, 2012; Siapara et al., 2015; Joobani, 2017; Mortensen, 2015; Shim & Stengel, 2017) as well as legacy media (Esser, 2009; Horten, 2011; Zhang, 2019; 2020; Morse, 2018a; 2018b).

There are also significant efforts to formulate theoretical interrelationships between media and war. Simon Cottle (2006, p. 9) stressed how the media do not simply produce more content on war but become involved in it in "active, performative ways" and "do things with conflicts". In particular, Cottle was instrumental in making a terminological choice in favour of mediatisation rather than mediation, at a time when the discipline still hesitated about it. In his view, mediation implied a neutral middle ground while mediatisation conveyed a "much stronger sense of media involvement" (ibid.). At the same time, he focused on a broader spectrum of phenomena than just armed confrontation. In Cottle, mediatised "conflict" functions as a broad umbrella category to shelter such different spheres as protest, war, environmental issues, and identity politics. It is mediatisation that provides the point of gravity while, as the author himself admitted, the concept does not receive much analytical development in return. It also forms a nexus of these disparate areas and allows us to discover how "mediatised conflicts" are often born at the intersection of multiple fields and actors. Thus, Cottle concluded that "[m]ediatized war, inevitably, will continue to be a battlefield in its own right, and one where journalists are expected by governments, military, and publics to pursue conflicting goals [...]" (ibid., p. 99).

Institutional approaches of the 2010s

Later studies developed this perspective in attempt to dig deeper into institutional relationships. Sarah Maltby (2012) approached the military–news media nexus using an extensive case study of the British army. She found that "the military increasingly engage with the media to achieve its own institutional goals and protect against vulnerabilities" (p. 265) and, on top of that, do so proactively. Their entire work is restructured "in a manner that conforms to media production" (p. 266). Mediatisation is evident in that the military increasingly uses news media in order to communicate with its personnel and their families (even to sustain morale), the government, and society at large. "[T]he media provides the rationale and interface for interactions between the military and their audiences, and the institutional activities of the military come to be organized around this fact" (p. 262).

Much of this work builds on assumptions and "simplistic notions regarding media effects", which is indicative of the mediatised military; as there are no means to measure these effects, therefore "positive media coverage tends to be equated with public support" (ibid., p. 259). The audiences with which the military communicates are those that exist in its imagination.

Using Erving Goffman's interactionist approach, Maltby (2013, p. 102) followed up on this analysis with a greatly expanded account of how "all military activity is assuming a media form" due to a performative element. Yet it is not only the military that adopts media logic; as the media follows the actions of the military and their centre of gravity, it adopts the military logic, too. Trying to outmanoeuvre the military's information management, the media enacts its counter-moves, which in turn leads to further counter-moves by the military, leading to the media's new counter-moves, etc. Later still, Maltby (2015) added the third component – the marketing logic – forming a tripartite process of mediatisation–militarisation–marketisation, of all involved.

Thomas Crosbie (2015) is more concerned with the ramifications of media coverage for the military, something he also calls "military mediatization". He focuses on the cases of scandals around military activities which, in his opinion, incur losses of personnel or entire weapons systems (such as cluster bombs) that cannot be used due to being publicly discredited (only in the Western context, one feels compelled to add). Borrowing concepts from systems theory "as a means of categorizing Hepp's (2009; 2012) molding forces" (Crosbie, 2015, p. 106), the scholar proposes considering the "feedback" to the scandals in order to "better account for the feedforward (the shaping of future organizational behaviour in response to media logics)" (Crosbie, 2015, p. 102). He demonstrates, with the example of the biggest US military scandal of the 2000s, i.e. the torture of detainees at Abu Ghraib, that the military is concerned with the mediation of scandal only to the extent that it can negatively affect its capabilities or monopoly on force.

Phases of mediatisation: The diffused war and the arrested war

Another remarkable theoretical arc is that of Andrew Hoskins and Ben O'Loughlin. Starting from empirical research into consequences of communication in the context of terrorism, particularly jihadism, the War on Terror and counterinsurgency, Hoskins and O'Loughlin (2009) followed Cottle's model of mediatised conflict where "those conducting war are aware of themselves as involved in a process being recorded and disseminated via media [...]" (ibid., p. 83).

This springboard helped them launch the concept of "diffused war" (Hoskins & O'Loughlin, 2010a; 2010b) characterised by "more diffuse causal relations between action and effect" (Hoskins & O'Loughlin, 2010a, p. 906). This leads to unpredictable outcomes of the actions (including those by the military), subverting the military's activity and its very premises. Under diffused war, terrorist groups and other non-state actors can reap asymmetrical benefits of the media ecology because user-generated content can easily be co-opted and reframed by their master narrative and "[t]he proliferation of digital media content and connectivities makes it impossible to know in advance what content will go viral [...]" (Al-Lami et al., 2012, p. 239). That came, however, with a caveat that "despite this process being 'on the edge of chaos', order is achieved" (Hoskins & O'Loughlin, 2011, p. 205), suggesting the presence of a "network gate" that controls the chaotic flows at a higher level.

In later work, Hoskins and O'Loughlin (2015) develop this into a full-fledged theoretical model of mediatisation of war. They define mediatisation as "the process by which warfare is increasingly embedded in and penetrated by media" (ibid., p. 1323). Grounded in their previous work, they distinguish three distinct phases of mediatisation of warfare: (1) the well-managed broadcast era war (the 1990s); (2) the diffused war unfolding in chaotic, unpredictable, and participatory media ecology (the 2000s); and (3) the arrested war, "a new paradigm in which professional media and military institutions have arrested the once chaotic social media dynamics". Thus, "[t]he mainstream has enveloped the extreme" and "[t]he centre has adapted and come back even stronger" (ibid., 1320–1321). Accordingly, the qualities associated with the diffused war, such as alternative or subversive content, virality, fragmentation of news markets, and citizen-centric accounts, are now "arrested by the mainstream" and eventually by the media: "[M]edia has enclosed war within its infrastructure. Media arrests war" (ibid., p. 1321). The "subverted citizen" becomes integrated into the mainstream, media strategy of personalisation of the soldier allows securing public support, the military becomes more independent in media-ops, and the virality and connectivity are mobilised to serve the "centre" as new and user-generated content is integrated into the mainstream media, now busy with its verification. Instead of embedded journalists, "soldiers themselves are embedded journalists recording their own experiences, accomplishments, and feelings" (ibid., p. 1327), be it in milblogs or through helmetcams – the content that is then appropriated by mainstream media.

Hoskins and O'Laughlin use the example of Russia's war against Ukraine and standoff with the West, in which "chaos is embraced as a way to seize, define, and arrest the conflict's meaning" (ibid., p. 1329). The difficulty of verifying the identity of "the little green men" who annexed Crimea, both confused the media and audiences while also offering them a certain spectacle and televisuality. As the Kremlin's troll factories jam social media with noise, the communication forms that were not so long ago lauded as makers of revolutions now become fully appropriated by the elites. As a result, the perception of the media's role returns to the "hypodermic needle" model. "Western policy-makers and journalists alike see the Ukraine crisis through the first phase of mediatization, of linear influence efforts, and are thrown when Russian strategists have embraced the second and third phases of mediatization" (ibid., p. 1331). The doctrine of the Kremlin's theorist of postmodern propaganda, Vladislav Surkov, is to "show the constructed nature of all news and therefore the contestability of any claim" (ibid.). Through difficulty to know for sure what is real and what is fake, the Kremlin manages to keep any opposition confused.

One can certainly question certain aspects of this theory; for example, what qualifies as "mainstream" and "centre", whether other empirical cases from the Donbas War would not lend better support to the theory, or to what extent the threshold between the three stages is clear-cut. Göran Bolin et al. (2016), particularly, pointed out that while the Russo-Ukrainian War (comprising both annexation of Crimea and the Donbas War) has been successfully arrested from the Russian side, the Ukrainian perspective looks certainly more diffused, with a swarm of individual and collective actors working independently in the same direction. On the other hand, the analysis of digital content documenting the Donbas war confirms the theory of arrested war inasmuch as videos shot on portable devices and posted online can either be attributed to media-ops units directly or are used by them for propaganda purposes (Horbyk, 2020).

In this section, I have outlined the key tenets of mediatisation theory, as well as origins of the mediatisation of war concept in works by McLuhan and Baudrillard. The more empirically grounded conceptualisations, however, date to the post-9/11 landscape of the 2000s and 2010s, in works on "mediatised conflict" by Cottle, the institutionalist perspectives of Maltby and Crosbie, and the diffused/arrested war proposed by Hoskins and O'Laughlin. What all these attempts have in common is that they propose alternative (often mutually complementary) explanations of how the military navigates a changing mediascape. Having established this, the following section will analyse the *empirical* studies of mediatisation of war.

Mission creep: Applied studies on mediatisation of war and military

Apart from the studies reviewed in the previous section – works seeking to generate theory, where empirical cases have the key task of illustrating and supporting the conceptual framework – the largest bulk of war mediatisation studies belongs to what can be termed applied studies of how warfare is integrated with the media. Rather than theory-driven, this type of research is case-driven and uses mediatisation theory as an interpretive model to be tested or used to explain the empirical findings.

It is only logical that the applied approach is numerically stronger compared to the theoretical. "Mediatisation" is mentioned in 195 articles (132 of them research articles) published in the field's leading *Media, War and Conflict* journal since its inception in 2008. This is a significant number judged by the total 408 items published by the journal from 2008 up to the first issue in 2021 (among them, 264 research articles). Almost 48 per cent of all pieces, and 50 per cent of research articles, refer to the term, which represents a strong position of mediatisation in the generic field of war and media. At the same time, not all studies that refer to mediatisation in some form claim to use it as the theoretical foundation, or else actually do it. A closer review reveals that a significant part of impactful research articles is dispersed across other journals, primarily *Journalism* and *Information, Communication and Society*, even though *Media, War and Conflict* dominates. These three journals seem to be the arenas to go to for those who wish to address the field's community.

Below follows a mapping of empirical studies that explicitly position themselves in the mediatisation camp. They can be loosely grouped in six categories, according to their focus and type of material or case.

Group 1: Mediatisation as representation

First of all, one branch of research brings mediatisation theory to the much older field of representation of war. This branch is still focused on the concept of "mass media", occasionally pulling in material from social media by way of comparison or backing for the main findings. It also tends to belong to the institutionalist approach within mediatisation studies. For example, Frank Esser (2009) was rather early with an empirically solid, quantitative study of how the media perceived their own role in the Iraq War through "media-on-media reports", or metacoverage. Thus, Esser spoke of "mediated wars" that are "almost entirely" perceived through mass media coverage driven by media logic to which "the political and military protagonists increasingly adapt their behavior" (ibid., p. 710).

Some scholars are sceptical regarding the scope of media influence. Even though mediatisation of war has greatly accelerated since the 1960s, the media are still reflective of the political environments in their countries, Gerd Horten (2011) posited. And whereas he suggested that the role of media in the Vietnam War is often exaggerated, this (mis)perception led to a total control over the media during the Gulf War while transformations during the 2003 Iraq War were ambiguous, complex, and multi-directional. However, it seems too shallow to define mediatisation as a one-way impact of the media. Rather, mediatisation implies a mutual integration of logics and practices, which in no way cancels the significance of the political system. As the politics is mediatised, the media also becomes politicised, which to a large extent explains the contradiction observed by Horten.

Using the material from Al-Jazeera's coverage of the 2008 Gaza War, Tal Morse (2018b, p. 398) developed "the analytics of mediatized grievability" (ibid., p. 385) that assesses whether the media humanises the dead, producing a witnessing text and commonality in time and space. This in particular shows how well mediatisation combines with other critical frameworks such as Judith Butler's notion of grievability. It can also overlap with other fields of research (this is already evident in Cottle, 2006), for example in Mohammad Kalantari's (2020) analysis of mediatised Shi'ism as a religious movement influenced by the media in the context of the Iran–Iraq War. Focusing mainly on conspiracy theories, Eileen Culloty (2020) suggested that mediatised conflict is especially challenging for the media by virtue of its uncertainty which creates space for conspiratorial thinking.

In some other studies, mediatisation functions at worst as a catchy-trendy concept; at best as a sign of recognition of the media-saturated society without deeper theoretical implications or connections to the core subject of the study. Stig Arne Nohrstedt (2016, p. 159), who wrote extensively on war journalism, suggested that the media "are being dragged into the wars […] irrespective of legal and territorial borders". Speaking of this perceived unidirectional dominance of the military over the media, he proposed an interesting "conceptual twin, the 'martialization', of conflict journalism" (ibid., p. 160). Reviewing the cases of the military's manipulation of embedded journalists and physically targeting independent journalists in war, Nohrstedt & Ottosen (2014) pointed out, from the West-centric perspective, the legal issues, the merger of news and entertainment, cooperation of filmmakers with the military, the role of computer games, and drone warfare.

Group 2: New and legacy media in war

The second branch of applied mediatisation of war studies combines the focus on the legacy and new media almost in equal shares, reflecting the realities of a hybrid media system. For Mette Mortensen (2015), a new culture of witnessing arises through visual, connective and shareable representation of conflict by the belligerents, legacy media and bottom-up actors – not unlike in Hoskins and O'Loughlin's diffused war.

Shixin Ivy Zhang (2019; 2020) also applied Hoskins and O'Loughlin's (2015) model in combination with actor-network theory to the Chinese context, finding that both professional media and users form the agenda together: the mainstream media appropriate social media content whereas users counter-set and expand the mainstream agenda. This, I believe, should be questioned for the lack of discussion of the users' uncertain identity in the age of troll farms; it may well be that much of the Chinese social media debate is in fact steered by authorities. In any case, Zhang's findings indicate the presence of a "network effect" of mutual benefits whereby the network enables users to communicate, and the users add value to the network. As a result, "the dividing line between views and news blurred" (Zhang, 2019, p. 10).

Beatriz Herrero-Jiménez et al. (2018, p. 153) spoke of "a new mode of political mediatization". The authors demonstrated not only how social media content from the Syrian War blended into coverage by legacy media, but also how European political parliamentary discourse shifted from believing in social media as a valuable tool of information and democracy to fearing it as a threat rife with extremist content and disinformation. It seems only appropriate to invoke the concept of *pharmakon* – a medium that is at once poison and cure – as developed by Jacques Derrida from Plato. New and social media have clearly become such *pharmakon* for the society that moved from techno-optimism to infodemic of fake news and conspiracy theories.

Group 3: Use of social and new media by involved actors

The third group of studies focuses on the use of social and new media by the military or other actors in war. Eugenia Siapara et al. (2015) employed and, to some degree, tested the three phases theory of Hoskins and O'Loughlin (2010b; 2015) based on the analysis of 3 million tweets around the 2014 Gaza War. While admitting the arrival of arrested war, this study is mainly built around the notion of diffused war. The empirical analysis though, it seems, points in the direction of arrested war indeed, as "most influential actors were news organizations and political leaders" (Siapara et al., 2015, p. 1314). There was also significant evidence for bot activity "including news aggregation, human user mimicking and automated retweets" (ibid., 1314).

As in some studies on traditional media coverage, mediatisation is often "missing in action" in works on social media in war where the concept is hardly used as an interpretive device. This "weak" (as opposed to "strong") form of mediatisation research is curiously found in scholarship on how social media are used by or around the military (Karlin & Matthew, 2012; Crilley, 2016; Shim & Stengel, 2017). David Shim and Frank Stengel (2017) highlighted how gender theory and feminist technoscience can be applied to visual self-presentation of the Bundeswehr. Here, mediatisation is understood as simply "representation of war in different media". Masculine and technocentric as these representations are, it is unclear how exactly mediatisation changes this traditional, millennia-old construction. A classic case of a representation study, it uses a Facebook photo album as a glossy illustrated magazine of sorts, almost as a substitute for legacy media content. As a result, mediatisation does less useful work in this study than it could; it never occurs in the final discussion or conclusions. This somewhat typical situation is hardly amended in Laura Shepherd's (2017) response, where mediatisation is once again used as synonymous with representation ("represented in the media or mediatised, to use the vocabulary of this research programme", ibid., p. 350). There is of course nothing wrong with using the term to mean something that differs from its use in much of the mediatisation theory debate – a semantic monopoly is the last thing scholarship needs – but it is still difficult to see how using mediatisation merely in lieu of representation, or in the sense of "something being in a media form", can advance knowledge. In any case, such conceptual *malentendus* testify to the early phase of the theory's development.

Groups 4 and 5: Arts and history

Some studies apply mediatisation theory in the context of literary and artistic representations of war. Syrine Hout's (2017) analysis of literary "fallout" from the 2006 war in Lebanon revealed how blogosphere, video-art and comic books augment representation of wartime experiences in books by Lebanese authors. Others approach mediatisation from a generally semiotic/(post)structuralist perspective, such as Amey (2014), who proposed a story-telling approach to the mediatisation of journalists' war coverage, or Hossein Joobani (2017) who defined Islamic State's terror strategy as "mediatisation of savagery" in a Baudrillardian sense.

There seem to be emerging the beginnings of a historical approach to mediatisation of the military and war, too. One example is a recent volume edited by Christoph Cornelissen and Marco Mondini (2021) on the mediatisation of war and peace around World War I and the Interbellum when traditional printed and new media (such as cinema) interplayed with the military conflict, caught up in clashing motives of the military and the press. As a rare exception, there is also a complete history of the mediatisation of one nation's military: Rafi Mann (2015) outlined a complex relationship between the Israeli Defence Forces and the press since 1948, while Michal Shavit (2016) focused on the case study of mediatisation of the IDF in 2000–2014, finding that media activities became the military's "interpretive grid" (ibid., p. 1).

Group 6: Digital war

One of the recent developments is the emergence of a fledgling field of digital war (Merrin, 2018) that captures the consequences of new technological affordances for war. The field refuses to treat developments in the media separately from those that affect military communication and weaponry, evident in the broad use of drones, robotics, AI, cyber-attacks, and so on. It is yet unclear what the relationship of this new field is to that of mediatisation of war and military. It is likely that it will specialise in different aspects of the problem, and the mediatisation of war approach will focus more on representations and military–journalist relations, while digital war will deal with mediated weaponry, communication infrastructures, and everyday media practices.

The seeds of the latter approach can already be found in such empirical studies as Olga Boichak's (2019) dissertation (cf. Boichak & Jackson, 2019), where she examined how mediated narratives mobilise networked publics, often reaching far beyond the homeland into the diaspora. A different study within an ongoing research project on the role of mobile phones in the Donbas War and the 2022 Russian invasion of Ukraine shows that the technology is deeply integrated into combat, erasing boundaries between the civilian and the military. Smartphones are used simultaneously to communicate with family, entertain, coordinate fire, wiretap the foe and the friend, map the minefields, etc. – and all of it while being officially banned at the front line (Horbyk, 2022).

This new field is rapidly crystallising around the eponymous *Digital War* journal founded by Andrew Hoskins and William Merrin under a tongue-in-cheek motto "There is no longer war, there is only digital war". The journal embraces in an interdisciplinary fashion a wide range of problems – from the use of drones and AI in warfare to digital technologies in military archaeology. In the first issue, Ben O'Loughlin provocatively suggested going further still, towards a "post-digital war" which is "to see how digital innovations have already been integrated into how militaries, media and societies wage, resist and understand war" (O'Loughlin, 2020, p. 123).

In this section, I reviewed the empirical studies that use a mediatisation framework in the context of war and the military, identifying key journals and developing a typology that consists of six groups of studies, focusing on (1) media representation, (2) use of new versus old media, (3) use of social and new media by various actors, (4) artistic representations of war, (5) history of war mediatisation, and (6) digital war. I will now analyse and discuss the results of this research field mapping in the next section.

Mapping the (battle)field: Disposition of forces, lines of attack

What does the field of war/military mediatisation look like, then? It is rapidly developing and has already produced relatively intensive debates and concepts with strong explanatory potential, such as "mediatized conflict" (Cottle, 2006), "mediatization of the military" (Maltby, 2012), "diffused war" vs. "arrested war" (Hoskins & O'Loughlin, 2010b, 2015), and "mediatized grievability" (Morse, 2018a, 2018b). Some of these concepts have stimulated discussion and inspired empirical applications. In particular, Simon Cottle's "mediatized conflict" and Hoskins and O'Loughlin's "diffused vs. arrested war" can be seen as central concepts in the field. It has also stimulated the trunking of a new branch that lays claim to a field of its own: that of digital war (Merrin, 2018). It has a particularly strong and already demonstrated potential to connect with other disciplines, theories, and fields such as feminist and gender theories, history, and studies of culture and religion. All of it points to a still young and developing field with potential for growth. As it appears in early 2022, the principal lesson of one and a half decades of studying the mediatisation of war and the military is that the boundaries between the military and the media, legacy and new media, and even war and peace have loosened and hybridised.

At the same time, there are several problems that impede the expansion and institutionalisation of the field.

Problem 1: Lack of conceptual consensus, clarity, and development

The key challenge for research on the mediatisation of the military lies in clarifying its relationship with other larger and rather crowded fields it partly overlaps with. First, the self-consciousness of the field is weak, and there is a lack of distinction from the broader area of war and journalism/media. Willingness to reflect thereupon is also lacking. Many studies simply use "mediatisation" as a more fashionable synonym of representation, which fails to harness the full potential of mediatisation theory as developed in media studies. Mediatisation is best thought of in terms of a three-way relationship between the military, the media and the audiences; yet many are preoccupied with only one element in the triangle.

Of course, it may reflect the fact that this theory is still far from its definitive form, and there is some unclarity and discussion as to what mediatisation should mean. But if mediatisation of war and the military is to become a robust branch capable of not only borrowing and applying mediatisation theory to individual cases but also of contributing to the theory and advancing it, it will have to clearly demarcate its boundaries and develop a consensus on its key notion. By contrast, a much younger and smaller digital war approach is already more assertive and self-conscious in carving out a space for itself as an independent field.

Problem 2: Lack of dialogue with overlapping fields

The second problem can be seen in the lack of dialogue with other fields that partly overlap with its scope. Mediatisation of war and the military is much more isolated from military and security studies, sociology of the military, and even military strategy and tactics with a focus on information warfare than it is from the study of war representation by journalists. At the same time, as the military and media logics fuse, scholars of this process must understand full well what the military logic, and the perspective of the military, is. Military studies would also be enriched by the critical and theoretical perspective of mediatisation studies. For example, Whyte et al. (2021), a new and well-researched volume on information warfare within security studies, does not mention mediatisation. Such leading journals in military studies as *International Security* and *Survival*, let alone the professional journal of the US Army, *Military Review*, do not return any results upon a "mediatisation" query. *Security Dialogue* and *Studies in Conflict and Terrorism* published some articles on media, yet even "mediation" is used there overwhelmingly in the legal sense. While not without difficulties, such dialogues would certainly be enriching for all participants.

From the perspective of media studies, mediatisation of war and the military is much preoccupied with the hybridisation of different areas – and simultaneously it lacks a connection with a key concept in current military theory: hybrid warfare (and its equivalents). Implying the weaponisation of all things civilian (including all sorts of media), this concept offers unique opportunities for the application of mediatisation theory.

Problem 3: Lack of empirical studies on the ground

At the same time, mediatisation is insufficiently used to critically study how new media and communication technologies blend into actual combat. This presents the third principal challenge to mediatisation of the military, coinciding with the need for more empirical, on-the-ground studies in spite of the tremendous difficulties of such work. In the words of Crosbie (2015, p. 105):

> For example, night-vision goggles and subvocal communications technology allow for extraordinarily mediated experiences in battlefields; remote sensors mediate the experiences of pilots and sailors (Adamsky, 2010; see also Mortensen, 2009); and drones allow officers in Syracuse, NY, to kill people in Afghanistan.
>
> (Bumiller, 2012)

As the scholar continues, "[t]hese are all fully mediated experiences and worthy of research" even though he believes they "should be analytically separated from instances of mediation where the process is affected by the logics of news media" (ibid.). The utility of such separation is perhaps less certain, but in any case the need to go beyond "news media" in mediatisation is urgent. To a large extent, this challenge is now to be answered by the emerging field of digital war.

Conclusion

Even though the beginnings of theoretical reflection on mediatisation of war can be found in works by McLuhan and by Baudrillard, the terms "mediatised conflict/war" became established in the mid-2000s, in part thanks to the effort of Cottle (2006). Key studies focused the debate on how the military adapts to transformations of news media (Maltby, 2012; Crosbie, 2015) and how virality and connectivity have shaken the constraints of media management in the diffused war (Hoskins & O'Loughlin, 2010b) and then became co-opted in the arrested war (Hoskins & O'Loughlin, 2015). Apart from these theoretical efforts, mediatisation informs a conceptual backdrop in many empirical war and media studies (many of them published in *Media,*

War and Conflict) that can be subsumed under six groups: (1) representation of war, (2) new versus legacy media in war, (3) new and social media use in war, (4) artistic mediation, (5) history of war mediatisation, and (6) digital war, which also lays claim to a field of its own concentrated around the eponymous journal.

Despite three key deficits – of conceptual consensus and development, of dialogue with adjacent fields, and of on-the-ground studies, the field is certainly dynamic and capable of generating highly productive concepts and models. The robustness of the field is evident from its capacity to produce new fields (such as digital war). Another promising direction stems from Niemeyer and Ericson's (2019) proposal to study temporalities of mediatisation, which begins to take form in recent studies on the history of military mediatisation. The focus on the *longue durée* returns us to the origins, back to the state where not only is war inseparable from communication, but communication becomes a form of war, as with the Trojan horse.

Bibliography

Adamsky, D. (2010). *The culture of military innovation: The impact of cultural factors on the revolution in military affairs in Russia, the US, and Israel.* Stanford, CA: Stanford University Press.

Al-Lami, M., Hoskins, A. & O'Loughlin, B. (2012). Mobilisation and violence in the new media ecology: The Dua Khalil Aswad and Camilia Shehata cases. *Critical Studies on Terrorism*, 5(2), 237–256. https://doi.org/10.1080/17539 153.2012.692509

Amey, P. (2014). Mediatization of armed conflicts. From discourse to narratives. In A. Vautravers & D. Donovan (Eds), *Information warfare* (pp. 122–132). Geneva: Webster University Press.

Arquilla, J. & Ronfeldt, D. (1996). *The advent of netwar.* Santa Monica, CA: RAND Corporation.

Badsey, S. (2016 [2010]). Media war and media management. In G. Kassimeris & J. Buckley (Eds), *The Ashgate research companion to modern warfare* (pp. 401–418). London & New York: Routledge.

Baudrillard, J. (1995). *The Gulf War did not take place.* Bloomington: Indiana University Press.

Boichak, O. (2019). Battlefront assemblages: Civic participation in the age of mediatized warfare. Ph.D. Dissertation. Syracuse University.

Boichak, O. & Jackson, S. (2019). From national identity to state legitimacy: Mobilizing digitally networked publics in eastern Ukraine. *Media, War & Conflict*, 13(3), 258–279. https://doi.org/10.1177/1750635219829161

Bolin, G. (2014). Institution, technology, world: Relationships between the media, culture, and society. In K. Lundby (Ed.), *Mediatization of communication* (pp. 175–198). Berlin: De Gruyter. https://doi.org/10.1515/9783110272215

Bolin, G., Jordan, P. & Ståhlberg, P. (2016). From nation branding to information warfare: The management of information in the Ukraine–Russia conflict. In M. Pantti (Ed.), *Media and the Ukraine crisis* (pp. 3–18). New York: Peter Lang.

Cavelty, M. D. (2016 [2010]). Cyberwar. In G. Kassimeris & J. Buckley (Eds), *The Ashgate research companion to modern warfare* (pp. 123–145). London & New York: Routledge.

Clausewitz, C. von. (2007 [1832]). *On war*. Oxford University Press.

Cornelissen, C. & Mondini, M. (Eds) (2021). *The mediatization of war and peace: The role of the media in political communication, narratives, and public memory (1914–1939)*. Berlin & Boston: Walter de Gruyter.

Cottle, S. (2006). *Mediatized conflict: Developments in media and conflict studies*. Maidenhead: Open University Press.

Crilley, R. (2016). Like and share forces: Making sense of military social media sites. In L. L. Shepherd & C. Hamilton (Eds), *Understanding popular culture and world politics in the digital age* (pp. 51–67). Abingdon: Routledge. https://doi.org/10.4324/9781315673394-4

Crosbie, T. (2015). Scandal and military mediatization. *Media, War & Conflict, 8*(1), 100–119. https://doi.org/10.1177/1750635214531108

Culloty, E. (2020). Conspiracy and the epistemological challenges of mediatised conflict. In S. Maltby, B. O'Loughlin, K. Perry & L. Roselle (Eds), *Spaces of war, war of spaces* (pp. 83–102). New York & London: Bloomsbury Publishing. https://doi.org/10.5040/9781501360282.ch-005

Der Derian, J. (2001). *Virtuous war: Mapping the military-industrial-media entertainment network*. New York: Basic Books.

Escudero, L. (1996). *Malvinas: El gran relato*. Barcelona: Gedisa.

Escudero Chauvel, L. (2014). *Media stories in the Falkland–Malvinas conflict*. Nottingham: CCC Press.

Esser, F. (2009). Metacoverage of mediated wars: How the press framed the role of the news media and of military news management in the Iraq Wars of 1991 and 2003. *American Behavioral Scientist, 52*(5), 709–734. https://doi.org/10.1177/0002764208326519

Hallin, D. C. (1986). *The uncensored war: The media and Vietnam*. Oxford University Press.

Herrero-Jiménez B., Carratalá, A. & Berganza, R. (2018). Violent conflicts and the new mediatization: The impact of social media on the European Parliamentary agenda regarding the Syrian War. *Communication & Society, 31*(3), 141–157. https://doi.org/10.15581/003.31.3.141-157

Horbyk, R. (2020). The visual regime of the soldiering self at the East Ukrainian frontline. [Preprint]. *SSRN*, 1–15. http://ssrn.com/abstract=4258884

Horbyk, R. (2022). "The war phone": Mobile communication on the frontline in Eastern Ukraine. *Digital War*, online first, 1–16. https://doi.org/10.1057/s42984-022-00049-2

Horten, G. (2011). The mediatization of war: A comparison of the American and German media coverage of the Vietnam and Iraq Wars. *American Journalism, 28*(4), 29–53. https://doi.org/10.1080/08821127.2011.10677801

Hoskins, A., & O'Loughlin, B. (2009). Pre-mediating guilt: Radicalisation and mediality in British news. *Critical Studies on Terrorism, 2*(1), 81–93.

Hoskins, A. & O'Loughlin, B. (2010a). Security journalism and "the mainstream" in Britain since 7/7: Translating terror but inciting violence? *International Affairs, 86*(4), 903–924. https://www.jstor.org/stable/40865002

Hoskins, A. & O'Loughlin, B. (2010b). *War and media: The emergence of diffused war*. Cambridge: Polity.

Hoskins, A. & O'Loughlin, B. (2011). Remediating *jihad* for western news audiences: The renewal of gatekeeping? *Journalism, 12*(2), 199–216. https://doi.org/10.1177/1464884910388592

Hoskins, A. & O'Loughlin, B. (2015). Arrested war: The third phase of mediatization. *Information, Communication & Society, 18*(11), 1320–1338. https://doi.org/10.1080/1369118X.2015.1068350

Hout, S. (2017). Artistic fallout from the July 2006 War: Momentum, mediation, and mediatization. *Arab Studies Quarterly, 39*(2), 793–814. https://doi.org/10.13169/arabstudquar.39.2.0793

Joobani, H. A. (2017). From caliphate to hyperreality: A Baudrillardian reading of the Islamic State's mediatization of savagery. *Asian Politics & Policy, 9*(2), 340–346. https://doi.org/10.1111/aspp.12314

Kaempf, S. (2013). The mediatisation of war in a transforming global media landscape. *Australian Journal of International Affairs, 67*(5), 586–604. https://doi.org/10.1080/10357718.2013.817527

Kalantari, M. R. (2020). The media contest during the Iran–Iraq war: The failure of mediatized Shi'ism. *Media, War & Conflict,* first published online 31 January 2020: https://doi.org/10.1177/1750635220902192

Karlin, B. & Matthew, R. A. (2012). *Kony 2012* and the mediatization of child soldiers. *Peace Review: A Journal of Social Justice, 24*(3), 255–261. https://doi.org/10.1080/10402659.2012.704222

Maltby, S. (2012). The mediatization of the military. *Media, War & Conflict, 5*(3), 255–268. https://doi.org/10.1177/1750635212447908

Maltby, S. (2013). *Military media management: Negotiating the "front" line in mediatized war.* London: Routledge.

Maltby, S. (2015). Imagining influence: Logic(al) tensions in war and defence. In M. F. Eskjær, S. Hjarvard & M. Mortensen (Eds), *The dynamics of mediatized conflicts* (pp. 165–184). New York: Peter Lang. https://doi.org/10.3726/978-1-4539-1620-9

Mann, R. (2015). Not just intermediaries: The mediatization of security affairs in Israel since 1973. In U. Lebel & E. Lewin (Eds), *The 1973 Yom Kippur War and the reshaping of Israeli civil–military relations* (pp. 81–120). Lanham, MD: Lexington Books.

McLuhan, M. (1968). *War and peace in the global village.* New York: Bantam.

McQuail, D. (2006). On the mediatization of war: A review article. *International Communication Gazette, 68*(2), 107–118. https://doi.org/10.1177/17480485006062227

Merrin, W. (2018). *Digital war: A critical introduction.* London & New York: Routledge.

Morse, T. (2018a). The construction of grievable death: Toward an analytical framework for the study of mediatized death. *The European Journal of Cultural Studies, 21*(2), 242–258. https://doi.org/10.1177/1367549416656858

Morse, T. (2018b). Mediatized war and the moralizing function of news about disruptive events. *Journalism, 19*(3), 384–401. https://doi.org/10.1177/1464884917693861

Mortensen, M. (2009). The camera at war: When soldiers become war photographers. In R. Schubart et al. (Eds.), *War isn't hell, it's entertainment: Essays on visual media and the representation of conflict* (pp. 44–60). Jefferson, NC: McFarland.

Mortensen, M. (2015). *Journalism and eyewitnesses: Digital media, participation, and conflict*. London: Routledge.

Niemeyer, K. & Ericson, S. (2019). From live-tweets to archives of the future: Mixed media temporalities and the recent French terrorist attacks. *Media, War & Conflict, 12*(2), 125–130. https://doi.org/10.1177/1750635219853891

Nohrstedt, S. A. (2016). "Mediatization" of war and "martialization" of journalism: The twins threatening democracy and human rights in the New Wars. In U. Carlsson (Ed.), *Freedom of expression and media in transition. Studies and reflections in the digital age* (pp. 155–164). Gothenburg: Nordicom.

Nohrstedt, S. A. & Ottosen, R. (2014). *New wars, new media, new war journalism: Professional and legal challenges in conflict reporting*. Gothenburg: Nordicom.

O'Loughlin, B. (2020). Towards a third image of war: Post-digital war. *Digital War, 1*(1), 123–130.

Rasmussen, V. M. (2007). *The risk society at war: Terror, technology and strategy in the twenty-first century*. Cambridge University Press.

Rid, T. (2016 [2010]). Small wars and telecommunication. In G. Kassimeris & J. Buckley (Eds.), *The Ashgate research companion to modern warfare* (pp. 433–452). London & New York: Routledge.

Scolari, C. & Rodriguez-Amat, J. R. (2018). A Latin American approach to mediatization: Specificities and contributions to a global discussion about how the media shape contemporary societies. *Communication Theory, 28*, 131–154. https://doi.org/10.1093/ct/qtx004

Shavit, M. (2016). *Media strategy and military operations in the 21st century: Mediatizing the Israel Defence Forces*. London & New York: Routledge.

Shepherd, L. J. (2017). "Social media, gender, and the mediatisation of war": A reply to Shim and Stengel. *Global Discourse, 7*(2–3), 348–352. https://doi.org/10.1080/23269995.2017.1337981

Shim, D. & Stengel, F. A. (2017). Social media, gender and the mediatization of war: Exploring the German Armed Forces' visual representation of the Afghanistan operation on Facebook. *Global Discourse, 7*(2–3,) 330–347. https://doi.org/10.1080/23269995.2017.1337982

Siapera, E., Hunt, G. & Lynn, T. (2015). #GazaUnderAttack: Twitter, Palestine and diffused war. *Information, Communication & Society, 18*(11), 1297–1319. https://doi.org/10.1080/1369118X.2015.1070188

Virilio, P. (2002). *Desert screen: War at the speed of light*. London: Continuum.

Whyte, C., Thrall, A. T. & Mazanec, B. M. (2021). *Information warfare in the age of cyber conflict*. London & New York: Routledge.

Zhang, S. I. (2019). Mediatization of conflict in the social media era: A case study of the Sino–Indian border crisis in 2017. *Journalism, 22*(10), 2618–2636. https://doi.org/10.1177/1464884919870329

Zhang, S. I. (2020). *Media and conflict in the social media era in China*. London: Palgrave Macmillan.

Part III

Evolving Areas and New Conceptualizations

8 Mediatisation's Tensions and Tendencies

The Context of Homes, Householders, and Emerging Screen Interactions

Deborah Chambers

Introduction

This chapter focuses on the home and householders as a demarcated but fluid field to attend to some of the inconsistencies and strengths of mediatisation. The notion of a "mediatised home" may be approached in terms of velocities and degrees of media's integration into home life. Equally, domestic mediatisation concerns how emerging media technologies and symbolic systems transform householders' micro-modes of remote communication to sustain work, education, caregiving, informal socialising, and entertainment from home. This is illustrated by the intensified household reliance on new screen technologies such as Zoom during COVID 19 lockdown conditions. The pandemic lends urgency to an enquiry into productive approaches, concepts, and methods for academic considerations of the mediatisation of home and the domestic mediatisation of householders' interpersonal exchanges beyond home.

Highlighting mediatisation's tendency towards media-centrism, the chapter's first section pinpoints constituents of mediatisation that can counterbalance this propensity. To enhance mediatisation studies of homes and households, positive solutions to media determinism are pinpointed, typified by the social constructionist perspective as an open, cross-disciplinary, multi-method, and *multiscalar* approach. This section also presents the concept of an "intermediating nexus" between scales as a conceptual tool to study the interdependencies between macro and micro-levels of mediatisation.

The second section considers key approaches to the mediatisation of home by addressing Karin Knorr Cetina's concepts of *scopic media* and *synthetic situations* in her analysis of screen-based remote communication. These concepts are drawn on to study how households are mediatised via video call technology such as Zoom during COVID 19 lockdowns, from 2020 onwards. This avenue of enquiry invites consideration of Eliseo Verón's sociosemiotic approach to mediatisation, outlined in the third section. His concept of *semiotic rupture* underscores a growing mismatch between the

DOI: 10.4324/9781003324591-12

production and recognition of mediated symbols arising from the complex conditions of interactive screen technologies.

Through the example of Zoom, as a new mode of social discourse production, the final section explores how the home and householders are mediatised by these new technological features of communication. Combining the work of Verón and Knorr Cetina, it explains that the scopic mediation of remote interpersonal communication from home, via Zoom, comprises a synthetic situation involving *semiotic ruptures*. These converging gadgets and software applications *are sense production devices* that transform the home and household by generating *unanticipated modes of exchange*. I show how these synthetic situations have intensified trans-domestic communication as a feature of domestic mediatisation.

Counterbalances to media-centrism

Introduced in the 1990s, mediatisation comprises a broad approach rather than a single theory (Couldry and Hepp, 2013, p. 197). Its objective is to attend to the growing sphere of influence of communication media, including their proliferating quantity and expanding range, as interconnected processes embedded across all socio-cultural, political, and economic spheres (Ekström et al., 2016). Mediatisation refers, then, to the mounting significance of media for the human condition, conveyed in the idea that everyday life is more and more "mediatised". As a meta-theory or paradigm, mediatisation invites meta-level theorisations of media's influence on society and culture. The most challenging features of mediatisation are its scope and breadth. Mediatisation encompasses but wavers between grand theories and small-scale empirical research. As a synthesising concept, its purpose is to explain spheres of action and social domains where socio-cultural values and practices are interwoven with media. But its broad range can seem nebulous and unwieldy. How mediatisation plays out in the context of the home and household poses challenges.

Two traditions place differing emphases on the notion of a "media logic": an institutional and a social-constructionist approach. The institutional approach detects a media logic within a wide range of processes that facilitate and organise communication and social practices (Hjarvard, 2014). Conceived as a meta-process, this paradigm has been queried for its media-centric and self-propelling emphasis which can neglect human agency and certain non-media-centric dynamics (Deacon and Stanyer, 2014). If "the media" are assigned an omnipotent agency, then underlying political, socio-cultural, and economic forces shaping media institutions can be overlooked (Murdock, 2017). Suggestive of media determinism, this could hamper studies of media transformations relating to home and household.

Within the social constructionist approach, Krotz identifies *media transformations* and *transformations in everyday life, culture, and society* as the nucleus of mediatisation research. Mediatisation's goal is to consider and understand "everyday life, culture and society" *in the context of* media transformations (Krotz, 2017, pp. 108–109). Relations between media and culture are determined, then, by the specific cultural field under study. Rather than assuming the influence of media over other domains, the social constructionist approach offsets media-centrism by guiding conceptual enquiries into levels, modes, and velocities of media proliferation in specific social spheres (Couldry and Hepp, 2013).

A positive feature of mediatisation studies is its flexibility, acting as a counterbalance against the pitfalls of media determinism. Krotz (2017) argues that mediatisation's strength lies in its lack of standardisation. It is continually open to other disciplines, perspectives, and methods. Research within the German Research Foundation's (Deutsche Forschungsgemeinschaft) priority programme "Mediatised Worlds" (2010–2016) reflects this openness by advancing mediatisation as a meta-process, structured around three perspectives: transformations, discontinuities and reflective developments, and formations and generations (Krotz et al., 2017).

A second corrective to media-centrism is offered by Ekström et al. (2016), who identify three transdisciplinary and transparadigmatic tasks for mediatisation's research agenda: *historicity*, *specificity*, and *measurability*. First, investigations of temporal transformation processes need to be historicised. Second, differences between specific circuits and contexts must be pinpointed. Third, to enable comparisons, scales of mediatisation need to be measurable. These tasks seek to counteract the potential theoretical and empirical imprecisions of mediatisation. However, macro-level perspectives that focus on public spheres aim to capture wider structural processes. Yet they tend to understate micro-social dynamics. This privileging of wider structural processes and macro-level interests can pose difficulties for measuring and analysing the micro-dynamics of home life. How does mediatisation manifest in the context of household routines? How is digitally enabled communication beyond the home managed by householders? And how is mediatisation encountered, propelled, or resisted by householders in the intimate surroundings of home?

A third counterbalance against tendencies towards a media-centric logic is an accent on micro- and macro-levels or scales of society, to ensure contextual and relational precision. These scales encompass interpersonal relations and social networks, institutional and organisational procedures, and the vicissitudes of the wider economy (Krotz, 2017; Sowinska, 2016). If domestic mediatisation is about how macro-level media forces circumscribe home life at a micro-social level, it is also about how householders imagine, negotiate, re-interpret, and challenge these mutable forces (Chambers, 2016). This scalar approach coincides with the three tasks for a mediatisation agenda set out by Ekström et al. (2016). As a corrective to its media-centric and self- driving emphasis, Hjarvard (2014) recommends mid-level analysis of specific media institutions and systems such as politics, sport, and delineated contexts such as the home to understand how media intercede and influence patterns of social interaction. Similarly, media-*centred* rather than a centrist approach to mediatisation is advocated by Hepp et al. (2015) who highlight the interconnections between media and wider social cultural transformations (see also Couldry and Hepp, 2013). This approach accents the role of social actors in steering mediatising trends and tendencies to stress the progressively complex and unpredictable repercussions of media orientation and media saturation.

A scalar and media-*centred* approach offers a productive means of identifying, navigating, and synthesising various levels of research by integrating small-scale contexts, themes, and issues with broader scale mediatising patterns, trends, and currents. It facilitates empirically grounded research and a non-media-centric perspective to consider how the "logics" of various institutions function contemporaneously: how their differing logics converge and intercede. Although assessing exactly how these levels intersect is a challenge, an open theory – ranging over macro- and micro-levels – holds promise for gauging the implications of differing yet integrated scales of research. Mediatisation can be viewed as both a broad, long-term process and an integrating approach capable of combining and synthesising research across disciplines, perspectives, and scales. The challenge is to find theoretical and empirical techniques sensitive enough to explain the roles, processes, and implications of media as transformative forces within and across the three levels.

A fourth, related counterbalance to media-centrism is mediatisation's employment of multiple methods of data gathering and analysis as a feature of the social constructionist approach. Mediatisation's methodologies range from quantitative large-scale survey data for detecting macro-level patterns of change, to small-scale ethnographic observations and interviews for capturing granular detail relating to householders' everyday experiences of mediatisation. To analyse the interplay between home and the public sphere, mediatisation's strengths lie in its theoretical and methodological openness, its inherently *multiscalar* modulations and the use of multiple, qualitative and quantitative, methods. The home is approached in mediatisation studies as a defined field of media engagement, characterised by recent digital transformations in digital media hardware, software, and content.

However, to date we lack a thorough understanding of the intersections and interdependencies between macro- and micro-level processes. More precise procedures are required, particularly for the study of domestic mediatisation. Where does each level begin and end? Macro-level changes involve the algorithmic learning of householders' interpretations and uses of media software and symbolic content. This comprises alterations in software such as computer gaming and video call platforms such as Zoom, in response to patterns of use. Despite mediatisation's defining features as a meta-process, rigorous procedures are required to guide analyses of this *contraflow* of multiple media forces.

The concept of "mediation" advanced by Silverstone (1999) has synergies with mediatisation research. For Silverstone, mediation is constituted by interconnecting practices between producers and receivers of media texts (Silverstone, 2013). Explaining the "double articulation of media", he stipulated the need to approach media as both *symbolic* and *material* forms (Silverstone and Haddon, 1996). The term "mediatisation" was later introduced as an integrating conceptual framework to address the pervasive quality of media within varied practices interconnected with, oriented to or dependent on media. If "mediatisation" denotes the pervasive integration of media in daily life as part of wider socio-cultural changes, the term "mediation" remains relevant for discerning media's role in transmitting and distributing information (Jansson, 2013, p. 281).

"Mediation" and "mediatisation" can be productively linked via the term *intermediating nexus*. This concept helps pinpoint mediatisation's differing scales to assess the coordinative forces of mediatisation as part of a meta-process. It points to two emphases. First, this nexus enables enquiries into macro-processes: media institutions, technologies, discourses, symbols, and practices which form "interconnected regimes of media related dependencies and normalizations" (Jansson, 2014, p. 273). Second, it concedes that mediatising forces originate beyond the media, steered by complex contraflows between macro-level political and economic currents (such as corporate deregulation and non-media socio-cultural forces) and micro-scale forces (such as households and families). The term "intermediating nexus" can circumvent assumptions that "the media" comprise one external, separate institution that transforms the field of home, households, and personal life as a one-way process. As a set of contraflows, mediatisation involves a "logic" but not a separate or single "logic". Its multiple logics correspond to political economic, social, cultural, spatial, and temporal domains.

Mediatisation of home and households

Reflecting mediatisation's openness, research on media transformations in the home and among householders draws on related models such as domestication theory. Domestication emphasises householders' agency in navigating the home's complex media ecology. Utilising qualitative methods, domestication theory offers empirically grounded research supported by guiding concepts to assess how householders enfold and navigate media within altered household routines. Domestication concepts variously adopted in mediatisation studies of homes and households include "media repertoire" (Haddon, 2016) and "double articulation" (Silverstone and Haddon, 1996). "Double articulation" pinpoints the dual attributes of media as both material objects and symbolic texts to explain how they are shaped in relation to their social contexts (see Hartmann, 2006). The physicality of media technologies renders media "objects" meaningful while their affordances facilitate the consumption of "media texts" as transmitters of meaningful messages. However, the symbolic dimensions of this articulation are yet to be centred in mediatisation studies of home. The work of Verón, discussed below, offers a corrective to this oversight.

Three types of research which show how scholars have employed mediatisation in studies relating to homes and households are identified by Krotz (2017): (1) panel studies from a systematic perspective, (2) comparative studies of media transformations in defined social contexts, and (3) emerging or changing types of media. First, the systematic perspective is exemplified by the qualitative panel study of old and new media uses by Jutta Röser and colleagues. Their longitudinal study, employing ethnographic methods, investigates 25 heterosexual families' domestication practices in middle-class German households over a decade (Röser et al., 2017). The domestic sphere is approached as a decisive field of mediatisation, as a context of media consumption and discernment, to evaluate householders' use of classic mass media and online-based media (Peil and Röser, 2014). Accenting the openness and integrative aspects of mediatisation research, these authors combine mediatisation and domestication approaches to examine the domestication of the Internet.

Their longitudinal study explores the interplay of old and new home-based media to consider the extent to which classic media such as radio, TV programmes and newspapers are accessed online. It highlights convergence in domestic media use (Müller and Röser, 2017). With the coexistence of old and new media and variations in media practices between families, convergence of media was slow in middle-class German homes between 2011 and 2013. While new and diverse "practices" of domestic media use evolve, these scholars confirm that far from replacing "classic media" with online-capable convergent technologies, these householders negotiate the meaning of new media technologies and their content within an existing media repertoire.

New media propel mediatisation across three fields: the use of domestic media repertoires, the significance of lifeworld caesuras for domestic media activity, and changes in gender relations with the Internet. Media convergence, indicated by intersecting uses of traditional and new media, is characterised by cloud services that integrate data, applications, and personalised content across formats and contexts to support multi-device and cross-platform media use (Peil and Spaviero, 2017; Peil and Mikos, 2017). Media convergence is reflected in related studies of the adoption and integration of new media alongside existing media (D'heer & Courtois, 2016; Stauff, 2015). This body of research shows that convergent media contexts demand certain skills and resources such as investment of time, money, and social capital or help from experts (Peil and Röser, 2014). Finding that the non-linear adoption of convergent media can be rupturing, Röser and colleagues employ the concept of "deconvergence" to explain the disruptions involved in householders' simultaneous use of classic and new media (Peil and Spaviero, 2017; Peil and Mikos, 2017; Müller and Röser, 2017).

Second, to determine the onset of mediatisation, comparative studies focus on specific social contexts to gauge the parallels and divergences between past and present modes of communication in everyday practices. This is exemplified by research on changes in the reception of television in the home supplemented by use of a second screen while watching the big TV screen. For example, Göttlich and colleagues (2017) studied the use of mobile, digital devices such as laptops, smartphones or tablet computers as second screens in relation to the big TV screen, finding that changes in how television is received and used involve new modes of use and reception. They also discovered that applications used parallel or interlinked with the TV programme generate new modes of co-orientation in media reception supported by communication within wider social networks. This qualitative research, based on interviews with householders, accents the differing media generations and socialisations affected by these changes. The emphasis is on the dynamics of new media and the theoretical issues raised.

In my own work, I take the multiscreen living room as an example of how digital media mobilise the emergence of new domestic multiscreen activities. Drawing on quantitative data about patterns of use of screen devices and streaming services from the UK's communications regulator Ofcom (2018), I show that second screens foster elaborate household negotiations of personal time, shared time, and "family time". These new modes of temporal synchronicity can transform the living room into a flexible temporal zone (Chambers, 2019). Referring to the concept of "polymedia" (Madianou and Miller, 2012), this temporal perspective shows that new digital screen relations operate within *polymediated timescapes*. Second screens can open up and extend household time to produce new domestic screen cultures differentiated as *intra-domestic* and *trans-domestic* screen time. As such, mediatisation facilitates household navigations of newly supported relationships within home zones.

A third mode of research, focusing on specific types of emerging and changing media, shares similarities with systematic research but ranges beyond the home and household. In mediatisation research on emerging and changing media, Karin Knorr Cetina and colleagues emphasise that personal interactions are increasingly conducted via screens. This mediatisation of the face-to-face setting demands a rethink about one of the most basic elements of sociality: *the social situation*. Knorr Cetina (2009; 2014) refers to Goffman (1964) who viewed physical co-presence as the ideal type of human interaction: one where an individual has access to others' "naked senses". In turn, other individuals gain access to one's own senses. Goffman perceived these co-present situations, steered by cultural rules, to be essential for generating empathy and trust. However, remote communication via interactive screens is radically different from in-person face-to-face interactions.

Two concepts are advanced by Knorr Cetina et al. (2017): "scopic media" and the "synthetic situation". They explain that interactive screen media give rise to new modes of scopic media. Examples of scopic media include the telescope or computer-controlled screens. They argue that interactive screen technologies reconfigure the face-to-face situation as a *synthetic situation*. In ethnographic detail, and long before the pandemic, Knorr Cetina examined how traders engage in stock, bond, and currency trading, as cross-border transactions. Involving the exchange of currencies between trading centres in different countries with different time zones to conduct trading, these transactions rely on six or more computer screens that display the market (Knorr Cetina, 2014; Knorr Cetina et al., 2017). Their relevance for mediatisation studies of homes and households is revealed by highlighting a growing mediatisation of interpersonal communication.

Knorr Cetina's mediatisation approach is of particular significance for the study of transformations in social interactions sustained by video sharing platforms – from Instagram to Zoom. These technologies rely on *scopic mediation*, involving the visual attentiveness of observing, staring, or viewing. During COVID 19 lockdown conditions, householders' screen-enabled formal and informal interactions from home soared in 2020 and 2021, sustained via video call technology such as Zoom, Teams, Skype, MS Teams, WhatsApp, House Party, and Facebook Messenger (Ofcom, 2021; Pew Research Centre, 2021). In "stay at home" circumstances, video calls were a lifeline for online households. They not only sustained informal socialising, caregiving, and entertainment across households and communities but also sustained communication between transnational families and friends across countries and time zones. This mode of communication now endures as a routine micro-mode of remote communication from home.

Mediatised societies are now adapting to digital situations rendered synthetic by digital screens. This gives rise to what Knorr Cetina calls *synthetic societies*: societies comprised of global microstructures where the spread of digital modes of coordination are microsociological in nature yet are potentially global in their span. This signals mediatisation's *intermediating nexus* of macro and micro-scales. Knorr Cetina's concepts of "synthetic situations'" and "scopic mediation" can be extended, then, as heuristic tools to assess the implications of this new mode of remote communication: one operated from the intimate space of home, as a key dimension of domestic mediatisation.

Video calls from home mediatise household interactions by reordering social situations. They cultivate embodied modes of trans-domestic communication as a key feature of home mediatisation. However, "stay-at-home" lockdowns highlight not only the intermediating nexus of media and the COVID 19 pandemic but also the *rupturing* effects of digitally enabled face-to-face communication. How the screen intermediates, as a synthetic agent, to reorder remote face-to-face interaction invites consideration of the sociosemiotic approach to mediatisation developed by Verón, to understand the transformed symbolic operations and interactive processes of screen-based interactions. This concerns the double articulation of media as symbolic texts as well as material objects, mentioned above.

A semio-discursive approach

Eliseo Verón's semio-discursive approach represents a strand of the social constructionist perspective advanced by Latin American mediatisation theories. Verón examines how media *construct* realities, including how television came to be pivotal for political communication (Verón, 1995; 2001). An overview of his evolutionary method is provided by Scolari and Rodriguez-Amat (2018). Reaffirming Silverstone's emphasis on the double articulation of media in domestication theory, Verón, focuses on "social texts" – sign systems such as speech, images, gestures, and objects – to study the social construction of reality within a social semiosis network. He emphasises that all social practices are based on a process of meaning construction, explaining that "social texts" contain rules of generation (grammars of production) and rules of reading (grammars of recognition and interpretation). Social discourses distributed in the semiotic network operate between these two sets of constraints. Verón argues that the rise of digital media leads to a *change in scale* between these conditions of production and recognition, as a feature of mediatisation. The growing intervention of technology within conditions of production intensifies the complexities of communication. New media devices intervene by *constructing reality*, thereby generating a growing mismatch between production and recognition.

Echoing the links with Goffman made by Knorr Cetina, Verón explains that this mismatch was previously absent from the basic elements of face-to-face interpersonal exchanges. The transformation of human communication, triggered by technological interventions in social discourse production, drives this mismatch which Verón calls a *rupture*. The notion of a rupture or *decalage* between production and recognition characterises the mediatisation process. Verón argues that mediatisation occurs when wider institutions, practices, and culture begin to be coordinated in direct correspondence to the media. He explains:

> The mediatization of society explodes the border between what is "real" in the society and its representations. One begins to suspect that the media are not just devices for reproducing what is "real," copied more or less accurately, but rather *devices of sense production*.
> (Verón, 2001, pp. 14–15, quoted in Scolari and Rodriguez-Amat, 2018, p. 12, my emphasis)

For Verón, semiotic ruptures that characterise mediatisation are activated by the chronological succession of institutionalised media: from clay tablets and papyrus to the Internet (also see Krotz, 2007). But the rise of "new media" accelerates these ruptures. His observations about the Web, until his death in 2014, focused on the contexts of access and circulation as features of mediatisation. This was even before the Web's imminent transformative potential was realised (Scolari and Rodriguez-Amat, 2018). This sociosemiotic emphasis corresponds with mediatisation's scalar approach, proposed above. Moreover, with the shift from hardware to inter- active, synchronised screen-based or audio-based software applications such as video call platforms, these digital technologies constitute *devices of sense production* that reconfigure bodily, spatial, and temporal encounters.

Showing how Verón's mediatisation work applies to the field of home and household, a valuable line of enquiry among Latin American scholars is the mediatisation of sound and audio-visual media studied by José L. Fernández (2008; 2012). Fernández examines how radio's new media form conjures ideas of body, space, and time. New media's combined elem- ents – devices, genres, discourse styles, and communicational exchanges – reconstruct reality by cultivating *unanticipated modes of exchange* within social practices. The portable radio transformed sport culture, fiction, information, and music. The frequency modulation in radio gave rise to radio theatre (Fernández, 2008; 2012). And post-broadcasting entails the operation of emergent mediatised forms of music (platforms such as SoundCloud) and on delivery (platforms such as Spotify) (Fernandez, 2014). This work suggests how Verón's original semio-discursive approach to mediatisation can be employed to address mediatisation of the home and household context.

The successive integration of technical affordances – for example from radio to television or smartphone to Zoom – generates new social practices that present opportunities yet also places constraints on discursive organ- isation, genres, and styles of communication. These constraints transform reality. Verón used the term "reading contracts" to conceptualise the rela- tionship between an addresser and addressee (Verón, 1985). Produced and circulated through digitally mediated communication, user contracts become ever more complex and obscure. In today's mediatised home, modes of exchange between human and nonhuman actors such as social media, smart home technology, and video call platforms encompass complex and conten- tious relations between corporations that own the software algorithms and flows of data, and householders who grapple with their complex scales of value and significance.

Emergent trans-domestic screen interactions

Verón's semio-discursive approach offers productive synergies with Knorr Cetina's studies of scopic media. By integrating home, technology, and household sociality as a field of mediatisation, their work helps to gauge how interactive screen technologies such as Zoom perform as a sense- producing technology. Reliance on this technology to support communica- tion with physically absent others during pandemic lockdowns initiated new domestic encounters and new modes of distant socialisation by fostering sociability, intimacy, and a sense of sharing time. Zoom has abidingly changed the scale of communication by supporting trans-domestic interpersonal interactions locally and globally. Enabling absent family, loved ones, friends or community members to appear to be in the same physical space as one another, this visual mode of exchange is immersive. It generates a powerful sense of an embodied encounter. Yet its scopic features require hyper-attention. The word "synthetic" advanced by Knorr Cetina, not only refers to the synthesising affordances of screen media. It also conjures the simulated dynamics of screen-based interactive media. These interactive screens mediatise human interactions across a range of social situations.

Qualitative studies of remote informal socialising during lockdowns confirm the significance of video call software's visual features. Users cherished the multisensory and affective mode of engagement afforded by video call apps (Heshmat and Neustaedter, 2021; Watson et al., 2021). But despite the valued sense of immersion, "viewing" in a video call requires much more effort than the "seeing" encounter of a co-present chat. Involving a dynamic screen performance and the interpretation of non-verbal cues, this synthetic situation can render the encounter more intense and more stressful than in-person exchanges. Interactive screens are sensed as less gratifying than in-person interactions (Greenwood-Hickman et al., 2021). Although designed to feel intuitive, video calling involves complicated, awkward media affordances which rupture communication flows, leading to unpredictable outcomes and user confusion over protocols. Verón's sociosemiotic approach foregrounds these intensified complexities of digital communication.

During lockdowns, when users craved a recovery of the atmosphere of co-present encounters, Zoom proved to be essential yet deficient. Users often find it difficult to turn-take in conversations and either inflate or misinterpret social cues such as tone and pitch of voice, facial countenances, and body language. These responses prompt heightened concentration. Householders wrestle with distractions, conversational challenges, and unreliable device connectivity leading to transmission delay, temporary screen freezes, and voice echoes. Often described as "confusing" and "chaotic" (Heshmat and Neustaedter, 2021) or "really intensive and draining" (Hardley and Richardson, 2020, p.1), video calling can generate feelings of information overload. Remote family members report that they feel like an observer rather than a participant (Heshmat and Neustaedter, 2021). The interactive scopic element of seeing one's own face while communicating can be perplexing alongside the multiple boxes of faces visible during group calls. Being constantly observed by others while watching the self and others can cause hyper-alertness, "zoom fatigue" and "nonverbal overload" (Bailenson, 2021). Some participants eventually "cleanse" themselves of the technology, in a manner reminiscent of the "demediatisation" described by Kopecka-Piech (2019).

This range of communicative challenges can lead to misrecognition in conversations and a *lack of control over exchanges*. The acute awareness of being watched as if on a stage, places pressure on video callers to engage performatively. Calculated decisions must also be made about camera orientation, positioning of the self, and home surroundings either to safeguard personal privacy or to present a home-specific mode of networked corporeality (Hardley and Richardson, 2020). By constructing reality within these synthetically generated situations, Zoom's scopic and synchronic affordances require householders to contend with new procedures of interaction involving new configurations of face, body, time, and space. Heshmat and Neustaedter (2021) found that swift changes between work and personal time in the home are often disrupting. And the use of video calls used for both work and social connections can interfere with domestic routines, leading to "contested spaces" (Lefebvre, 1991). Decisions must be made about what time video calls can be made and which family member can use the dining room or kitchen table for a Zoom meeting (Shortt and Izak, 2020). Impinging on the moral economy of the household, this can cause conflicts between work time and family time in the home. It can generate tensions between household members. The technology generates ruptures and dissonances which are absent in co-present face-to-face communication that transform domestic dynamics.

Research evidence indicates that when women are outnumbered in group meetings, men tend to speak two-thirds longer than women. Men also tend to adopt a power dynamic while women tend towards a rapport dynamic (Mendelberg et al., 2014). For video calls where participants contend with audio lag and overlapped speech, the negative effects of such gendered communicative styles may be magnified to impede women's conversational exchanges (Wang and Roubidoux, 2020). Zoom's face-detection algorithm is reported to manifest a racial bias by apparently erasing faces with dark pigmentation when a virtual background is applied on the app. Users have noticed that Zoom appears to remove the head of Black people when using a virtual background (Hern, 2020; see Noble, 2018). Coupled with the burden placed on women during lockdowns to take responsibility for maintaining social contacts as part of affective kin-work, emerging evidence suggests that synthetic situations may exacerbate *socially* and *algorithmically* coded racial and gender disparities (Power, 2020; Ryan and El Ayadi, 2020).

By steering users' affective reactions, reality is continuously (re)constructed as processes of textual (mis)interpretation that initiate unanticipated modes of exchange as *semiotic ruptures* to users' agency. These rupturing experiences encountered in the heart of the home not only highlight the frictions built into the technology's interface. Such synthetic situations also accentuate relations of power and the ethical dimensions of scopic communication systems. Overall, the mediatisation of home via video call technologies such as Zoom forms part of an assemblage of scopic media that transforms the household into a dynamic and evolving site of simulation and trans-domestic exchange. Such dissonances reveal that video calling breaches the apparent ease, simplicity, and transparency of co-present interpersonal exchanges.

Conclusion

This chapter has examined some of the strengths and limitations of mediatisation for the analysis of media transformations within the demarcated context of home and household. After identifying certain drawbacks of a media-centric approach that invites media determinism, the first section outlined the advantages and weaknesses of a social constructivist approach. Four features of mediatisation were identified to counterbalance tendencies towards media-centrism. The first is its openness, flexibility, and lack of rigid standardisation. The second is mediatisation's transdisciplinary and transparadigmatic missions that guide its research agenda: historicity, specificity, and measurability (Ekström et al., 2016). The third is a multiscalar approach to facilitate media-*centredness* rather than media-centrism. The fourth corrective is a commitment to multiple methods. However, mediatisation calls for procedures to analyse the interdependencies between macro- and micro-scale processes. Combining Silverstone's concept of "mediation" with "mediatisation", I introduced the concept of "intermediating nexus" to guide analyses of the intersections between mediatising levels.

The second section pinpointed three types of study that advance our understanding of the mediatization of home and households: longitudinal studies of media convergence and deconvergence in the home from a systematic perspective; comparative studies that assess media transformations in defined social contexts; and emerging or changing types of media. The latter approach, represented by Knorr Cetina's theorisation of *scopic mediation*, draws attention to the mediatisation of the face-to-face situation as a *synthetic situation*. It opens up avenues for studying the use of video call technology such as Zoom to sustain trans-domestic interactions during COVID 19 lockdown conditions. Involving local, regional or global microstructures, this approach calls for a rethink about householder interactions in relation to the discourses, symbols, and flow of screen-enabled interaction.

The third section introduced Verón's sociosemiotic approach to explain its value in pinpointing the *unanticipated modes of exchange* arising from converging gadgets and software applications as *sense production devices* that reconfigure bodily, spatial, and temporal dynamics. This sociosemiotic emphasis reminds us that mediatisation – encountered at meso- and micro-scales – involves transformations in the technological and symbolic dynamics of relational communication practices. Verón's concept of *semiotic rupture* underlines the growing mismatch between production and recognition resulting from the escalating technological complexities of conditions of production. This concept has been elaborated to explain the misrecognition involved in householders' navigation and interpretation of media affordances as a feature of mediatisation.

The final section combined Verón's semiotic approach with Knorr Cetina's work on synthetic situations to consider the transformative features of video call technology in the home. Verón's notion of a semiotic rupture – accenting a digital separation between production and recognition – combined with Knorr Cetina's concepts of scopic mediation and synthetic situations, helps us to understand the semiotic ruptures and misinterpretations involved in what is now an established mode of *trans-domestic* interpersonal communication. Synchronised scopic media generate a new attentional regime and attentional integration, one that implies new embodied co-ordinations and new interactional protocols.

Drawing on Verón, the idea that screen-based digital communication technologies present a smooth, effortless, and efficient transition from co-present to screen-based personal interaction must be interrogated. In the context of homes and households and initiated under pandemic conditions, video call participants must now cope with complexities which can extend yet also destabilise household agency. These relatively new modes of home-oriented communication call for a reconsideration of the transformations involved in householder interactions, particularly given predictions of an evolving metaverse: one that steers us towards a new virtual ecosystem (Lee et al., 2021). The metaverse comprises a media logic that conjures the vision of an immersive Internet as a vast, integrated, and shared realm. But the ruptures and dissonances involved in the home use of video call technology under pandemic conditions already reveals the complications that householders must grapple with to communicate beyond the confines of home. Mediatisation is equipped to track these dramatic changes.

References

Bailenson, J., "Nonverbal overload: A theoretical argument for the causes of Zoom fatigue." *Technology, Mind and Behaviour*, 2 (1) (2021) https://doi.org/10.1037/tmb0000030

Chambers D., *Changing Media, Homes and Households*. London: Routledge, 2016.

Chambers, D., "Emerging temporalities in the multiscreen home." *Media, Culture and Society*, 43 (7), 1180–1196, 2019.

Couldry, N. and Hepp, A., "Conceptualizing mediatization: Contexts, traditions, arguments." *Communication Theory*, 23 (3), 191–202, 2013.

Deacon, D. and Stanyer, J., "Mediatization: Key concept or conceptual bandwagon?" *Media, Culture & Society*, 36 (7), 1032–1044, 2014.

D'heer, E. and Courtois, C., "The changing dynamics of television consumption in the multimedia living room." *Convergence*, 22 (1), 3–17, 2016.

Ekström, M., Fornäs, J., Jansson, A. and Jerslev, A., "Three tasks for mediatization research: Contributions to an open agenda." *Media, Culture and Society*, 38 (7), 1090–1108, 2016 .

Fernández, J.L. (ed.), *La Construcción de lo Radiofónico*. Buenos Aires, Argentina: La Crujía, 2008.

Fernández, J.L., *La captura de la audiencia radiofónica*. Buenos Aires, Argentina: Liber, 2012.

Fernández, J.L. (ed.), *Postbroadcasting: Innovación en la Industria Musical*. Buenos Aires: La Crujía, 2014.

Goffman, E., "The neglected situation." *American Anthropologist*, 66 (6), 133–36, 1964.

Göttlich U., Heinz, L. and Herbers, M.R., Mediatisierte Medienrezeption: Neue Integrationswege der Ko-Orientierung? In F. Krotz, C. Despotović and M.M. Kruse (eds), *Mediatisierung als Metaprozess. Medien, Kultur, Kommunikation* (pp. 163–183). Wiesbaden: Springer VS, 2017.

Greenwood-Hickman, M.A., Dahlquist J. and Cooper J,. "'They're going to Zoom it': A qualitative investigation of impacts and coping strategies during the COVID-19 pandemic among older adults." *Front Public Health*, 9, 2296–2565, 2021.

Haddon, L., The Domestication of Complex Media Repertoires. In K. Sandvik, A.M. Thorhauge and B. Valtysson (eds), *The Media and the Mundane: Communication across Media in Everyday Life* (pp. 17–30). Göteborg: Nordicom, 2016.

Hardley, J. and Richardson, I., "Digital placemaking and networked corporeality: Embodied mobile media practices in domestic space during Covid-19." *Convergence*, 27 (3), 625–636, 2020.

Hartmann, M., The Triple Articulation of ICTs: Media as Technological Objects, Symbolic Environments and Individual Texts. In T. Berker, M. Hartmann, Y. Punie and K.J. Ward (eds) *Domestication of Media and Technology* (pp. 80–102). Maidenhead: Open University Press, 2006.

Hepp, A., Hjarvard, S. and Lundby, K., "Mediatization: Theorizing the interplay between media, culture and society." *Media, Culture & Society*, 37 (2), 314–324, 2015.

Hern, A., "Twitter apologises for 'racist' image-cropping algorithm." *The Guardian*, 21 September 2020. https://www.theguardian.com/technology/2020/sep/21/twitter-apologises-for-racist-image-cropping-algorithm

Heshmat, Y. and Neustaedter, C., "Family and friend communication over distance in canada during the COVID-19 pandemic." *Designing Interactive Systems Conference*, pp. 1–14, 2021. https://doi.org/10.1145/3461778.3462022

Hjarvard, S., Mediatization and cultural and social change: An institutional perspective. *Mediatization of Communication*. Handbooks of Communication Science, 21, 199–226, 2014.

Jansson, A., "Mediatization and social space: Reconstructing mediatization for the transmedia age." *Communication Theory*, 23 (3), 279–296, 2013.

Jansson A., Indispensable Things: On Mediatization, Space and Materiality. In K. Lundby (ed.), *Mediatization of Communication*. Handbooks of Communication Sciences, vol. 21, pp. 273–296. Berlin: De Gruyter Mouton, 2014.

Knorr Cetina, K., "The synthetic situation: Interactionism for a global world." *Symbolic Interaction*, 32 (1), 61–87, 2009.

Knorr Cetina, K., Scopic Media and Global Coordination: The Mediatization of Face-To-Face Encounters. In K. Lundby (ed.), *Mediatization of Communication*. Berlin: de Gruyter, pp. 39–62, 2014.

Knorr Cetina, K., Reichmann, W. and Woermann, N., Dimensionen und Dynamiken synthetischer Gesellschaften. In F. Krotz, C. Despotovic and M-M Kruse (eds), *Mediatisierung als Metaprozess*. Wiesbaden: Springer VS, pp. 35–57, 2017.

Kopecka-Piech, K., *Mediatization of Physical Activity: Media Saturation and Technologies*. Lanham, MD: Rowman and Littlefield, 2019.

Krotz, F., "The meta-process of 'mediatization' as a conceptual frame." *Global Media and Communication*, 3 (3), 256–260, 2007.

Krotz, F., "Explaining the mediatisation approach." *javnost – the public*, 24 (2), 103–118, 2017.

Krotz, F., Despotovic, C. and Kruse, M.M., *Mediatisierung als Metaprozess.* Wiesbaden: Springer VS, 2017.

Lee, L.H., Braud, T., Zhou, P., Wang, L., Xu, D., Lin, Z. and Hui, P., "All one needs to know about metaverse: A complete survey on technological singularity, virtual ecosystem, and research agenda." *Journal of Latex Class Files*, 14 (8), 1–67, 2021.

Lefebvre, H., *The Production of Space*. Malden, MA: Blackwell, 1991.

Madianou, M. and Miller, D., *Migration and New Media: Transnational Families and Polymedia*. London: Routledge, 2012.

Mendelberg, T., Karpowitz, C.F. and Oliphant, J.B., "Gender inequality in deliberation: Unpacking the black box of interaction." *Perspectives on Politics*, 12, 18–44, 2014.

Müller, K.F. and Röser, J., Convergence in Domestic Media Use? The Interplay of Old and New Media at Home. In S. Sparviero, C. Peil and G. Balbi (eds), *Media Convergence and Deconvergence*. Global Transformations in Media and Communication Research – A Palgrave and IAMCR Series. Cham: Palgrave Macmillan, 2017.

Murdock, G., "Mediatisation and the transformation of capitalism: The elephant in the room." *Javnost*, 24 (2) 119–135, 2017.

Noble, S.U., *Algorithms of Oppression*. New York: New York University Press, 2018.

Ofcom, *The Communications Market 2018: Narrative Report*. https://www.ofcom.org.uk/research-and-data/multi-sector-research/cmr/cmr-2018/report. 2018.

Ofcom, *Online Nation, 2021*. https://www.ofcom.org.uk/__data/assets/pdf_file/0013/220414/online-nation-2021-report.pdf. 2021.

Peil, C. and Mikos, L. Konvergierende Medienumgebungen, in L. Mikos and C. Wegener (eds.), *Qualitative Medienforschung. Ein Handbuch*. pp. 209–218. Konstanz: UVK, 2017.

Peil, C. and Röser, J., The Meaning of Home in the Context of Digitization, Mobilization and Mediatization. In A. Hepp & F. Krotz (eds), *Mediatized Worlds*. pp. 233–249. Basingstoke: Palgrave Macmillan, 2014.

Peil, C. and Sparviero, S., Media Convergence Meets Deconvergence. In S. Sparviero, C. Peil and G. Balbi (eds), *Media Convergence and Deconvergence: Global Transformations in Media and Communication Research*. pp. 3–30. Cham: Palgrave Macmillan, 2017.

Pew Research Center, *The Internet and the Pandemic*. https://www.pewresearch.org/internet/2021/09 /01/the-internet-and-the-pandemic/. 2021.

Power, K., "The COVID-19 pandemic has increased the care burden of women and families." *Sustainability: Science, Practice and Policy*, 16 (1), 67–73, 2020. https://doi.org/ 10.1080/15487733.2020.1776561

Röser, J., Müller, K., Niemand, S. and Roth, U., Häusliches Medienhandeln zwischen Dynamik und Beharrung: Die Domestizierung des Internets und die Mediatisierung des Zuhauses 2008–2016. In F. Krotz, C. Despotovic and M.M. Kruse (eds), *Mediatisierung als Metaprozess*. pp. 139–162. Wiesbaden: Springer VS, 2017.

Ryan, N.E. and El Ayadi, A.M, "A call for a gender-responsive, intersectional approach to address COVID-19." *Global Public Health*, 15(9), 1404–1412, 2020.

Scolari, C. and Rodriguez-Amat, J., "A Latin American approach to mediatization: Specificities and contributions to a global discussion about how the media shape contemporary societies." *Communication Theory*, 28 (2), 131–154, 2018.

Shortt, H. and Izak, M., The Contested Home. In M. Parker (ed.), *Life After Covid-19: The Other Side of the Crisis*. Bristol University Press, 2020.

Silverstone, R., *Why Study the Media?* London: Sage, 1999.

Silverstone, R., *Media and Morality: On the Rise of the Mediapolis*. Cambridge, UK: Wiley, 2013.

Silverstone, R. and Haddon, L., Design and the Domestication of Information and Communication Technologies: Technical Change and Everyday Life. In R. Silverstone and R. Mansell (eds), *Communication by Design: The Politics of Information and Communication Technologies*. pp. 44–74. Oxford: Oxford University Press, 1996.

Sowinska, M., "Die Medien überfluten uns. Alltagstheorien über Medienwandel." *Kommunikation.medien*, 6 (6) 1–22, 2016.

Stauff, M., "The second screen: Convergence as crisis." *ZMK Zeitschrift für Medien- und Kulturforschung*, 6 (2), 123–144, 2015.

Verón, E., L'analyse du 'contrat de lecture': Une nouvelle méthode pour les études de positionnement des supports presse. *Les Médias. Expériences, recherches actuelles, applications*. pp. 203–230. Paris: Institut de Recherches et d'Études Publicitaires, 1985.

Verón, E., *Semiosis de lo ideológico y del poder / La mediatización*. Buenos Aires, Argentina: UBA, 1995.

Verón, E., *El cuerpo de las imágenes*. Bogotá, Colombia: Norma, 2001.

Wang, S.S. and Roubidoux, M.A., "Coronavirus disease 2019 (COVID-19), video-conferencing, and gender." *Journal of the American College of Radiology*, 17 (7), 918–920, 2020.

Watson, A., Lupton, D. and Michael, M., "Intimacy and sociality at a distance in the COVID-19 crisis: The sociomaterialities of home-based communication technologies." *Media International Australia*, 178 (1), 136–150, 2021.

9 Mediatisation and Platform Labour
Blind Spots and Connections

Rafael Grohmann

Labour and work issues are relatively under-represented in mediatisation research (Pallas & Fredriksson, 2013; Chan & Humpfreys, 2018; Jansson & Fast, 2019; Hepp, 2020), and this is an important theoretical challenge. The research agenda on mediatisation and work has developed a rich debate on how media and work are related, around discourses, practices, institutions, and interactions. The current state of the world of work reveals the importance of understanding the changes in the relations between media and society, in a context of deep mediatisation (Hepp, 2020). This means dialectically understanding how the media – as connection infrastructures (Couldry, 2020) – interplay in production processes. As Jansson (2017) argues, mediatisation research needs to focus on contradictions that involve everyday life, inequalities, and struggles for autonomy. There are also connections between work, mediatisation, and capitalism (Murdock, 2017).

In the context of deep mediatisation, some crucial terms by which to understand work issues are datafication and platforms. We live in a media environment engaged with algorithms, data, and platforms. The automation of media, in processes related to artificial intelligence, also depends on human work (Casilli, 2019; Grohmann & Araújo, 2021). This means that the mediatisation of work faces new challenges in relation to this media scenario, with infrastructure, materiality, and new forms of interaction.

I argue that platformisation (Poell, Nieborg & Van Dijck, 2019) can be considered a current stage of mediatisation, or at least an alternative perspective for understanding deep mediatisation. Platformisation (Casilli & Posada, 2019; Grohmann & Qiu, 2020) affects labour at different levels, such as mechanisms of rentier capitalism (Murdock, 2017; Sadowski, 2020), datafication of labour (Couldry & Mejias, 2019; Chen & Qiu, 2019), algorithmic management (Mateescu & Nguyen, 2019) and the use of social media and other digital infrastructures by workers to organise and build alternatives (Soriano et al., 2020; Hepp, 2020). In all these processes media and communication play a crucial role.

This chapter theorises about the platformisation of labour – as an element of mediatisation – based on relations between financialisation, datafication, and neoliberalism. Thus, it discusses: (a) algorithms, data, and platforms;

DOI: 10.4324/9781003324591-13

(b) platform labour and its typologies and characteristics; (c) algorithmic management as a central element of the platformisation of labour; and (d) alternatives to the current scenario.

Algorithms, Data and Platforms

An algorithm is a basic unit of computing aimed at solving problems, an automated set of instructions (Van Dijck, Poell & De Waal, 2018) that transforms "data into desired results" (Gillespie, 2018, p. 97). Although the notion of an algorithm is older than that of a computer, algorithmic logics have progressively governed more and more dimensions of social and media life over the past 30 years, by what Gillespie (2018) understands as "public relevance algorithms". Thus, relations with food, transportation, love, and work also go through algorithmic mediations. Our relationships and interactions change due to and along with the algorithms.

Algorithms are produced, like any technology (Vieira Pinto, 2005), by human work, for example in the tech industry, but they are also the result of interactions of people with them in everyday life. However, it is a false symmetry to understand that both activities are at the same level, because of the power relations involved in the tech industry producing and extracting value from technologies. We cannot underestimate the role and responsibility of the "Cloud Empire" (Couldry & Mejias, 2019) in the classification and automation of social processes, which are taken, in turn, as an imperative that is not only technological but also financial and political. As Wajcman (2019) shows in research on Silicon Valley engineers, there are conceptions of the world and ideologies involved in the construction of technological artefacts. This means that, from an institutional point of view, the tech industry is also changing in this current period.

Thus, these algorithms are not built in a vacuum or in a neutral way – as an algorithmic imaginary of neutrality and objectivity makes you want to believe (Bucher, 2017; Pasquale, 2015). There is an algorithm politics (Beer, 2017), which has a role in social ordering processes, related to cultural, ideological, and financial contexts. They originate socially from certain places and only show some perspectives to the detriment of others. This reveals their biases, with the possibility of automating inequalities (Eubanks, 2017).

But automation and systematisation of processes by algorithms only happens with the supply and accumulation of data. It is from this "invisible work of data" (Denis, 2018) that the algorithms work. Data and algorithms are part of society's infrastructure (Murdock, 2017) in the context of digital platforms. There is a mantra that has been repeated in the business field – "data is the new oil". From the point of view of financial importance, this is true. However, data are not natural products, but they need to be appropriated and constructed, in what Morozov (2018) calls data extractivism. They act, therefore, in the capitalist mode of production in processes of documentation, mining, filtering, and extracting. And like the algorithms, they are treated as a "scientific paradigm" (Van Dijck, 2014), naturalising the "data gaze" (Beer, 2019) as something neutral, objective, and unquestionable.

Algorithms and data are part of datafication – which involves deep mediatisation – involving the growing centrality of data in everyday life and, I add, in the capitalist mode of production, both in its production and in its circulation, being, at the same time, an expression of digital infrastructures, mediatisation, and financialisation.

Thus, I argue that data extraction is not mere information gathering, but value and resource extraction, and therefore algorithms and data are part of platform capitalism (Srnicek, 2016) and platform labour As Sadowski (2019, p. 7) states, "when data is treated as a form of capital, the imperative to collect as much data, from as many sources, by any means possible intensifies existing practices of accumulation and leads to the creation of new ones". The accumulation of data is also financial and an expropriation of the resources of others, when "data is taken without meaningful consent and fair compensation for the producers and sources of that data" (Sadowski, 2019, p. 7). Zuboff (2019) adds the role of data surveillance – of the most varied types – in capitalism, considered to be a new logic of accumulation based on tracking, classification, and profiling.

It is not possible to conceive the datafication process without financialisation, from a process of creating a surplus not explained by the power of human labour, presenting a new standard of accumulation and extraction of value in capitalism, with an increasing asymmetry between the production and circulation of capital, in addition to the appropriation and reconfiguration of its flows (Lapavitsas, 2013). Thus, financialisation is, at the same time, a structural component of the capitalist mode of production when it acts as an agent of circulation of meanings for the sedimentation and fixation of neoliberal rationality throughout all spaces. These changes in the capitalist accumulation process are reflected in changes in the work and media processes, including circulation technologies (Harvey, 2018).

This financialisation–datafication overlap updates "the historical fact that the financial market and technology have joined hands to erect their bios, a new existential orientation related to the planetary process of capital modernisation" (Sodré, 2014, p. 258), with an articulation that accelerates the circulation of capital. Some examples of these connections are the "uberisation of money" – which connects peers in a network without the need for government, banking or financial mediation – and the appropriation of digital platforms in relation to the derivative technique (Arvidsson, 2016; De Marchi, 2016).

As stated by Van Dijck, Poell and De Waal (2018), platforms are fuelled by data, automated and organised through algorithms. Thus, algorithms and data are at the base of their structures. In addition, they are formalised by ownership relationships, guided by business models, and governed by terms of agreement. They are neither neutral nor free of value, and they have norms inscribed in their architectures and affordances. If Srnicek (2016) focuses on the changes that took place from the capitalist order, including the ways of extracting value, Van Dijck, Poell and De Waal (2018) understand this scenario as taking a broader set of elements, from commodification to selection and curation of content – thus configuring themselves as complementary approaches.

Platforms – in their most varied types – are, on the one hand, the realisation of the accumulation and extraction of value from data mechanisms and algorithmic mediations; on the other hand, they mean their more visible face (or friendly interface), infiltrating social practices, on the one hand, with the promise of offering personalisedsed services and, on the other, causing dependence on their infrastructure on the Web (Helmond, 2015) and in various sectors of society.

In addition, platforms are digital infrastructures that act, at the same time, as means of production and means of communication (Williams, 2011), serving both to work and to interact, being a locus of communication and work activities. Platforms act as production processes in the circulation of capital, as a means of communication; they contribute to the acceleration of this circulation, reducing the rotation time, reducing the dead time and accelerating production and consumption (Harvey, 2018). This is the context for understanding what creates "platformisation" and how this affects the world of work.

Platformisation of Labour

The relations between media and labour are not new, nor is the process of digitisation. This has been a field discussed for at least 20 years by scholars around the world, such as Fígaro (2001) and Bölin (2012), involving topics such as active audience, media work(ers), transformations in the world of work with digitisation, production and consumption circuits. The emergence of digital platforms is a continuation of the process of transforming the relationship between media and labour. The novelty is the entry of new infrastructures – including data algorithms – and their ability to generalise to all sectors of society.

Nieborg & Poell (2018, p. 4276) define platformisation as "penetration of economic, governmental, and infrastructure extensions of digital platforms into the web and app ecosystems". This process affects sectors such as cultural production (Nieborg & Poell, 2018), public health, education, journalism, work, and urban transport (Van Dijck, Poell & De Waal, 2018). Platformisation of labour better describes the current scenario of digital and platform labour than "uberisation", which has been circulated in different spheres as a metaphor, but which does not cover the multiplicity of work activities mediated by platforms beyond Uber itself, as there are a variety of value extraction logics (Srnicek, 2016) and work characteristics (Casilli, 2019; Graham & Woodcock, 2018).

Instead of "uberisation", then, it is about understanding platformisation of labour as the dependence that workers and consumers have on digital platforms – with algorithms, data, and capital – together with changes that involve the intensification of flexibilisation of labour relations and contracts and the imperative of an entrepreneurial rationality (Dardot & Laval, 2016) as the ways of justifying the ways of being and appearing of capital.

Van Doorn (2017) defines platform labour as work activities that are mediated, organised, and governed by means of digital platforms, being, therefore, a more restricted definition than that of Fuchs and Sandoval (2014), for whom all work activities today involve a digital aspect. On the one hand, this last definition allows us to see how global production chains happen. On the other hand, its breadth does not allow us to understand the specifics of work activities. These are activities marked by technological sub-subordination and subjected to measurement of performance.

It turns out that platform labour does not take place in the abstract, but from different forms of appropriation of value (Bolin, 2016), depending both on the characteristics of the work platforms and on gender, race, and territory relations (Van Doorn, 2017), such as migrant work, for example. The working class is not uniform in its composition, being, by definition, complex and heterogeneous. This would not be different with platform labour and their workers.

Work activities are located spatially and socially in the face of global value chains, and these inequalities shape the platformisation of labour. As Casilli (2019) points out, in the Global South, platform labour often presents itself as the only possible alternative for the "future of the work". In Europe and the United States, the current scenario of platform labour is inserted in the context of the gig economy that intensified since the economic crisis of 2008 (Huws et al., 2019). However, in Latin America and, specifically, in Brazil, the gig economy and informal work have historically been the norm, not the exception, acting as ways of managing the survival of the working class.

Thus, there are geographies of platform labour, with concentrated demand and geographically dispersed supply, with an international division of digital labour (Fuchs & Sandoval, 2014). As stated by Graham and Anwar (2019), platforms implant a labour market that has the possibility to operate on a global scale and help platforms "operate unboundedly, and allow them to reconfigure the geography of their production networks for almost zero cost. Workers meanwhile can sell their labour power globally, but still are tethered to the locales in which they go to bed every night" (Graham & Anwar, 2019). That is, the circulation and extraction of value from platform labour occur in unequal ways in different countries and regions, with class relations and obeying the parameters of global financialisation-datafication.

Therefore, platform labour: (a) is based on mediations of gender, race, territory, among other social and intersectionalities, with differences in appropriation of value; and (b) cannot be reduced to work in delivery and ride-hailing sectors. Hence it is possible to think of typologies of digital labour platforms. From the classifications proposed by Scholz (2016), Schmidt (2017), Graham and Woodcock (2018), and Casilli (2019), I propose the following types of digital labour platforms: (a) platforms that require the worker in a specific location (such as Uber or Deliveroo); (b) micro-work platforms (such as Amazon Mechanical Turk, Appen, Lionbridge), that is, the work of training data for the "artificial intelligence"; and (c) freelance platforms (such as Workana and Fiiver), which combine tasks from painting to design and coding.

Each of these types reveals different relationships with platform labour, with possibilities for different working conditions (and profiles of workers, based on social markers), production processes, appropriation of value, algorithmic management of work, and ways of controlling work and workers. This does not mean that, within the typology, there is uniformity or homogeneity, since, for example, domestic work platforms (such as TaskRabbit and Care.com) have a predominantly female characteristic (Hartmann et al., 2019).

The dynamics of platformisation of labour, in general, involve, according to a study by Huws et al. (2019) in 13 European countries, precarious work, reduced worker autonomy, and flexibility only for the employer. Thus, in its different typologies, the platformisation of labour combines two essential dimensions: (a) datafication of work activities, with (b) neoliberal rationality – as interconnected elements of datafication-financialisation.

Algorithmic Management of Work

Data, as Srnicek (2016) argues, presents key functions in platform capitalism, such as giving competitive advantages to algorithms and allowing the outsourcing of workers. Thus, datafication – as a aspect of deep mediatisation – acts as a work management and control mechanism, which is also a component of an accumulation logic based on the usurpation of workers' data, which are, at the same time, fixed and circulating capital (Fuchs, 2017).

In this sense, it is central to understand the algorithmic management of work, as "practices of supervision, governance and control conducted by algorithms in workers remotely" (Möhlmann & Zalmanson, 2017), with the algorithms reconfiguring the activities of and being a crucial component of platform labour. Their forms of pressure and control are different depending on the type of work platform, with specificities, for example, in the activities of a delivery worker and a "data trainer" at Amazon Mechanical Turk (Gray & Suri, 2019).

The characteristics of algorithmic management, according to Möhlmann and Zalmansson (2017), are: (a) permanent tracking and evaluation of workers' behaviour and performance; (b) automation of decisions through algorithms; and (c) less algorithmic transparency, with workers not having access to the set of rules that govern the algorithms.

Surveilled labour (Couldry & Mejias, 2019) is part of the context of algorithmic management, with the monitoring of workers' interactions, scheduling of work activities considered smart, and the management of workers' behaviour through data. The automation of decisions in the algorithmic management of work affects even workers in situations of unemployment, as there is an intensification of the automation of the systems of hiring and selection of workers, with algorithmic biases of gender and race occurring in these processes (Eubanks, 2017).

To these aspects, I add as aspects of the algorithmic management of work: (a) management of data and metadata through global platforms impacting workers and local laws; (b) work gamification, understood from Woodcock (2019) as the application of game elements from business imperatives, as a "gamification from above", redesigning temporalities and spatiality; (d) intensification of feelings of autonomy and independence at work amid the fact that the boss is supposed to be a "system", an "app", not a "person"; that is, the algorithmic imaginary of neutrality and objectivity acting in strong relationship with the neoliberal ideology of entrepreneurship involving performance management, effectiveness, and evaluation logic.

Gamification and permanent tracking are the realisation of a worker quantified from performance and performance metrics managed by algorithms, with management techniques going beyond the subject of "transcending themselves by the company" or "motivating themselves more and more to satisfy the customer" (Dardot & Laval, 2016, p. 331). It is about transcending and motivating yourself from your own metrics, such as self-healing and self-guiding mechanisms seen as an entrepreneurial spirit. It is the automated "new reason in the world" – managed from algorithmic and financial logic.

There is also a grammar of capital in circulation that is an auxiliary force of financialisation and datafication, as a visible face of neoliberal rationality. This happens from the sedimentation and crystallisation of meanings in games of repetition and actualisation, as true "mantras", in a grammar that legitimises the ways of being and appearing of capital in the different instances of social life. They are prescriptions that, when circulated, are positioned as totalising and taken as natural. Based on keywords that function as "slogans", narratives are stitched up that not only justify neoliberal rationality, but present it as the only possible one, in a "capitalist realism" (Fisher, 2011). This is updated based on a Silicon Valley ideology and capitalist rhetoric about the platform economy (Codagnone, Karatzogianni & Matthews 2019) – as images of neoliberal rationality.

Thus, from the sedimentation of these meanings that, for example, the fact that a "private global wage company disguised in the form of unregulated work [...] appropriates the most value generated by the services of drivers becomes naturalised" (Antunes, 2018, p. 35), behind the facade of a platform. These are the ways to legitimise the productive reorganisations of capital from technological oligopolies and their platforms, projecting crystallised meanings of "disruption" and "exemplary image".

Understanding totalisation of neoliberal rationality means, on the one hand, recognising a spread of its way of thinking and acting in all instances of everyday life, also materialised in platform labour (as articulations between datafication and financialisation), then undermining, possibilities of resistance and alternative projects of society that do not pass, to a certain extent, through the circulation of capital and mechanisms of neoliberal rationality. As Brown (2016, p. 103) wrote, "the neoliberal triumph of homo economicus as the exhaustive figure of the human is undermining the practices and the imaginary of democracy, overcoming the subject who governs himself through moral autonomy".

The alternatives to the current scenario of platform labour have become more of an attempt to mitigate the logic of datafication-financialisation, as they can live peacefully with these processes. As Brown (2016) affirms, neoliberal politics can even stagnate, but the effects of neoliberal rationality would still be accelerated, which is why even opponents of such economic policies can also "organise themselves through neoliberal rationality" (Brown, 2016, p. 280).

Alternatives

There are three main movements for the construction of alternatives to the contemporary scenario of labour: (a) regulation of labour on digital platforms; (b) collective organisation of workers; (c) construction of other logics of work organisation, such as platform cooperativism. These are attempts to mitigate the collapse of the working class in the face of platform capitalism. This means saying, on the one hand, that the "circulation of struggles" (Dyer-Witheford, 2015) does not cease to exist. They are the struggles in the scope of the circulation of capital. According to Harvey (2018, p. 56), they both "constrain and facilitate certain forms of thought and action". On the other hand, the constraints and limits of these struggles encounter the tentacles of neoliberal rationality, with the possibility of co-optations and reappropriations. These are the tensions and contradictions in the work organisation in the context of the platformisation of labour. Thus, by pointing out the limits of these movements, I am not minimising them, but as Sandoval (2019) states, recognising the possibility of offering a solidary critique when facing the tensions and ambivalences.

The movements around labour regulation include: (a) regularising workers on digital platforms as employees of corporations who insist on calling them "self-employed"; and (b) guidelines for decent work on digital platforms based mainly on parameters of the International Labour Organisation (ILO). As an example of this last movement, there is the Fairwork project (Graham & Woodcock, 2018), which intends to institute decent and fair work principles on digital platforms, creating pressure mechanisms on the platforms to improve the working conditions of its employees. The principle are: (a) payment; (b) working conditions, involving protecting the health and safety of the worker; (c) fair contracts; (d) fair management; and (e) fair representation.

The workers' collective organisation movements, in turn, have shown: (a) unionisation of workers from digital platforms, in traditional formats or outside the logic of traditional unionism; (b) collective organisation of workers in areas such as media, arts, and entertainment, ranging from the creation of a game workers union in the United Kingdom (Game Workers Unite) to the Youtubers union in Germany, including workers from companies like Buzzfeed, Fast Company, and Vox (Cohen & De Peuter, 2018), including freelancers; and (c) internationalist/global protests and strikes involving digital platforms. As Dyer-Witheford, Kjosen and Steinhoff (2019) point out, in this circuit, workers' struggles are against algorithmic management and surveillance at work. And collective organisation is also facilitated by communication on digital platforms, which then acts as a mobilising force for work and workers. This is true for both platform workers who require a specific location and micro-workers, with one example being Turker Nation, from Amazon Mechanical Turk workers.

Platform cooperativism (Scholz, 2017), in turn, which has already been problematised by Grohmann (2018) and Sandoval (2019), is the promise of another logic of work organisation mediated by platforms, involving collective ownership, transparency of data, co-determined work, and rejection of excessive vigilance in the workplace. On the one hand, there are already existing initiatives with potential. On the other hand, there are traces of the logic of datafication-financialisation of capitalist platforms and discourses that permeate dimensions of entrepreneurial rationality. Both coexist in a deepening of tensions and contradictions involving cooperativism, also involving dilemmas between structural precariousness and commercialisation. For Sandoval (2019, p. 18), it is necessary to face these dilemmas beyond neoliberal capitalism: "as a co-operative movement of people around the globe, platform co-operative could use its collective political voice to demand structural reforms that would improve the conditions for alternative co-operative projects to flourish". For the author, facing the entrepreneurial neoliberal rationality "requires not a co-operative entrepreneur, but social solidarity and a global co-operative movement" (Sandoval, 2019, p. 18).

Therefore, these movements represent attempts to face and mitigate the impacts of the dominant platformisation of labour. The confrontation, as the above experiences show, requires local movements on global scales. As Huws (2014) states, new forms of work control also require new ways of organisation and resistance. The totalisation of neoliberal rationality makes it extremely difficult, but it does not prevent attempts or fissures, even if minimal – with limits, dilemmas, and contradictions – of alternatives to the scenario of platform labour.

Conclusions

The platformisation of labour presents challenges to mediatisation research. This means understanding the platform as an aspect of deep mediatisation, and its mechanisms as, at the same time, media/technology, and culture/society. If the focus of mediatisation research is on change, it is necessary to analyse the transformations in the world of work brought about by platform labour as means of communication and production.

There are other possible dimensions of this research agenda. Datafication, as an aspect of mediatisation, is intertwined with aspects such as surveillance and algorithmic management. Alternatives to the dominant platforming are also important elements, such as collective workers' organisation and platform cooperativism. In addition, there is the role of infrastructure and algorithms in restructuring work. This means understanding mediatisation research in its connections to debates on platform capitalism, data as capital, and political economy. The role of mediatisation research can be to connect debates from the most different areas.

The research agenda can be improved in a variety of ways. One example is the development of more research on the work behind artificial intelligence as part of a media ecosystem. The dominant narratives about artificial intelligence tend to make human labour invisible in the data production process for automation. I understand the role of the media ecosystem in this process in two ways. First, as media processes between the workers themselves and between them and the platforms, in the sense that interactions with the platforms are work relations. Second, the media industries, including social media companies, need the labour of training data for artificial intelligence to power their systems. For example, the circulation of advertising depends on evaluation of the campaigns by these workers. Other examples can be the emergence of new ways of working – in the influencer industry, in the tech industry – that present changes in ways of working and consuming media.

This research agenda is not new, as media and work are historically related. In the last two decades, the world of work has been affected by digitalisation. Platformisation is only the current historical moment, the result of previous processes. If mediatisation research focuses on change, platformisation symbolises transformations in the world of work. The challenges of mediatisation research lie in understanding changes and continuities in relation to media and society – in this case, the work, towards the future of the increasingly central role of (automated) media.

References

Antunes, R. (2018). *O Privilégio da Servidão: O novo proletariado de serviços na era digital*. São Paulo: Boitempo.

Arvidsson, A. (2016). Facebook and finance: On the social logic of the derivative. *Theory, Culture & Society*, V. 33, n. 6.

Beer, D. (2017). The social power of algorithms. *Information, Communication & Society*, V. 20, n. 1.

Beer, D. (2019). *The Data Gaze*. London: Sage.

Berardi, F. (2012). *The Uprising: On Poetry and Finance*. Cambridge, MA: MIT Press.

Bolin, G. (2012). The labour of media use: The two active audiences. *Information, Communication & Society*, V. 15, n. 6.

Bolin, G. (2016). *Value and the Media: Cultural Production and Consumption in Digital Markets*. London: Routledge.

Broussard, M. (2018). *Artificial Unintelligence*. Cambridge, MA: MIT Press.

Brown, W. (2016). *El Pueblo Sin Atributos*. Barcelona: Malpaso.

Bucher, T. (2017). The algorithmic imaginary: Exploring the ordinary affects of Facebook algorithms. *Information, Communication & Society*, V. 20, n. 1.

Casilli, A. (2019). *En Attendant les Robots: Enquête sur le travail du clic*. Paris: Seuil.

Casilli, A. & Posada, J. (2019). The Platformisation of Labour and Society. In: *Society and the Internet*. Oxford: Oxford University Press, pp. 293–306.

Chan, N. & Humphreys, L. (2018). Mediatization of social space and the case of Uber drivers. *Media and Communication*, V. 6, n. 2.

Codagnone, C., Karatzogianni, A. & Matthews, J. (2019). *Platform Economics: Rhetoric and Reality in the "Sharing Economy."* London: Emerald.

Chen, J. & Qiu, J. (2019). Digital utility: Datafication, regulation, labour, and Didi's platformisation of urban transport in China. *Chinese Journal of Communication*, V. 12, n. 3, 274–289.

Cohen, N. & De Peuter, G. (2018). "I work at Vice Canada and I need a union": Organizing Digital Media. *Labour Under Attack: Anti-unionism in Canada*. Nova Escócia: Fernwood, pp. 114–128.

Couldry, N. (2020). *Media: Why It Matters*. London: Polity.

Couldry, N. & Hepp, A. (2017). *The Mediated Construction of Reality*. London: Polity Press.

Couldry, N. & Mejias, U. (2019). *The Costs of Connection*. Palo Alto, CA: Stanford University Press.

Dardot, P. & Laval, C. (2016). *A Nova Razão do Mundo*. São Paulo: Boitempo.

De Marchi, L. (2018). Como os algoritmos do Youtube calculam valor? Uma análise da produção de valor para vídeos digitais de música através da lógica social de derivativo. *MATRIZes*, V. 12, n. 2.

Denis, J. (2018). *Le travail invisible des données: Eléments pour une sociologie des infrastructures scripturales*. Paris: Presses de Mines.

Dyer-Witheford, N. (2015). *Cyber-Proletariat: Global Labour in the Digital Vortex*. London: Pluto Press.

Dyer-Witheford, N., Kjosen, A. & Steinhoff, J. (2019). *Inhuman Power: Artificial Intelligence and the Future of Capitalism*. London: Pluto Press.

Eubanks, V. (2017). *Automating Inequality*. New York: St. Martin's Press.

Figaro, R. (2001). *Comunicação e trabalho*. São Paulo: Annablumme.

Fisher, M. (2011). *Capitalist Realism: Is There No Alternative?* Winchester: Zero Books.

Fontes, V. (2017). Capitalismo em tempos de uberização: Do emprego ao trabalho. *Marx e o Marxismo*, V. 5, n. 8.

Fuchs, C. (2017). *Social Media: A Critical Introduction*. Abingdon: Routledge, 2017.

Fuchs, C. & Sandoval, M. (2014). Workers of the world unite! A framework to critically theorising and analysing digital labour. *TripleC*. V. 22, n. 2.

Gillespie, T. (2018). *Custodians of the Internet: Platforms, Content Moderation and the Hidden Decisions That Shape Social Media*. New Haven, CT: Yale University Press.

Graham, M. & Woodcock, J. (2018). Towards a fairer platform economy: Introducing the Fairwork Foundation. *Alternate Routes*, V. 29.

Graham, M. & Anwar, M. (2019). The global gig economy: Towards a planetary labour market? *First Monday*, V. 24, n. 4.

Gray, M. & Suri, S. (2019). *Ghost Work: How to Stop Silicon Valley from Building a New Global Underclass*. Boston: Houghton Mifflin Harcourt.

Grohmann, R. (2018). Cooperativismo de plataforma e suas contradições: Análise de iniciativas da área de comunicação no Platform.Coop. *Liinc em Revista*, V. 14, n. 1.

Grohmann, R. & Araújo, W. (2021). Beyond Mechanical Turk: e Work of. Brazilians on Global AI Platforms. In: Verdegem, P. (ed.), *AI For Everyone? Critical Perspectives*. London: University of Westminster Press.

Grohmann, R. & Qiu, J. (2020). Contextualizing platform labour. *Contracampo: Brazilian Journal of Communication*, V. 22, n. 1, 1–15.

Hartmann, H., Hegewisch, A. & Childers, C. (2019). *Women, Automation and the Future of Work*. London: IWPR.

Harvey, D. (2018). *A Loucura da Razão Econômica*. São Paulo: Boitempo.

Helmond, A. (2015). The platformisation of the web: Making web data platform ready. *Social Media & Society*, V. 1, n. 2.

Hepp, A. (2020). *Deep Mediatisation*. London: Routledge.

Huws, U. (2014). *Labour in the Global Digital Economy*. New York: Monthly Review Press.

Huws, U., Spencer, N.H., Coates, M. & Holts, K. (2019). *The Platformisation of Work in Europe*. Brussels: Foundation for European Progressive Studies.

Jansson, A. (2017). *Mediatization and Mobile Lives: A Critical Approach*. London: Routledge.

Jansson, A. & Fast, K. (2019). *Transmedia Work: Privilege and Precariousness in Digital Modernity*. London: Routledge.

Lapavitsas, C. (2013). *Profiting without Producing: How Finance Exploits Us All*. New York: Verso.

Mateescu, A. & Nguyen, A. (2019). Algorithmic management in the workplace. *Big Data & Society*. https://datasociety.net/wp-content/uploads/2019/02/DS_Algorithmic_Management_Explainer.pdf

Möhlmann, M. & Zalmanson, L. (2017). Hand on the wheel: Navigating algorithmic management and Uber drivers' autonomy. *International Conference on Information Systems (ICIS 2017)*. Seul.

Morozov, E. (2018). *Big Tech: A ascensão dos dados e a morte da política*. São Paulo: Ubu.

Murdock, G. (2017). Media materialities: For a moral economy of machines. *Journal of Communication*, V. 68, n. 2.

Nieborg, D. & Poell, T. (2018). The platformisation of cultural production: Theorizing the contingent cultural commodity. *New Media & Society*, V. 20, n. 11.

Noble, S. (2018). *Algorithms of Opression: How Search Engines Reinforce Racism*. New York: NYU Press.

Pallas, J. & Fredriksson, M. (2013). Corporate media work and micro-dynamics of mediatization. *European Journal of Communication*, V. 28, n. 4.

Pasquale, F. (2015). *The Black Box Society*. Cambridge, MA: Harvard University Press.

Poier, S. (2018). My boss is an app: An auto-ethnography on app-based gig economy. *Émulations*, n. 28.

Poell, T., Nieborg, D. & Van Dijck, J. (2019). Platformisation. *Internet Policy Review*, V. 8, n. 4.

Roberts, S. (2019). *Behind the Screen: Content Moderation in the Shadows of Social Media*. New Haven, CT: Yale University Press.

Rosenblat, A. (2018). *Uberland: How Algorithms Are Rewriting the Rules of Work*. Berkeley: University of California Press.

Sadowski, J. (2019). When data is capital: Datafication, accumulation and extraction. *Big Data & Society*, V. 3, n. 1, 1–9.

Sadowski, J. (2020). The internet of landlords: Digital platforms and new mechanisms of rentier capitalism. *Antipode*, V. 52, n. 2.

Sandoval, M. (2019). Entrepreneurial activism? Platform cooperativism between subversion and co-optation. *Critical Sociology*, V. 46, n. 6, 801–817.

Schmidt, F. (2017). *Digital Labour Markets in the Platform Economy: Mapping the Political Changes of Crowd Work and Gig Work*. Bonn: Friedrich-Ebert-Stiftung.

Scholz, T. (2016). *Uberworked and Underpaid*. London: Polity Press.

Scholz, T. (2017). *Cooperativismo de Plataforma*. São Paulo: Fundação Rosa Luxemburgo.

Sodré, M. (2014). *A Ciência do Comum*. Petrópolis: Vozes.

Soriano C., Grohmann R., Chen, Y., Karatzogianni, A., Qiu, J., Cabanes, J., Alves, P. & Dey, A. (2020). Digital Labor Solidarities, Collective Formations, and Relational Infrastructures. *AoIR Selected Papers of Internet Research*.

Srnicek, N. (2016). *Platform Capitalism*. London: Polity.

Van Dijck, J. (2014). Datafication, dataism and dataveillance: Big data between scientific paradigm and ideology. *Surveillance & Society*, V. 12, n. 2.

Van Dijck, J., Poell, T. & De Waal, M. (2018). *The Platform Society*. New York: Oxford University Press.

Van Doorn, N. (2017). Platform labour: On the gendered and racialised exploitation of low-income service work in the "on-demand" economy. *Information, Communication & Society*, V. 20, n. 6, 898–914.

Vieira Pinto, A. (2005). *O conceito de tecnologia*. v. 1. Rio de Janeiro: Contraponto.

Wajcman, J. (2019). How Silicon Valley sets time. *New Media & Society*, V. 21, n. 6.

Williams, R. (2011). *Cultura e materialismo*. São Paulo: Ed. UNESP.

Woodcock, J. (2019). *Marx at the Arcade: Consoles, Controllers, and Class Struggle*. Chicago: Haymarket Books.

Zuboff, S. (2019). *The Age of Surveillance Capitalism*. London: Profile Books.

10 The End of Media?

From Mediatisation to Datafication

Anne Kaun

In this chapter I engage with the question of whether the field of media and communication studies is experiencing a disappearance of the notion of mediatisation. It might seem provocative and ignorant to contribute a chapter on the end of mediatisation to a volume that is explicitly outlining the current challenges of this subfield. But it is exactly the move away from mediatisation that I see as its biggest challenge. In what follows I will outline first the process of disappearance and second discuss some potential reasons for the coming end of mediatisation research. One of the reasons for this disappearance I situate in the changed notion and character of media that is fundamental to the turn towards datafication.

My own entrance to the field of mediatisation research was as an interested outsider. In 2011 and 2014, I wrote two reports mapping the then current approaches to mediatisation for one of the main Swedish funding bodies, that captured the general and growing interest in this line of research. Later on, I was watching the evolving field from the sidelines. While I never claimed to have contributed to the theoretical development myself, I followed the academic production and institutionalisation with interest. Some of the central European media and communication scholars were invested in developing a general theory of mediatisation and contributed to the institutionalisation as a subfield through conferences, workshops, and a temporary working group that was later turned into a standing section within a professional association. Colleagues based in the USA approached me from time to time to inquire about this field that has this funny sounding name. They were asking if it is worth ploughing through hundreds of papers that were published with mediatisation in the title and produced a rather high threshold for entering the discussion in the first place. Some of the central disputes of the field were alienating to me and seemed exclusively academic without much bearing on the most pressing social, political, and economic issues related to media.

However, in recent years it seems that the notion of mediatisation is increasingly being sidelined by the notion of datafication that is focusing on the specific process of turning our social lives into data points. Powering algorithms and artificial intelligence, the emergence of big data seems to

DOI: 10.4324/9781003324591-14

have replaced the discussion of the mediatisation of our lives. This move from mediatisation to datafication could be considered merely as a strategic shift that reflects general tendencies of academia to move from one buzz-word to the other to legitimise funding for research projects and groups. In this chapter I am taking the theoretical and conceptual arguments developed in mediatisation research seriously and think that there is more to the changing outlook of mediatisation studies than mere academic strategising. The change in terminology and methodology is growing out of the increasing dominance of data-based media technologies that occupy our attention, experiences, political organising, and governance.

A brief history of mediatisation research

Research using the terminology of mediatisation emerged more vividly in the early and mid-2000s. Several publications that are now standard reading in many media and communication studies programmes contributed important knowledge on the social changes related to media that are increasingly entangled with our social, political, cultural, and economic spheres of life (for an overview see Kaun & Fast, 2014). From the outset the term mediatisation has been contested and there has been constant discussion regarding the diverse ways of conceptualising mediatisation (Couldry & Hepp, 2013; Hjarvard, 2013; Jensen, 2013) including a strong critique of the overall status of mediatisation as a key term or bandwagon concept (Deacon & Stanyer, 2014); and in return a further concretisation and differentiation of the term (Hepp, Hjarvard & Lundby, 2015).

Sonia Livingstone, for example, has addressed changing foci and terminology in the field of media and communication research that more generally reflect the ubiquity of media with relevance for "almost every dimension of social life", mediatisation being one of these changing concepts. According to her the field has moved between different self-chosen labels, from mass communication to media and communication studies, that reflect the conceptual development within the field as well as the changing social context that the field engages with. In that sense, concepts such as mediatisation and datafication not only serve as a theoretical tool to understand current social phenomena but also a definition of the object of the field that reflects its evolution over time (Bolin & Forsman, 2000).

However, most approaches share an understanding of mediatisation as the "broader consequences of media and communications for everyday life and across social space" (Couldry & Hepp, 2013, p. 195). This understanding assumes a broader consideration of the role that media play in everyday life, institutions, and culture more generally, moving beyond former approaches towards media effects on the individual level. The interest in these broader approaches towards media change became more prevalent in the 2000s with increasing speed and accessibility of the internet, broad use of smart mobile phones and the emergence of large platforms that enhanced the integration of media into our lives. This, it was argued, required new theoretical and methodological engagements that were often grounded in earlier attempts to go beyond the audience–production–text line of thought, for example, proposed by Roger Silverstone and Jesus Martin-Barbero. It is, however, striking that the emergence of the mediatisation concept in the late 2000s was largely happening outside of the Anglo-American context that has been interpreted by Couldry and Hepp (2013) as a sign of the true internationalisation of the field. However, Sonia Livingstone refers to a number of transnational confusions, as the terms mediatisation as well as mediation do not travel that easily between different languages. Livingstone establishes the general distinction between "mediation (*Vermittlung*) [which] ordinarily references the legal/regulatory term for seeking discursive solutions to disputes, [and] *Mediatisierung* (mediatisation) and *Medialisierung* (medialisation) refer to the metaprocess by which practices of the everyday and social relations are increasingly shaped by mediating technologies and media organisations" (Livingstone, 2009, p. 4). In a similar vein, Kirsten Drotner suggests a distinction when she argues that "the more general term is mediation while the more specific term is medialisation and mediatisation" (my translation, Drotner, 2006, p. 19). She further argues that in the Scandinavian context mediation is not a real synonym or alternative to mediatisation, as the term remains fuzzy as to what meaning making in media-saturated societies might encompass. Furthermore, she states that "mediation is a key term in learning studies (...), and hence its application in the present context is likely to obscure more than illuminate the possible learning resources involved in digital meaning-making practices" (Drotner, 2008, p. 71). Consequently this chapter also focuses on mediatisation rather than mediation.

In the Scandinavian context, we can more generally still distinguish between a broad and a narrow definition of mediatisation, with the broad understanding being grounded in cultural studies approaches (Fornäs, 1994; 1995; 2000; Hannerz, 1990; Jansson, 2002) and the narrow understanding (e.g. Hjarvard, 2008a; 2008b; 2008c; Lundby, 2008; 2009; Strömbäck, 2008a; 2008b) being more firmly based in social science-oriented approaches (Fornäs & Kaun, 2011).

Following the broader definition of mediatisation, Johan Fornäs et al. remind their readers of epistemological and methodological difficulties with grasping the complexity of mediatisation:

> There is in world history, in the modern era, and most particularly in its current late-modern phase, an accelerating growth, spread, diversification and interlacing of communications media across the globe. Media use constitutes increasingly greater parts of everyday life for a growing number of people around the world. This historical process of mediatisation draws a widening range of activities into the sphere of media, making mediation an increasingly key feature of society and everyday life. All contemporary major social and cultural issues directly

implicate uses of media. Debates on war, science, ethics, ecology, gender identities, ethnic communities, generation gaps and socialization – all immediately raise questions of media power. Media no longer form a distinct sector, but are fully integrated in human life. This paradoxically means that their enormous influence can never be adequately "measured", since there is no media-free zone with which to compare their effects.

(Fornäs, Becker, Bjurström & Ganetz, 2007, p. 1)

Implicit in the quote above is a critique that was raised against a too narrow understanding of what media-related change might mean, namely the idea of comparing unmediated phenomena with mediated ones (e.g. Couldry, 2008). Similarly, André Jansson emphasises a cultural perspective on mediatisation that foregrounds the role of media representations for the development of cultural frameworks and reference points, both on the individual as well as collective level. He argues that "the mass media provide a means for individuals to map out and elaborate their positions in time and space" (Jansson, 2002, p. 14). He continues by stating that

the term mediatization refers to the process through which mediated cultural products have gained importance as cultural referents and hence contribute to the development and maintenance of cultural communities. In other words, the mediatization of culture is the process that reinforces and expands the realm of media culture.

(Jansson, 2002, p. 15).

The cultural approaches to mediatisation have all embedded the process of mediatisation in larger processes of culturalisation, globalisation, and commercialisation, and in that sense aim to reach beyond the unidirectional approaches that are partly implied by a narrower perspective. While the concept becomes more complex and inclusive of structural coherent processes of social change that are interrelated, it potentially becomes shallow and fuzzier, as has been suggested in a number of critical accounts.

In contrast, the narrower social science-oriented approach concerns specific shifts in the organisation of sectors in society based on media logics. Stig Hjarvard (2008b, p. 113) suggests for example the following definition of mediatisation:

By mediatization of society, I understand the process whereby society to an increasing degree is submitted to, or becomes dependent on, the media and their logic. This process is characterized by a duality in that the media have become *integrated* into the operations of other social institutions, while they also have acquired the status of social institutions *in their own right*.

Two aspects are especially important in the definition above. First, there is the institutionalisation of media and consequently the adaptation of media institutional logics by other sectors or domains. Second, this is a process that is accelerated over time. The procedural character of mediatisation is one of the main distinctions from mediation that has been considered as a more static process by, for example, Jesper Strömbäck (Strömbäck, 2008b; Strömbäck & Nord, 2008). Additionally, Stig Hjarvard makes a distinction between indirect and direct mediatisation, suggesting that "direct mediatization refers to situations where formerly a non-mediated activity converts to a mediated form, i.e., the activity is performed through interaction with a medium" (Hjarvard, 2008b, p. 114). One of his main examples is the introduction of computer-mediated chess and online banking as direct or strong forms of mediatisation. Indirect mediatisation in contrast takes place "when a [given] activity is increasingly influenced with respect to form, content, or organization by mediagenic symbols or mechanisms" (Hjarvard, 2008b, p. 115). Here he refers to processes of media increasingly surrounding other everyday experiences such as eating or driving. Another example is the knowledge of Danes about the U.S. and its dependence on media representations. However, the distinction between direct and indirect mediatisation is rarely clear-cut. Both forms are often intermingled, and they appear in combination. However, Hjarvard argues that the distinction is analytically relevant since direct or strong mediatisation stands for the process of replacing a formerly non-mediated activity by a mediatised activity. Media here act as a necessary interface for social interaction. Indirect mediatisation is much more subtle and general, and refers to "the general increase in social institutions' reliance on communication resources" (Hjarvard, 2008b, p. 115).

What the broad and narrow approach share is an understanding of mediatisation as encompassing all kinds of processes of change that are media-induced or related to a change in the media landscape over time. This also includes changes in the media landscape over time that are linked to other large-scale processes of social change (for a terminological discussion of media ecology versus media landscape see Bolin (2014)). In recent years, mediatisation has become to be understood increasingly as a sensitising concept that emphasises the role of media in social change rather than a way to conceptualise causal explanations (Hepp, 2020). Here the notion of deep mediatisation has been central to further the discussion of media-related change. In terms of methodological approaches to study mediatisation, Andreas Hepp has proposed both diachronic and synchronic ways that encompass both longer historical analyses and more focused accounts of current, more specific changes. Hence, Hepp proposes different temporal layers of mediatisation that can and should be considered methodologically as well.

Further developing earlier approaches to mediatisation research, Nick Couldry and Andreas Hepp put forward three factors and research streams that characterise mediatisation research in their editorial introduction to the special issue "Conceptualizing mediatization: Contexts, traditions, arguments" of the journal *Communication Theory*: first, there is a growing importance of media to people in general (including the normalisation of internet access, the spread of mobile phones and the explosion of social media). Second, there is increasingly diverse research considering the open-ended consequences of media in society beyond the nexus of production–text–audience since the 1980s. Third, the field of media and communication studies saw new approaches to power emerging that recognise its repro-duction in, as the authors write, "huge networks of linkages, apparatuses, and habits within everyday life" (e.g. Actor Network Theory) (Couldry & Hepp 2013, p. 194). Couldry and Hepp ultimately argue that the concept of mediatisation makes it possible to study the consequences of media beyond simple media effects. This openness of the concept has invited numerous research projects.

In recent years, the field of mediatisation research has moved towards incorporating contemporary phenomena such as the shift to digital and data-based media. Andreas Hepp, for example, has suggested considering mediatisation as a sensitising concept that is based on the understanding of media as a process that is constantly changing since especially digital media are permanently in beta version. According to him datafication constitutes a new phase of deep mediatisation that has intensified this flexibility and dynamic in the process of change. He argues that deep mediatisation reflects

> how important media are as means of communication and as an influence on the social construction of reality. This social construction is under-stood as an ongoing, multilevel process. Consequently, mediatization research's perspective on that process places an emphasis on dynamics and interrelations, moves beyond simple causal logic.
>
> (Hepp, 2020, p. 57)

Furthermore, he proposes to understand mediatisation as a moulding force of media reflecting a multi-level phenomenon. Media are part of what constitutes liquid modernity. Liquid modernity was partly made possible by commercial, digital media as an "omnipresent factor in this liquid life". That means they contribute to the experience of fluidity and ever-changing social constituents, while being themselves characterised by fluidity and constant change. Hepp argues further that those earlier approaches to link mediatisation to the dispersal of media logics into other sectors and domains becomes tricky in late modernity, as media logics are difficult to discern and identify. The procedural character of the media obscures media logics. Hence the ongoing process of articulation stands in a stark contrast to a static idea of media logic that is translated or adopted by other domains. According to Hepp, the procedural character of the media has been intensified with digitalisation, and digital media are predominantly in a process of constant change. In that sense, Hepp and other researchers of mediatisation argue that there are new processes of change emerging with digital media and datafication, including calls for new methodological approaches. However, there are also calls to a cautious consideration of earlier approaches to studying media-related practices as well as media-related change. Sonia Livingstone (2019), for example, argues that we have learned important lessons from audience studies that also have implications for researching datafied societies. For instance, early audience research as well as the public discourse have underestimated the critical capacities of audiences. Scholars of datafication research should not fall into the same trap, but take the audience or user perspective seriously when engaging with datafication and its consequences. Part of the question of emerging media technologies requires us to rethink approaches to studying how we conceptualise media in the first place.

Conceptualising media within mediatisation research

An important aspect of developing an understanding of the notion of mediatisation is the underlying understanding of what constitutes media in the first place. According to Marian Adolf (2017), different mediatisation approaches vary fundamentally in how media are defined. Göran Bolin has argued already in 2014 that the institutional approach within mediatisation research necessarily privileges mass media, as they are institutionalised media. The constructivist approach is broader in scope and also includes non-institutionalised media, including alternative media as well as the combination of different media ensembles.

However, there is a different temporal connection between the definition of media as to when mediatisation as a process started as well as epistemological and ontological assumptions. The initial approaches of mediatisation research draw on earlier medium theory including works by Marshall McLuhan, Harold Innis or Joshua Meyrowitz.[1] For example, Marshall McLuhan's well known quotes and metaphors such as "the medium is the message" or "the global village" reflect the idea that media "extended our central nervous system [itself] in a global embrace" (McLuhan, 2008 [1964]) and that media constitute "settings or environments for social interaction" (Meyrowitz, 1997). Medium theory, just as mediatisation, aims to establish a holistic approach to understand media, beyond studies focusing on media content or media reception only. Medium theory suggests an analysis of the societal implications of a media ecology. Core questions of medium theory, according to Joshua Meyrowitz (1997, p. 61), are "[h]ow do the particular characteristics of a medium make it physically, psychologically, and socially different from other media and from face-to-face interaction, regardless of the particular messages that communicated through it?" Following these central questions, Meyrowitz (1995), for example, discusses the impact of printing and literacy on enhanced secularisation and the decreasing power

of the church, since the technology and the printed material led to a democ-
ratisation of religious interpretations and engagement. Deuze's (2010; 2011)
concept of media life can be interpreted as a further development of early
medium theory. He suggests that life is not only lived *with* but also and primarily *in* the media. Hence, living in the media is analysed as a necessary
survival strategy. Deuze's (2010, p. 5) conclusion is that

> living a media life is not just having access to all kinds of devices we use
> to mediate our lives. Nor is it just about knowing how and when to use
> such equipment. A media life is just as much about our orientation to
> media as it is about media and what we do with them.

Deuze understands a media life as a life lived in the media that is crucial for
success in all spheres of life and all institutions. It is "in other words: necessary for its successful reproduction and survival" (Deuze, 2010, p. 6). At the
same time, the notion of media has continuously been broadened within
media and communication research, towards encompassing not only cultural techniques such as "doors" (Siegert, 2013), but also elemental media
such as fire (Peters, 2015). While these broad approaches to media are
mainly situated in media theory and are rarely considered in mediatisation
research, they point to important changes in how we think what constitutes
media. Similarly, the process of datafication has broadened the field of media
and communication studies towards both computational methods and new
forms of engagement by users and audiences. This begs the question whether
datafication requires us to rethink the fundamental ideas that are at the
heart of mediatisation research, or if this process is merely a continuation of
already existing tendencies.

Datafication: old wine in new bottles?

Since around 2013, there has been an increasing interest in the process of
datafication that is defined as the conversion of increasing aspects of our lives
into data, namely the conversion of social action into online quantified data
through, for example, social networking platforms (Mayer-Schönberger &
Cukier, 2013; van Dijck, 2014). This process in turn allows for anticipatory
practices of prediction and prognosis on new scale. According to Jose van
Dijck, datafication emerged as new paradigm in both science and society
that is based on the ideology of dataism, namely the idea that big data
allow for a more accurate way of approaching social reality that is objective
and neutral. Social media data are here considered as objective traces of
social action facilitated by large-scale platforms that act in neutral ways
(van Dijck, 2014). The ideology of dataism is also reflected in what Nick
Couldry and Ulises Mejias (2019) have termed "data colonialism", namely
an emerging order "for the appropriation of human life so that data can be
continuously extracted from it for profit. This extraction is operationalized

via data relations, ways of interacting with each other and with the world facilitated by digital tools" (Couldry & Mejias, 2019, p. xiii). These data relations that increasingly form an important way of generating profits link our social actions intimately with capitalism, and contribute to continuous surveillance and monitoring of our behaviours and interactions. This has led to the decreasing autonomy of individuals while a rapidly growing social quantification sector has emerged that among others includes social media platforms as well as smart home appliances. Datafication according to Couldry and Mejias constitutes one of the most important ways of producing value by appropriating human life through converting it into data.

Sofie Flensburg and Stine Lomborg provide a systematic review of datafication research since the introduction of term in 2013. They argue that research consists predominantly of theoretical contributions conceptualising emerging social, economic, and cultural changes in relation to the process of datafication. Methodologically, most studies rely on qualitative inquiries and rarely employ computational methods to explore datafication (Flensburg & Lomborg, 2021). At the same time, there has been an urge to reconsider fundamental methodological approaches within media and communication studies, in order to grasp the changes that go hand in hand with datafication (Lomborg, Dencik & Moe, 2020). This has involved innovative digital and computational methods (Puschmann, Ausserhofer & Slerka, 2020; Rogers, 2020) as well as revising "traditional" methods such as grounded theory (Mattoni, 2020).

Since the first discussions of datafication as an important and increasingly dominant social process, several publications have emerged that engage, for example, with the question of what the consequences of datafication are for audiences and the formation of public spheres (Møller Hartley, Bengtsson, Schjøtt Hansen & Sivertsen, 2021), audience experiences of metrification and demetrification (Bolin & Velkova, 2020), as well as studies of the datafication of specific domains, among others health (Ruckenstein & Dow Schüll, 2017) and education (Jarke & Breiter, 2019). Furthermore, media and communication studies more generally have seen a move towards studying technologies rather legacy media, including a focus on data, artificial intelligence, and algorithms, while the theoretical and empirical interest has moved towards questions of materialities, forms of hidden labour, and broader ecologies of how technologies emerge and evolve. This move has also been prepared within mediatisation research, for example by discussions of how mediatisation relates to notions of media ecologies and media landscapes (Bolin & Hepp, 2017).

These shifts actualise the question of whether datafication constitutes a completely new development or if it constitutes a further development of the process of mediatisation and is, to follow Andreas Hepp's (2020) words, one layer of deep mediatisation. Stine Lomborg, Lina Dencik and Hallvard Moe (2020) argue that the object of media and communication studies has fundamentally shifted with digital media that make the traditional distinction between production, reception, and distribution increasingly meaningless. At the same time, this shift poses a fundamental question to media and communication studies. They argue:

> if anything digital can be media, it fundamentally challenges taken-for-granted notions in our field: What are media institutions to be studied when the networked media can be anything from babysitter apps to rifles and where are the "texts" in these media that audience studies till hold as defining criteria.
>
> (Lomborg, Dencik & Moe 2020)

Hence, the process of datafication based on digital media forces us to rethink the foundation of media and communication studies; for example, moving from content-centric analyses towards ways of data production and extraction (Turow & Couldry, 2018, quoted in Lomborg, Dencik & Moe 2020). At the same time, it seems apt to revisit mediatisation research that similarly evolved in connection with large shifts within the discipline. However, there have only been rare attempts to bring mediatisation and datafication research into dialogue with each other. Instead, it seems that datafication has emerged as a new bandwagon concept that attracts increasing numbers of scholars within media and communication studies very much like mediatisation research did previously. While Hepp argues that datafication emerges as a new period of deep mediatisation, I would like to argue that the focus on data not only reflects a new way in which media technologies are intertwined and – in Hepp's terms – moulded with our everyday lives, but that also the basic understanding of what media are has changed.

Concluding remarks: the end of media – the end of mediatisation?

Developing the argument above, namely that the move towards datafication both in society and research, also implies a different understanding of what media are and do, I suggest linking the discussion to a shift from media's traditional logic of representation towards the dominance of an operational logic that is fostered by datafied and automated media. Here I am following Mark Andrejevic (2020), who argues that we have experienced a weakening of the classical understanding of what media are and do in society. This weakening is expressed in a shift from representational logics to operationalism. Operationalism refers to the displacement of narrative accounts and explanations by automated responses. Automated responses based on large amount of data do not seek to understand but to act, which was already anticipated and discussed by Nick Couldry in 2014. Relying on big data analytics, his argument goes, often promotes an anti-hermeneutic – an anti-interpretative – approach to the social. In that sense they are not representational, but operational. This shift is based on the process of datafication and the large amount of information that is continuously produced with and through digital media. This amount of information can no longer be sorted, categorised, and organised manually, but requires automated methods. Hence, cultural tasks of categorising and organising content and information are increasingly delegated to automated, algorithm-based systems.

Andrejevic further argues that the "collapse of representation into operationalism makes it harder for humans to see how decisions are being made and this discerns the reasons for their consequences. The fantasy of operationalism is the subtraction of the moment of human judgement" (Andrejevic, 2020, p. 20). While representations – the fundamental logic of traditional media – are part of the domain of the subject allowing for recognition of the other and the self, the operational logic of automated media produces an absence of an object of representation. The subject and subjectivity are increasingly managed through nudges and modulations to produce desired behaviours that are disconnected from symbolic norms and roles. According to Andrejevic there are specific expressions of this operational logic, namely "the consumer whose needs are met before they arise, the citizen whose actions are shaped by the nudges of 'libertarian paternalism', the criminal whose actions are pre-empted before they can take shape, and a future that is deprived of the possibility of history" (Andrejevic, 2020, p. 134). The operational logic of automated media goes hand in hand with a form of *framelessness*, namely the contemporary tendency to capture and save everything with the hope of producing a totality of information and data points.

Following Andrejevic's points, I argue that the process of datafication contributes to the end of a representational logic of media and a shift towards an operational logic. This also constitutes a fundamental shift of the role and meaning of media as we know them. To a certain extent one could argue that datafication represents the end of media. Consequently, rather than arguing that datafication is a new layer of the process of mediatisation, it might rather be the end of mediatisation that is implicated in the end of media.

Rethinking the theory of mediatisation in the light of datafication provokes some foundational questions about the nature and character of the process of mediatisation, such as whether the process of datafication is fundamentally reshaping mediatisation research. However, the most pressing issue is the need to develop a deeper understanding of what these shifts imply for our social worlds. What does it mean that we increasingly engage with automated media that follow operational rather than representational logics? What does this shift mean for our possibilities of recognising others and ourselves? These are still open questions that need our attention and challenge researchers within media and communication studies to fundamentally rethink their objects and methods of inquiry.

In this contribution, I am engaging with the question whether the process of datafication is fundamentally reshaping mediatisation research.

With a focus on the question of how media logics are shifting in and with datafication, I argue that rather than speaking of datafication as a continuation of mediatisation as process, it constitutes a fundamental shift that is based on the decreasing importance of traditional media that are based on the logic of representation, and the increasing importance of automated media that are based on the logic of operationalism. In that sense, the end of media as we know them constitutes one of the most important challenges within mediatisation research.

Note

1 How closely related medium theory and mediatisation are was discussed, among other things, at a workshop on "Media Evolution and Cultural Change: Discussing Medium Theory and Mediatization", on 3 September 2011 at the University of Bremen, with keynote speakers Joshua Meyrowitz, Stig Hjarvard, Andreas Hepp, and Fredrich Krotz.

References

Adolf, M. (2017). The Identity of Mediatization: Theorizing a Dynamic Field. In O. Driessen, G. Bolin, A. Hepp, & S. Hjarvard (Eds.), *Dynamics of Mediatization: Transforming Communications* (pp. 11–34). Basingstoke: Palgrave Macmillan.

Andrejevic, M. (2020). *Automated Media*. London: Routledge.

Bolin, G. (2014). Institution, Technology, World: Relationships between the Media, Culture, and Society. In K. Lundby (Ed.), *The Mediatization of Communication* (pp. 175–198). Berlin and Boston: De Gruyter Mouton.

Bolin, G., & Forsman, M. (2000). Medien- und Kommunikationswissenschaft in Schweden: Zergliederung oder Ko-Existenz? *Montage/AV, 9*(1), 187–201.

Bolin, G., & Hepp, A. (2017). The Complexities of Mediatization: Charting the Road Ahead. In O. Driessens, G. Bolin, A. Hepp, & S. Hjarvard (Eds.), *Dynamics Of Mediatization: Institutional Change and Everyday Transformations in a Digital Age* (pp. 315–331). Cham: Springer International Publishing.

Bolin, G., & Velkova, J. (2020). Audience-metric continuity? Approaching the meaning of measurement in the digital everyday. *Media, Culture & Society, 42*(7–8), 1193–1209. doi:10.1177/0163443720907017

Couldry, N. (2008). Mediatization or mediation? Alternative understandings of the emergent space of digital storytelling. *New Media and Society, 10*(3), 373–391.

Couldry, N. (2014). Inaugural: A necessary disenchantment: Myth, agency and injustice in a digital world. *The Sociological Review, 62*, 880–897.

Couldry, N., & Hepp, A. (2013). Conceptualizing mediatization: Contexts, traditions, arguments. *Communication Theory, 23*(3), 191–202. doi:10.1111/comt.12019

Couldry, N., & Mejias, U. (2019). *The Costs of Connection: How Data Is Colonising Human Life and Appropriating It for Capitalism*. Stanford, CA: Stanford University Press.

Deacon, D., & Stanyer, J. (2014). Mediatization: Key concept or conceptual bandwagon? *Media, Culture & Society*, 36(7), 1032–1044. doi:10.1177/0163443714542218

Deuze, M. (2010). Survival of the mediated. *Journal of Cultural Science*, 3(2), 1–11.

Deuze, M. (2011). Media life. *Media, Culture and Society*, 33(1), 137–148.

Drotner, K. (2006). Fra skolebog til læringsressource: Didaktikkens medialisering. *Gymnasiepædagogik*, 59, 15–25.

Drotner, K. (2008). Boundaries and Bridges. Digital Storytelling in Education Studies and Media Studies. In K. Lundby (Ed.), *Digital Storytelling, Mediatized Stories. Self-representations in New Media* (pp. 61–81). New York: Peter Lang.

Flensburg, S., & Lomborg, S. (2021). Datafication research: Mapping the field for a future agenda. *New Media & Society*, https://doi.org/10.1177/1461444821 1046616.

Fornäs, J. (1994). Medier, kommunikation och kultur. In U. Carlsson, C. von Feilitzen, J. Fornäs, S. Ross, & H. Strand (Eds.), *Kommunikationens korsningar. Möten mellan olika traditioner och perspektiv i mediaforskningen* (pp. 47–67). Göteborg: Nordicom.

Fornäs, J. (1995). *Cultural Theory and Late Modernity*. London: Sage.

Fornäs, J. (2000). The crucial in between: The centrality of mediation in cultural studies. *European Journal of Cultural Studies*, 3(1), 45–65.

Fornäs, J., Becker, K., Bjurström, E., & Ganetz, H. (2007). *Consuming Media: Communication, Shopping and Everyday Life*. Oxford and New York: Berg.

Fornäs, J., & Kaun, A. (2011). Medialisering av kultur, politik, vardag och forskning: Slutrapport från Riksbankens. Jubileumsfonds Forskarsymposium i Stockholm, 18–19 Augusti 2011.

Hannerz, U. (Ed.) (1990). *Medier och kulturer*. Stockholm: Carlssons.

Hepp, A. (2020). *Deep Mediatization*. London: Routledge.

Hepp, A., Hjarvard, S., & Lundby, K. (2015). Mediatization: Theorizing the interplay between media, culture and society. *Media, Culture & Society*. doi:10.1177/0163443715573835

Hjarvard, S. (2008a). *En verden af medier. Medialiseringen af politik, sprog, religion og leg*. Frederiksberg: Samfundslitteratur.

Hjarvard, S. (2008b). The mediatization of society: A theory of the media as agents of social and cultural change. *Nordicom Review*, 29(2), 105–134.

Hjarvard, S. (2013). *The Mediatization of Culture and Society*. London and New York: Routledge.

Hjarvard, S. (Ed.) (2008c). *The Mediatization of Religion: Enchantment, Media and Popular Culture, Northern Lights 2008*. Bristol: Intellect.

Jansson, A. (2002). The mediatization of consumption: Towards an analytical framework of image culture. *Journal of Consumer Culture*, 2(1), 5–31.

Jarke, J., & Breiter, A. (2019). Editorial: The datafication of education. *Learning, Media and Technology*, 44(1), 1–6.

Jensen, K. B. (2013). Definitive and sensitizing conceptualizations of mediatization. *Communication Theory*, 23(3), 203–222. doi:10.1111/comt.12014

Kaun, A., & Fast, K. (2014). *Mediatization of Culture and Everyday Life*. Södertörns högskola.

Livingstone, S. (2009). The mediation of everything. *Journal of Communication*, 59(1), 1–18.

Livingstone, S. (2019). Audiences in an age of datafication: Critical questions for media research. *Television & New Media, 20*(2), 170–183.

Lomborg, S., Dencik, L., & Moe, H. (2020). Methods for datafication, datafication of methods: Introduction to the Special Issue. *European Journal of Communication, 35*(5), 203–212.

Lundby, K. (2008). Introduction: Digital Storytelling, Mediatized Stories. In K. Lundby (Ed.), *Digital Storytelling, Mediatized Stories. Self-representation in New Media* (pp. 1–17). New York: Peter Lang.

Lundby, K. (2009). *Mediatization: Concept, Changes, Consequences.* New York: Peter Lang.

Mayer-Schönberger, V., & Cukier, K. (2013). *Big Data: A Revolution That Will Transform How We Live, Work, and Think.* Boston: Houghton Mifflin Harcourt.

Mattoni, A. (2020). The grounded theory method to study data-enabled activism against corruption: Between global communicative infrastructures and local activists' experiences of big data. *European Journal of Communication, 35*(3), 265–277.

McLuhan, M. (2008 [1964]). *Understanding Media. The Extension of Man.* London and New York: Routledge.

Meyrowitz, J. (1995). Mediating Communication: What Happens? In J. Downing, A. Mohammadi & A. Sreberny-Mohammadi (Eds.), *Questioning the Media. A Critical Introduction* (pp. 39–53). Thousand Oaks CA, London and New Delhi: Sage.

Meyrowitz, J. (1997). Shifting worlds of strangers: Medium theory and changes in "them" versus "us". *Sociological Inquiry, 67*(1), 59–71.

Møller Hartley, J., Bengtsson, M., Schjøtt Hansen, A., & Sivertsen, M. (2021). Researching publics in datafied societies: Insights from four approaches to the concept of 'publics' and a (hybrid) research agenda. *New Media & Society.* doi:10.1177/14614448211021045

Peters, J. D. (2015). *The Marvellous Clouds: Towards a Philosophy of Elemental Media.* Chicago: University of Chicago Press.

Puschmann, C., Ausserhofer, J., & Slerka, J. (2020). Converging on a nativist core? Comparing issues on the Facebook pages of the Pegida movement and the Alternative For Germany. *European Journal of Communication, 35*(3), 230–248.

Rogers, R. (2020). Deplatforming: Following extreme internet celebrities to Telegram and alternative social media. *European Journal of Communication, 35*(5), 213–229.

Ruckenstein, M., & Dow Schüll, N. (2017). The datafication of health. *Annual Review of Anthropology, 46*, 261–278.

Siegert, B. (2013). Cultural techniques: Or the end of the intellectual postwar era in German media theory. *Theory, Culture and Society, 30*(6), 48–65.

Strömbäck, J. (2008a). Four phases of mediatization: An analysis of the mediatization of politics. *The International Journal of Press/Politics, 13*(3), 228–246.

Strömbäck, J. (2008b). Medialisering och makt. En analys av mediernas politiska påverkan. *Statsvetenskaplig Tidskrift, 110*(4), 385–406.

Strömbäck, J., & Nord, L. W. (2008). Media and Politics in Sweden. In J. Strömbäck, M. Ørsted, & T. Aalberg (Eds.), *Communicating Politics: Political Communication in the Nordic Countries* (pp. 103–124). Göteborg: Nordicom.

van Dijck, J. (2014). Datafication, dataism and dataveillance: Big data between scientific paradigm and ideology. *Surveillance & Society, 12*(2), 197–208.

11 Demediatisation, Counter-Mediatisation, Media De-Saturation

Studying Media Reversals in Everyday Life

Katarzyna Kopecka-Piech

Demediatisation revisited

In his book *The Mediatisation of Culture and Society* (2013), Stig Hjarvard argues that, given the entanglement of media transformation with other ongoing changes, nothing is inevitable, including *de*-mediatisation (italics in original) (Hjarvard, 2013, p. 155). This may mean the surrender of any social institution to a control logic other than the media logic. One gets the impression that, less than a decade later, a sizable part of the academic community around mediatisation studies has not only forgotten this possibility, but has at times begun to contest it.

Meanwhile mediatisation has a wave shape – sometimes the role of the media is strengthened, sometimes weakened (Fornäs, 2016). Revolution is accompanied by evolution – that which changes rapidly and forces radical transformation is accompanied by a slow transformation, perhaps less spectacular, but nevertheless significant. First, because it shows the consequences of revolution. Second, because it constitutes a counterbalance to what is common and mass. And third, because in the context of the number of other transformations, it could be the forerunner of many more significant transformations.

To some extent, the problem with including non-usage in mediatisation research may have stemmed from the assumption that non-usage is something pathological and abnormal, undesirable and in need of a closer look and rectification (Selwyn, 2003; Kaun & Schwarzenegger, 2014). As Pepita Hesselberth (2018) writes, non-usage was burdened with the label of deficiency, maladjustment, possibly phobia. The approach of treating refusal and opting out as aberration originated largely from research on involuntary non-usage, rooted in the digital divide (Brennen, 2019). It ignored refusal media resulting from a conscious decision, e.g. a deliberate strategy as a result of one's own life or social project. As Bonnie Brennen (2019) enumerates, the reasons for opting-out are numerous: from ethical, to political, religious, cultural, simple time-saving, concerns about privacy and security, to the desire for independence and domination over technologies.

DOI: 10.4324/9781003324591-15

Kaun and Schwarzenegger (2014) believe that the study of disconnection provides a better understanding of mediatisation, because it is two sides of the same coin. Similarly, as Tero Karppi (2021) writes, focusing on undoing – illuminates qualities of activity. However, going further, it can be said that the study of disconnection allows us to see not only what the state of mediatisation is at any given moment, but also how it changes and undulates as a process; how in some spheres it reverses and begins to constitute an alternative enclave, undergoing "re-figuration" (Hepp, 2019, p. 109).

With the growing importance of mediatisation – as a paradigm, framework, research programme or approach – it is somewhat surprising that these issues are often separated from mediatisation as a key contemporary media studies concept. The integration of these studies in the spirit and assumptions of mediatisation theory could bring much to the development of media studies. However, research on disconnection, more on what is absent than present in human and social practice, has largely moved outside the field of mediatisation. This has probably happened for several reasons. One is the marginalisation of the significance of such motives, practices, discourses, and effects. A second is the dominant discourse of perpetual development towards increasing dependence of individuals and societies on media technologies. The third is the growing importance of metaprocesses that are super-processes in relation to mediatisation: datafication, platformisation, algorithmisation and, increasingly, intelligent artificialisation, which makes mediatisation only a narrow slice of complex, trans-sectoral metaprocesses that, to be fully understood, must be analysed from a different perspective and at different levels.

Mediatisation studies are dominated by the discourse and paradigm of continuous development towards intensification of meaning and media dependency, whether taking the shape of a utopian, dystopian or neutral vision. Let us note that the constructive critique of mediatisation also sets definitional boundaries based on one direction of change, albeit taking into account its sometimes possible non-linearity (Ekström et al., 2016). In their article postulating changes in mediatisation studies (Ekström et al., 2016), the authors, in setting the agenda, defined mediatisation as processes of growth, multiplication, and increasing of different dimensions of communication. However, any strengthening and broadening of impact is as important as the marginalised processes of retreat, diminution, and decline. Significantly, however, among further formulated demands, the authors reported abandoning the idea of the constant and steady growth of mediatisation and being attentive to sub-processes, which may reveal, for example, the contradictions of mediatisation (Ekström et al., 2016).

Despite occasional exhortations (also Kopecka-Piech, 2019), what remains on the margins is what constitutes a counterbalance to the dominant discourse and practice: alternative action that contests the established order, not only in the hope of changing it and returning to it at another time (the already famous "disconnect to reconnect") (Digital Detox, 2019), but because of a completely different life project: not based on media as an essential means of everyday action, but something additional and not essential. There are many reasons for this, motives and models of non-usage, and they do not only concern orthodox communities (Hesselberth, 2018), but millions of people worldwide (Brennen, 2019). Despite the fact of mediatisation transforming reality, especially at the macro level – which is rarely contested – a demediatisation transformation is taking place at the micro level of some users' everyday lives. Both transformations have different scopes, scales, possibilities; both are variable, non-linear, and paradoxical.[1]

The paradoxical nature of demediatisation stems from the fact that, as a response to mediatisation, it is entangled in it, hence it responds to the logic or moulding forces of mediatisation. But ultimately, demediatisation means diminishing the power of mediatisation (Kopecka-Piech, 2019), slowing down the growing importance of media and its consequences in everyday life (Müller, 2019). Non-users contribute to changing the nature and conditions of mediatisation, being an alternative rather than mainstream course of issues and changes. In the lives of these people, a denaturalisation of media takes place – what was natural so far, appearing as necessary, sometimes indispensable, becomes artificial and superfluous, and thus leads to the transformation of many spheres of people's lives.

Demediatisation is discreet, composite, residual and crawling. It means a defragmentation of mediation. It takes place through desaturation (Kopecka-Piech, 2019). It cannot be overlooked that technological desaturation, that is, non-possession and/or voluntary inaccessibility, changes the lives of individuals, and with increasing numbers, can change the lives of communities.[2] Although the change is not mass (even if such individuals are scattered across the globe), it provides a reference point or aspiration for others, an inspiration for change in different dimensions and scope that enter into relationships with similar trends and changes.

In turn, when we treat technologies as objects which we know people are connected to on the basis of dependence and dependency (Humayun & Belk, 2017), it becomes clear that the presence and availability of ownership of these objects or their absence in the human environment, determines the conditions of human life and functioning. Thus, the absence of technology (technological desaturation) (Kopecka-Piech, 2019) must be analysed similarly to the non-occurrence of certain processes and practices (processual desaturation), which results in changes in the temporal structure of everyday life (temporal desaturation). It is about properties shaping the media environment and activity in this environment. Technological desaturation is also supported by the results of Humayun and Belk's (2017) research, according to which people want objects (which they own and use) – to need them and to depend on them. They don't, however, want to be owned and needed by technologies. This is why, as the authors write, there is a strong trend to abandon digital technologies in favour of analogue ones. Whether (some) media are not mandatory in people's lives should be the focus of mediatisation studies (Ekström et al., 2016), as should the search for answers to the question of why this happens and what effects it has at the individual and collective level.

Demediatisation within mediatisation studies

Discussion of issues of reverse processes within mediatisation studies is still rarely undertaken. Does the theory fail in this regard both within the institutional, constructivist, and material-technological approaches? It seems that in each of them there is space to ask the question about what is not there or what is there that opposes dominant practices or discourses. Years ago, both researchers and critics of mediatisation called for these aspects to be taken into account. The aim of the research was to capture and explore responses to mediatisation pressures (Pallas, 2016). Some of the most prominent critics of mediatisation have signalled that the acceptance and abandonment of media technologies should be an equally important subject of mediatisation research (Deacon & Stanyer, 2014).

To be sure, these exhortations are not easily adopted and even more difficult to put into practice. Mediatisation has been associated with connection, interaction, and communication since the dawn of the concept. Progressive mediatisation is therefore synonymous with an increasing number of mediated technologies, contents, and processes. The few studies on media resistance in everyday life have so far been based on the concept of mediatisation.[3] André Jansson's research on counter-mediatisation, Tilo Grenz's research on de-mediatisation, and Katarzyna Kopecka-Piech's research on media technology desaturation are exceptions to this rule. Andreas Hepp (2019) has also drawn some attention to certain themes in his latest book *Deep Mediatisation*.

As Jansson (2017) notes, mediatisation on the one hand liberates users, and on the other, makes them dependent. Counter-mediatisation is a reaction against the dominant order of mediatisation, an expression of emancipation, also for the victims of mediatisation (Jansson, 2017). As Jansson (2018) states, many studies indicate that the normalisation of media technologies in everyday life is usually not unequivocally experienced positively, and people feel discomfort due to the dependence on media and the blurred temporal and spatial boundaries associated with their use.

Kopecka-Piech (2019) attempts to show how the use of media technologies in a seemingly mundane part of everyday life, such as physical activity, can result in frustration, discouragement, and ultimately abandonment of some media technologies, bringing back a sense of comfort and fulfilment from unmediated self-care and being active. Media saturation, which quantitatively and qualitatively becomes a method of measuring mediatisation, helps to illustrate how transformation and then re-transformation occurs at both the individual and collective level of this sphere of life.

Grenz, also in collaboration with Heiko Kirschner and Michaela Pfadenhauer, tried to fill the gap in the questioned and neglected side-effects of media and to illustrate how, in response to the unintended consequences of mediatisation, also in everyday life, users develop counter-strategies: discourses and practices of withdrawal, privatisation, and anonymisation, which together constitute demediatisation (Grenz & Kirschner, 2015). Pfadenhauer and Grenz (n.d.) therefore postulate the need to explore measures and strategies directed against mediatisation tendencies. Some of them may respond to the unintentional effects, uncontrolled and chaotic processes, resulting, for example, from the fact that we cannot predict the effects of technological progress (Grenz, 2013).

Hepp (2019), citing Cindy Roitsch's (2017) findings, states that users, feeling numerous pressures and challenges, start to adopt demarcation practices. They set boundaries by restricting certain media or withdrawing from them. The author argues for a normative approach to the management of mediatisation, recognising that users have the right to live autonomous and meaningful lives, although, on the other hand, for him this does not mean freedom from living in a figuration that threatens this, but obtaining it within its framework. It may not always prove to be a feasible project, especially if real human needs and values were to take centre stage again. However, Hepp does report a specific catalogue of digital media tasks and demands on them: self-determination, formability, supportiveness, promotion of knowledge (Hepp, 2019, p. 196), the third of which, he points out, is particularly rarely addressed in mediatisation studies. In the last sentence of his book, the author states that the aim of critical mediatisation studies should be, among other things, to reflect on alternative responses to the existing situation.

In the context of the few non-usage studies within mediatisation research, one could ask whether the problems of media use – anxiety, stress, frustration, discomfort and dissatisfaction – as well as the restriction of their freedom, autonomy and free development, should not arouse the interest of mediatisation researchers as intensely as the growing, new possibilities, increasing complexity of communication and ever newer uses of technology. Especially since, as researchers point out, unplugging from digital technologies in some societies (e.g. the USA) is no longer a niche idea, but a mainstream movement (Brennen, 2019). Isn't growing voluntary non-use and at the same time growing algorithmised practices, which increasingly exploit the unaware, sufficient reason to explore the withdrawal transformations brought about by mediatisation?

Emerging trends supporting demediatisation

There is an extensive catalogue of other arguments for exploring the issue at hand. These are the numerous movements, trends, fashions and tendencies that strengthen demediatisation. Recent decades have witnessed the development of many phenomena that foster and complement it, and are based on technological, health, public-political, business-economic, psychological-mental, existential-spiritual, artistic, environmental, and art-cultural grounds.

Let us look at demediatisation trends from the perspective of the five key trends that characterise the contemporary, mediatised media environment, namely differentiation; connectivity; omnipresence; and the rapid pace of both innovation and datafication (Hepp & Hasebrink, 2018). The authors point out that we need to be mindful of the non-linearity and internal contradiction of these trends. So, let's look at them as less obvious, looking for the hidden and the paradoxical responses to the dominant, the easily accessible. How, then, do the trends prevailing in the media environment compare to the reverse trends within it, outside it and at the intersection with it?

The response to media differentiation is undoubtedly unification, homogeneity and less media diversity. An emanation of such trends is minimalism, which aims to simplify everyday life (as well as make savings). Digital minimalism is its example: minimum devices, functionalities, applications – only what is necessary. This philosophy is about selecting and optimising activities to enhance what is important to the user, giving the satisfaction of avoiding the rest (Newport, 2019). Digital minimalism accompanies desaturating practices in some families (Kopecka-Piech, 2022). It is also favoured by other trends such as digital and physical decluttering (Humayun, 2020).

Connectivity can be understood, as the authors do, primarily as the interconnection of technologies (Hepp & Hasebrink, 2018), but it is also the connection of people to technology and people to each other using technology. All dimensions of connectivity are reduced with technological isolation, which is even material and physical in nature. We see this with the rise of trends such as the off-the-grid movement, in which people renounce the use of technology[4] and even electricity. However, you don't need such radical examples to observe disconnectivity. There is, for example, the growing popularity of interlocking and blocking materials, infrastructure and equipment called disconnection devices (Portwood-Stacer, 2012). These range from Faraday boxes and signal jammers in public and private spaces, to Wi-Fi blocking furnishing materials and other solutions that people use to prevent devices and people from connecting through them. At the software level, a good example are any apps that restrict, block the use of other apps or the devices themselves. They are used to learn how to manage screen time, and sometimes to fight against addiction. On the other hand, an artistic expression of opposition to hyperconnectivity, and above all to the resulting surveillance based on face recognition, can be found in artistic works.[5]

The omnipresence of media, i.e. the saturation of the physical environment with infrastructure and technological devices, handheld access and constant online presence, has some of the most significant medical and psychological consequences. Based on constant exposure to electromagnetic fields, a certain group of people (1.5–13.3% of the population) (Hedendahl et al., 2015) develops an entity called electromagnetic hypersensitivity, which resembles an allergy, but is a complex set of symptoms and disorders. It results in people isolating themselves as much as possible from radiation, i.e. not only not using the devices or staying in the network field, but staying as far away as possible from all transmitting and receiving infrastructures. Such extreme consequences are rare in the population. However, we often observe psychological actions aimed at limiting the significance of technology in everyday life, including the creation of internet-free spaces, Wi-Fi-free zones (public, such as cafes and meeting places, or private), as well as the implementation of specific rules and practices, like mindfulness, media dieting, and digital detoxing (Syvertsen & Enli, 2020), which entails the dynamic development of a free time industry based on media rejection (e.g. recreation, tourism) (Pawłowska-Legwand & Matoga, 2021).

The rapid pace of innovation representing the pressure to create, generate, sell, and buy ever newer technology has lived to see a response in the form of the sustainability movements growing in strength and reflected in media practices and analysis (Kuntsman & Rattle, 2019). They, increasingly, point to how a reduction in the consumption of appliances and electricity itself can contribute to slowing down environmental degradation, including the pollution of some regions with electromagnetic debris. In this vein, there are also many governmental and non-governmental organisations educating on media restriction; and informal movements that promote in society attitudes of detachment, reserve, and restriction of media in life. This fits in with the consumption described by Mariam Humayun and Russel Belk as post-digital consumption (2017). It involves interacting with disconnected objects that are simultaneously disentangled from corporate-controlled consumption.

A key trend is datafication – and thus the basis of surveillance capitalism (Zuboff, 2019): the modern manipulation and exploitation of unwitting users to generate profits, both financial and political. Datafication finds a response in a range of movements opposing this kind of exploitation, from less radical ones indicating active opposition and protest, to more radical ones using sabotage and hacktivism (Andersson, 2016; Casemajor et al., 2015; Portwood-Stacer, 2013). Datafication is the most profound trend and, at the same time, a transprocess that determines the course and effects of mediatisation, but also of demediatisation, echoed not only by media scholars but also by documentary filmmakers.[6]

In summary, the oppositional tendencies described are complex and convergent: social, cultural, technological, economic, psychological, environmental, health. They overlap and complement each other as well as reinforce the general trend of technological breakaway. In the context of such outlined trends, in opposition to the socio-technological mainstream, it is impossible not to notice that some of them are of growing importance in terms of the complex transformation taking place. They constitute a counterbalance to the mainstream of mediatisation. They do not take place in isolation from the dominant transformations in various dimensions of life, but complement and intensify attitudes, activities, and media changes.

In the context of demediatisation, the ability to analyse obsolescence and reversal in particular, becomes important. What are the negations and paradoxes of deep mediatisation and its dominant trends? What is lost when the degree of media saturation and its ubiquitous qualitative effects result in reaching a point of safety that for each sphere of human life (and even the individual in question) can be determined elsewhere? Where do we draw the boundaries of the safety of the technologisation of everyday life? What criteria should be used (medical, psychological, ethical, economic)?

These are questions that mediatisation studies answer to a limited extent or face the charge of normativism. Although, for example in the institutional approach it is assumed that mediatisation is a non-valued process, the loss of independence by the media to, for example, political institutions, is already treated as undesirable. Therefore, within mediatisation studies, it is necessary to debate the ethical dimension of the processes that entangle contemporary human beings with the risk of losing privacy, independence, and perhaps even human nature. Müller (2019) writes explicitly about the need to include the concept of the responsible user within mediatisation studies and responsible mediatisation management, which takes into account the support of users in their efforts to use media well. Not everyone can afford not to use, as this requires social capital, knowledge, and competence (Karppi, 2021). So, the question of freedom and liberty arises; the possibility of self-determination, including self-restriction, the conditions and effects of which should interest researchers as much as the effects of the lack of media access and communicative freedom.

Demediatisation from the outside of the mediatisation approach

As written by Ekström et al. (2016) and echoed by Corner (2018), many mediatisation scholars do not know that they are studying mediatisation. Similarly, many scholars of demediatisation do not know that they are studying demediatisation. Let's look at where, beyond a direct link to the mainstream of mediatisation studies, reverse tendencies are finding recognition and successfully uncovering their complex nature.

Let us start from the fact that the processes and phenomena analysed here do not have a stable notion (Hesselberth, 2018), are sometimes referred to by a whole range of terms which do not always coincide as concepts,[7] come from different traditions, and are studied from different perspectives. We are therefore dealing with:

- disconnection
- non-use/non-usage
- disuse
- abstinence

- rejection
- refusal
- opting-out
- resistance
- limiting
- departing
- detoxing
- dieting
- fasting
- restraint
- demarcation
- unplugging
- withdrawal
- avoidance
- non-consumption
- disengagement
- reducing
- disentanglement
- temperance
- non-uptake
- push-back.

Most of the studies conducted so far abstract from mediatisation theory, locating themselves in other paradigms and concepts. Indeed, mediatisation theory considers counter- phenomena as a manifestation of undurable containment only (Hepp & Hasebrink, 2018). But what about non-users who voluntarily, constantly, and significantly reduce their use of media technologies? What about the life change of such individuals? Disconnection may testify to the great importance of media in people's lives, but at the same time it testifies to the effects of media and the need for media absence (whether temporal, spatial or permanent). This means that there are boundaries, states, conditions, the crossing of which triggers reverse processes. Since they do not occur in a vacuum and are reinforced by other tendencies, they intensify and gain individual and social, if only economic, significance.

It is impossible to include here all the projects and findings in the field of non-usage media to date. It is worth mentioning some of them, which bring findings concerning demediatisation in its broadest sense and which do not abstract from the insufficient nature of previous approaches in media studies, especially the so-called disconnection studies.

Interest in research on reverse trends has particularly increased with the coining of the term digital disconnection, which is most fully defined by Pepita Hesselberth (2018, p. 1995) as the "tendency toward voluntary psychic, socio-economic, and/or political withdrawal from mediated forms of connectivity".

Kuntsman and Miyake (2019) point out that media disengagement is not an isolated phenomenon, but a set of practices, motivations, and effects. At the same time, they believe that disengagement should be a starting point for, among other things, new conceptualisations so that it can begin to constitute a norm rather than an aberration or paradox.

The research of Tine Syvertsen and Gunn Enli (2020) on digital detox shows what a response to media and mediated pressure and communication overload is, which is experienced by users in their daily lives who also feel a lack of authenticity. For them, real life and digital life are not the same thing, which, as the authors point out, does not correspond with the popular notion adopted in media studies.

In turn, Paul C. Adams and André Jansson (2021) proposed that disconnection should be distinguished from disentangling. The latter does not refer to a temporary or escapist practice, but is a conscious restoration of boundaries that have been violated, boundaries between human life and all external systems, including the technological. As the authors write, cutting ourselves off from the media would mean cutting ourselves off from society, and we would still be dependent on functioning within the systems that these media construct. Here, however, the question arises as to what this functioning within the cut-off would look like and what it should look like. This is why the authors define disentangling as an area of normative reflection, a rethinking of the digital world in which we function. This world requires reflection not only on progressive mediatisation, but also on the phenomena that bring us back to reflection, of which disconnection is one.

From this direction, come the reflections of Simone Natale and Emiliano Treré (2020), who point out the non-constructive character of disconnection as an individual practice, which is part of the rules of commodification of mediatised practices and their consequences in terms of anxiety and stress. The authors postulate "disconnection-through-engagement". They consider the knowledge and use of technologies and platforms dominating the media environment, as an attitude of reaction and critique. Thus, they go a step further than Adams and Jansson, moving from a reflection on the problematisation of entanglement with technology to action, which in their view can take the form of hybridity, anonymity or hacking. As such, they need not, in the authors' view, be the domain of IT-savvy individuals, but the everyday reality of all users, including non-experts.

Conclusions: the need for a research programme

What emerges from the above reflections on the nature of demediatisation, its presence within and beyond mediatisation studies, is the need to formulate a research programme that does not abstract from the marginal or non-mainstream, while locating the analysis within mediatisation theory.

First, the need arises to recognise creeping demediatisation, not to question variability and reversibility, and to make an effort to explore it, which is also a response to the demand to intensify audience research in mediatisation studies (Hepp, 2019; Livingstone, 2019), and this means both usage and non-usage research. Second, it seems important to define what should be studied and how. The imperative of connectivity and the regime of connectedness is already and will increasingly be challenged due to the range of everyday activities that have been embraced by digital technologies, bringing with them deep and major changes (Adams & Jansson, 2021). The role of mediatisation studies is to identify the logic or moulding forces shaping demediatisation, to raise questions about the causes, motives, practices, discourses, effects, and ethics of practices that are opposite to the dominant ones, in specific fields, over time, in comparison between populations, regions, and taking into account other variables as well. And, significantly, the task is also to identify those elements external to the media environment (trends, movements, tendencies) which, together with demediatisation, constitute interdependent transformations.

It seems that research on voluntary non-usage is justified within the developing theory of deep mediatisation (Hepp, 2019). Two of the three accounts of media logic – the interaction approach and the technology approach (Hepp, 2019) – are concerned with ordinary users, and influencing them is about adaptation. Non-usage is a type of adaptation to the conditions imposed by the media environment, and as such falls within the broad spectrum of influence and responses to it. This raises the question of the mechanisms of this adaptation. Voluntary non-usage should also form part of the study of media ensembles and media repertoires (Hepp, 2019), and specifically it is important to determine how media ensembles and repertoires are reduced – by what criteria and by what rules. How also does change permeate between media ensembles and repertoires, and thus the micro and meso levels? This in turn translates into an examination of the communication practices and habitus of individual figurations. Which of them, how and why do they become unmediated: either looking back or returning to their origins in the life of the individual? How do they enter into relations with other practices? Focusing research on voluntary non-usage is a response to non-mediacentric research (Moores, 2016; Morley, 2007) in a literal and profound sense. In what domains of everyday life, why and with what effect, are media beginning to play subordinate roles, through their new marginalised nature, transforming these fields and people's lives? From the perspective of deep mediatisation theory, the opportunity arises to explore the figurations (Hepp, 2019) of individuals limiting, separating, opting out, etc., as well as non-user significant presence in particular mediatised domains; especially when individual actors become supra-individual actors (Hepp, 2019, p. 107).

In the context of datafication and the growing role of big data, non-usage research is also an avenue to explore what escapes the processes of monitoring, analysis, dataveillance, and surveillance. We observe the increasing intrusion of technology, software, and algorithms, as well as artificial intelligence into our lives, which induces resistance and opposition, even from those who created this world.[8] Disconnection becomes a form of response and critique of technologies that dominate humans (Treré et al., 2020). The right to disconnect becomes a personal right for each individual. In this sense, demediation will naturalise. What is needed is an exploration of the logic or forces shaping disconnection. And these will be shaped in the era of not only surveillance capitalism but also post-digital consumption (Humayun & Belk, 2017).

Two important calls by critics of mediatisation return in this context. The first is a call to work for the measurability of mediatisation (Ekström et al., 2016). It has much in common with the call for a focus on demediatisation. It is the measurement (which is quantitative in nature but which, based on mixed methodology, flexibly combines with qualitative characteristics) that has highlighted an emerging demediatisation trend in everyday life research, focused on amateur physical activity (Kopecka-Piech, 2019). Fatigue, discouragement, unease, and frustration caused by the use of technology on a daily basis in this sphere, has led people to abandon technology, and the observation of this phenomenon quantitatively and qualitatively is possible through the use of indicators, measuring different degrees of media technology saturation: technological and processual. This is perfectly complemented by a temporal indicator: time technology saturation, used, among others, to measure the degree of saturation of family daily life (Kopecka-Piech, 2022). Desaturation is an impulse to improve measurement methods and develop new indicators which will also allow us to capture the quantitative aspect of demediatisation and conduct comparative research.

The next postulate concerns conceptual and definitional issues. Just as efforts are made to distinguish mediatisation from mediation, a distinction should be made between demediation and demediatisation. While the former signifies a process of leaving media mediation, the latter signifies a deeper transformative trend that, confronting mediatisation, is changing it and will continue to do so in the face of the many challenges posed by digital technology. Transformation occurs starting from the "micro-resistance" (Ribak & Rosenthal, 2015) at the individual level, sometimes temporal and ephemeral – sometimes deeply life-transforming and permanent. It takes place also at the meso level, within social opposition and even struggle against elements of a technologised system. It penetrates to the level, which does not know divisions and borders, of existential, normative reflection on the mediatised world, in the centre of which a human being should be. This requires "renegotiating the social contract" by working on forms beyond the control of the logic of mass connectivity and imparing it (Hesselberth 2018, p. 2007). Issues on normative nature are also posed by Hepp (2019), asking, in a way, how mediatisation can be shaped so that a good life, i.e. an autonomous and meaningful one, is possible; how to counter discourses that cover up the risks and harms of digital media use. Hepp gives numerous examples of actions at the micro and meso level. It seems important also at the level of academic research to focus on the issue of the multifaceted comfort and discomfort resulting from a particular media influence and reaction to it. Not only does a social response (if only in the form of a critical discourse on these issues) and a political response in the form of managing mediatisation seem necessary, but also cognition and assistance to the ordinary user who has to take up the daily challenge of micro-managing their mediatised life.

Hence, reflection naturally leads us to the ethical responsibility of researchers. Don't media scholars have a responsibility to make the public aware and educate them? Shouldn't researchers participate in the education process, teaching users strategies to negotiate their own non-usage, reflexive, and conscious use? As Natale and Treré (2020) point out, media scholars should move away from a naïve approach to users and educate them on how to effectively take care of their autonomy, privacy. and anonymity online and advocate for the creation of easy-to-use tools to do so. In this sense, it is difficult not to agree with the authors, going back to the works of the 1970s (Weizenbaum, 1976), concerning the fear of the effects of progressive computerisation – the greatest challenges of computer science are not of a technological nature, but of an ethical nature. When we listen to the voice of the creators of artificial intelligence projects, we have no doubt that crossing dangerous ethical, or perhaps even natural, boundaries is near, if it has not already happened.[9]

Contemporary mediatisation studies, not only investigating the sphere of computer mediated practices and discourses, but also using such tools for that purpose, should take a closer look at the ethical aspects of disconnection, so that, as representatives of the humanities and social sciences, they can take care of the human nature of technology now and in the future, as if in opposition to the boundless intentions of some computer studies. Their announcements are (no longer) a myth, but a successively implemented programme. Since "mediatisation is not on automatic pilot" (Hepp, 2019, p. 194), this means that with a concerted effort we can begin to take the reins.

Notes

1 On the paradoxicality of disconnection see Hesselberth (2018).
2 Imagine the daily life of a large group of inhabitants of radio quiet zones like Green Bank in the USA or Sant'Antonio, Reggello in Italy, which is an enclave for people suffering from electromagnetic hypersensitivity and who do not use computers or mobile phones.
3 Although it is worth noting the presence of such studies in research on the mediatisation of business or politics. One of the more interesting ones is Tilo Grenz's (2013) study on de-mediatisation of online poker, which highlights the processes of stopping the momentum of mediatisation: de-optionalisation, dequantification, deacceleration. The business area was also addressed by Esben Karmark (2010), author of studies on the "demediatisation of LEGO" and "mediatisation balance" of the company in the context of branding. In turn Julie Firmstone and Stephen Coleman (2015) worked on "civic demediatisation". The

concept applies to public communication, where communication through traditional channels is losing ground to the rise of social media.
4 See the Geomedia 2021 conference programme for an illustration of the richness of the topic, https://www.geomedia.uni-siegen.de/wp-content/uploads/2021/05/geomedia-2021-program-with-Abstracts-0505.pdf.
5 See for example Adam Harvey's anti-drone clothing (Howarts, 2013).
6 See for example: *iHuman*, Tonje Hessen Schei, 2019; *Social Dilemma*, Jeff Orlowski, 2020; *China's World Takeover*, Walid Berrissoul, 2020; *After Truth: Disinformation and the Cost of Fake News*, Andrew Rossi, 2020; *The Great Hack*, Karim Amer and Jehane Noujaim, 2019.
7 The same is true of the nomenclature of non-users, who are variously called: media deniers, resisters, disengagers, rejectors, refusniks, etc.; of course, often not defining such people in the same way, but drawing attention to the nuances of their non-doing practice; and the roots in the case of negative terms often drawing on the discourse of digital divide (Hesselberth, 2018).
8 See for example *Social Dillema* (documentary), Jeff Orlowski, USA, 2020.
9 One of the leading developers of artificial intelligence projects, Jürgen Schmidhuber, chief scientist of Nnaisense, claims that "A new form of life is emerging". Asserting that he has no responsibility, just as Albert Einstein's parents did not, he concedes that humanity is not the crowning glory of creation, and that this something that is emerging will leave us behind, surpass us, and change the universe. Statement in *iHuman* (documentary), directed by Tonje Hessen Schei, Norway, 2019.

References

Adams, P. C., & Jansson, A. (2021). Introduction: Rethinking the Entangling Force of Connective Media. In Adams, P. C., & Jansson, A. (Eds.), *Disentangling* (pp. 1–20). Oxford: Oxford University Press.
Andersson, L. (2016). No Digital "Castles in The Air": Online Non-Participation and the Radical Left. *Media And Communication*, 4(4), 53–62.
Brennen, B. (2019). *Opting Out of Digital Media*. London: Routledge.
Casemajor, N., Couture, S., Delfin, M., Goerzen, M., & Delfanti, A. (2015). Non-Participation in Digital Media: Toward A Framework of Mediated Political Action. *Media, Culture & Society*, 37(6), 850–866.
Corner, J. (2018). "Mediatisation": Media Theory's Word of the Decade. *Media Theory*, 2(2), 79–90.
Deacon, D., & Stanyer, J. (2014). Mediatisation: Key Concept or Conceptual Bandwagon?. *Media, Culture & Society*, 36(7), 1032–1044.
Digital Detox (2019), Digital Detox Retreats, https://www.digitaldetox.com/experiences/retreats
Ekström, M., Fornäs, J., Jansson, A., & Jerslev, A. (2016). Three Tasks for Mediatisation Research: Contributions to an Open Agenda. *Media, Culture & Society*, 38(7), 1090–1108.
Firmstone, J., & Coleman, S. (2015). Public Engagement in Local Government: The Voice and Influence of Citizens in Online Communicative Spaces. *Information, Communication & Society*, 18(6), 680–695.
Fornäs, J. (2016). Media Times: The Mediatisation of Third-Time Tools: Culturalizing and Historicizing Temporality. *International Journal of Communication*, 10(20), 5213–5232.

Grenz, T. (2013). Reflexive Mediatisation: Insights into the Frictional Interplay between Customers and Providers. KIT Working Paper. http://pfadenhauer.org/blog/wp-content/uploads/2014/01/working-paper-reflexivity-and-frictional-interplay.pdf

Grenz T., & Kirschner, H. (2015). Mediatisation, Risks and Antidotes in the Reflexive Modernity. 12h ESA Conference, Prague, 25–28.08.2015.

Hedendahl, L., Carlberg, M., & Hardell, L. (2015). Electromagnetic Hypersensitivity: An Increasing Challenge to the Medical Profession. *Reviews on Environmental Health*, *30*(4), 209–215.

Hepp, A. (2019). *Deep Mediatisation*. London: Routledge.

Hepp, A., & Hasebrink, U. (2018). Researching Transforming Communications in Times of Deep Mediatisation: A Figurational Approach. In *Communicative Figurations* (pp. 15–48). Cham: Palgrave Macmillan.

Hesselberth, P. (2018). Discourses on Disconnectivity and the Right to Disconnect. *New Media & Society*, *20*(5), 1994–2010.

Hjarvard, S. (2013). *The Mediatisation of Culture and Society*. New York: Routledge.

Howarts, D. (2013). *De Zeen*, https://www.dezeen.com/2013/06/23/stealth-wear-anti-drone-clothing-by-adam-harvey/

Humayun, M. (2020). Offline Is the New Luxury? Consuming Digital Detoxing. In J. Argo, T. M. Lowrey & H. Jensen Schau (Eds.), *Advances in Consumer Research*, Duluth, MN: Association for Consumer Research, pp. 987–993.

Humayun, M., & Belk, R. (2017). Being Dumb in the Age of Smart: Analogue Object Entanglements. In A. Gneezy, V. Griskevicius & P. Williams (Eds.), *Advances in Consumer Research*, vol. 45. Duluth, MN: Association for Consumer Research, pp. 117–122.

Jansson, A. (2017). *Mediatisation and Mobile Lives: A Critical Approach*. London: Routledge.

Jansson, A. (2018). Mediatisation as a Framework for Social Design: For a Better Life with Media. *Design and Culture*, *10*(3), 233–252.

Karmark, E. (2010). Challenges in the Mediatisation of a Corporate Brand: Identity-Effects as LEGO Establishes a Media Products Company. In M. Morsing (Ed.), *Media, Organizations and Identity*. London: Palgrave Macmillan, pp. 112–128.

Karppi T. (2021). Undoing the Outside: On Defaults and Off-Facebook Activity. In Tero Karppi, Urs Stäheli, Clara Wieghorst & Lea P. Zierott (Eds.), *Undoing Networks*. Minneapolis: University of Minnesota Press.

Kaun, A., & Schwarzenegger, C. (2014). "No Media, Less Life?" Online Disconnection in Mediatized Worlds. *First Monday*, *19*(11), https://doi.org/10.5210/fm.v19i11.5497.

Kopecka-Piech, K. (2019). *Mediatisation of Physical Activity: Media Saturation and Technologies*. Lanham, MD: Rowman & Littlefield.

Kopecka-Piech K. (2022). Family Digital Well-Being: The Prospect of Implementing Media Technology Management Strategies in Polish Homes. *Media, Biznes, Kultura*, *12*(1), 67–80.

Kuntsman, A., & Miyake, E. (2019). The Paradox and Continuum of Digital Disengagement: Denaturalising Digital Sociality and Technological Connectivity. *Media, Culture & Society*, *41*(6), 901–913.

Kuntsman, A., & Rattle, I. (2019). Towards a Paradigmatic Shift in Sustainability Studies: A Systematic Review of Peer Reviewed Literature and Future Agenda Setting to Consider Environmental (Un) Sustainability of Digital Communication. *Environmental Communication, 13*(5), 567–581.

Livingstone, S. (2019). Audiences in an Age of Datafication: Critical Questions for Media Research. *Television & New Media, 20*(2), 170–183.

Moores, S. (2016). Arguments for a Non-Media-Centric, Non-Representational Approach to Media and Place. In P. Adams, J. Cupples, K. Glynn, A. Jansson & S. Moores (Eds.), *Communications/Media/Geographies*. Routledge Studies in Human Geography. New York: Routledge, pp. 132–159.

Morley, D. (2007). *Media, Modernity and Technology: The Geography of the New*. Abingdon: Routledge.

Müller, K. F. (2019). Managing Mediatisation: How Media Users Negotiate a Successful Integration of (New) Media in Everyday Life. In Tobias Eberwein, Matthias Karmasin, Friedrich Krotz & Matthias Rath (Eds.), *Responsibility and Resistance*. Wiesbaden: Springer, pp. 111–130.

Natale, S., & Treré, E. (2020). Vinyl Won't Save Us: Reframing Disconnection as Engagement. *Media, Culture & Society, 42*(4), 626–633.

Newport, C. (2019). *Digital Minimalism: Choosing a Focused Life in a Noisy World*. Penguin.

Pallas, J. (2016). Mediatisation. In C. E. Carroll (Ed.), *The Sage Encyclopedia of Corporate Reputation*. Thousand Oaks, CA: Sage Reference. https://sk.sagepub.com/reference/the-sage-encyclopedia-of-corporate-reputation/i5698.xml

Pawłowska-Legwand, A., & Matoga, Ł. (2021). Disconnect from the Digital World to Reconnect with the Real Life: An Analysis of the Potential for Development of Unplugged Tourism on the Example of Poland. *Tourism Planning & Development, 18*(6), 649–672. DOI: 10.1080/21568316.2020.1842487.

Pfadenhauer M., & Grenz T. (n.d.). Mediatisation as a Business Model III: Counter-Strategies and Turning Points in the Mediatisation Process, Mediatized Words, http://www.mediatisiertewelten.de/en/projects/3rd-funding-period-2014-2016/mediatisation-as-a-business-model-iii.html

Portwood-Stacer, L. (2012). Anti-Consumption as Tactical Resistance: Anarchists, Subculture, and Activist Strategy. *Journal of Consumer Culture, 12*(1), 87–105.

Portwood-Stacer, L. (2013). Media Refusal and Conspicuous Non-Consumption: The Performative and Political Dimensions of Facebook Abstention. *New Media & Society, 15*(7), 1041–1057.

Ribak, R., & Rosenthal, M. (2015). Smartphone Resistance as Media Ambivalence. *First Monday, 20*(11), https://doi.org/10.5210/fm.v20i11.6307

Roitsch, C. (2017) Kommunikative Grenzziehung. Herausforderungen und Praktiken junger Menschen in einer vielgestaltigen Medienumgebung. Doctoral thesis, University of Bremen.

Selwyn, N. (2003). Apart from Technology: Understanding People's Non-Use of Information and Communication Technologies in Everyday Life. *Technology In Society, 25*(1), 99–116.

Syvertsen, T. (2020). *Digital Detox: The Politics of Disconnecting*. Bingley, UK: Emerald Group Publishing.

Syvertsen, T., & Enli, G. (2020). Digital Detox: Media Resistance and the Promise of Authenticity. *Convergence*, *26*(5–6), 1269–1283.

Treré, E., Natale, S., Keightley, E., & Punathambekar, A. (2020). The Limits and Boundaries of Digital Disconnection. *Media, Culture & Society*, *42*(4), 605–609.

Weizenbaum, J. (1976). Computer Power and Human Reason: From Judgment to Calculation. San Francisco: W. H. Freeman.

Zuboff, S. (2019). *The Age of Surveillance Capitalism: The Fight for a Human Future at the New Frontier of Power*. New York: Public Affairs.

Part IV
Conclusions

12 Limitations and New Directions for the Development of Mediatisation as a Research Field

Katarzyna Kopecka-Piech and Göran Bolin

The aim of this book has been to discuss the key challenges related to mediatisation research, and to highlight and critically examine the methodological, technological, and ethical problems that the field is facing. A further aim has been to consider the criticisms raised against mediatisation research and to map critical positions, both from within the field itself as well as from outside of it. The ambition has been to identify limitations, gaps, and deficiencies, but also to discuss problematic aspects of particular approaches, to highlight contradictions and paradoxes, and to take note of under-represented areas. In this final chapter, we wish to summarise the ways in which the book's contributors have addressed these topics.

We will first discuss some of the limitations observed, and some lesser explored research areas, to then set mediatisation research in relation to other societal processes.

Limitations and less explored researched topics

In the preceding chapters several major limitations in the development of mediatisation studies were identified. One of these is the failure to fill important research gaps, where many topics remain unexplored or require deeper study. Many of the chapter authors identify biases and limited diversity, e.g. in sports, where there is seemingly a greater interest in big events, involving men (Frandsen, in this volume), or fragmentation in the study of a particular sphere, e.g. culture (Nybro Petersen, in this volume). Some point to overgeneralisations (Lundby, in this volume), and hold that some of the changes are not studied deeply enough, while other types of changes are completely ignored. Another limitation is the dominance of the Anglo-American or broadly Western perspective, which is insufficiently complemented by a recognition of the situation in the Global East and South. This calls for better contextualisation of research, which should include considerations of historical and cultural specificities, and to be clear about the possible limitations of research findings. As can be inferred from Knut Lundby's chapter, the geographical diversity of research sites not only increases the richness of the

DOI: 10.4324/9781003324591-17

findings, but also means a choice of different research problems, methods, and concepts, enriching mediatisation research in its broadest sense.

Some authors mention several less explored research topics among those most commonly in focus in mediatisation research. It can be argued that new research trends start in niches and then spread to the mainstream, which are undeniable additions to existing research, but there are also more thoroughly explored areas that could provide new insights Sports, for example, has been mediatised almost "naturally" since time immemorial, and there has been some significant research carried out, providing some models of trends in media use and impact, and of methodological capture of these phenomena in research (Frandsen, in this volume). It is therefore important to both build on the already existing output of the field of mediatisation research and find inspiration and new research problems, and to research methods among new, so far unexplored niches of sectors where media operate.

At the same time, one should acknowledge that social life is penetrated by the influence of media and communication in different ways. Some parts of social and individual life are already deeply integrated with the media (as in the case of sports, politics, education); some remain in a relationship, but are not entirely penetrated by media (e.g., family life); while others could, at least in principle, exist without the media – yet the media affects them anyway, albeit indirectly. In the same way as the Christian Bible impacted on the lives of those who could not read during the Middle Ages, media technologies such as the smartphone or the computer are of fundamental importance for those who do not use them and have wide-reaching consequences also for refusniks. In that sense there is no "outside of the media" any longer (see also Kopecka-Piech in this volume). This means that spheres of life seemingly unaffected by the operations of media technologies can also be adjusted to the workings of the media, as technologies, organisations or sign structures. Therefore, this raises the question of which media elements and forces are influencing mediatisation processes across societal spheres, and the variation in this regard points to the necessity to observe which fields change with what dynamics and how fields influence each other. There are few studies in which we learn how the mediatisation of one sphere intersects with the mediatisation of other societal spheres.

Mediatisation as a meta-process among others

Furthermore, several authors emphasise that mediatisation is but one of several meta-level processes, and the preceding chapters frequently mentioned the importance of also taking other meta-processes, such as commercialisation, globalisation, individualisation, etc., into consideration. This analysis of media transformations in connection with general phenomena and trends is already firmly established in mediatisation studies (Krotz, 2007). However, there are also new processes that are beginning to enter the debate: datafication, platformisation, algorithmisation, etc. These processes are accompanied by trends such as the attempts to "de-mediatise" everyday life by developing avoidance strategies, and so forth (Kopecka-Piech, in this volume), as well as the increased focus on infrastructures of the media in what could be called the "infrastructural turn" (Grenz, in this volume). Because of their scale and dynamics, these new and growing processes and trends not only make it impossible to study mediatisation in isolation, but the widened scope and the holistic approaches might also lead to a risk of displacing the media perspective to the benefit of a more technologically oriented one, and through this raise questions about the foundations and status of mediatisation studies. Some authors argue that we might be drifting towards datafication studies, which forces us to redefine phenomena and reorient some studies, sometimes leading to what in this volume Anne Kaun, following Mark Andrejevic, terms operationalism; that is, the drive towards functionality and applicability of the technological systems at the cost of explanation and understanding of how the systems themselves work. The mediatised world is full of paradoxes; phenomena "hidden under the surface" (Grenz in this volume) that require decoding and interpretation. Some of them are not only symbolic, but also material (Kannengießer & McCurdy, in this volume) and need to be investigated with methods relevant to that. What we are witnessing might thus be an ongoing evolution towards processuality and materiality.

The fact that mediatisation research is currently facing the challenge of addressing the dynamic trends and (meta)processes of datafication, algorithmisation, platformiation, and the development of artificial intelligence suggests a return to the age-old question in media and communication studies: what do we mean by media today and how do the different dimensions of media need to be analysed in order to understand the situation? Still, media convergence and network communication prove challenging to conceptualisation and empirical understanding. As one author noted, we are dealing with a "media-related" phenomenon rather than simply "media"; we need to study not only the effects of transformation but also the transformation of the elements that construct mediatisation. At the same time, however, the body of work in mediatisation studies is rich enough to build on, and as some authors emphasise, what is needed is an awareness and good knowledge of that body of work, which some studies lack. The field has grown out of several decades of tradition, which is not completely outdated, but needs updating and transformation in itself. The latter should focus more on empirical grounding, and less on abstract considerations or internal disputes over theory.

Integrative approaches

A second point raised among the authors is the importance of adopting an integrative perspective. The complexity of the media landscape means that research on the micro, meso and macro levels must complement each other. This is best illustrated by the mediatisation of work and economics in the era of big tech and the gig economy (Grohmann, in this volume), in which the economic-financial and psychological-social spheres have a direct influence on each other. At the same time, however, shying away from the past and previous media studies output may prove counterproductive. As Line Nybro Petersen argues in this volume, the sometimes more than half-century-old classical output of communication sciences is for the most part still conceptually valid and analytically effective, and its application allows mediatisation studies to build further on already existing research traditions.

These reflections point to the need for a smooth oscillation in mediatisation analysis between micro and macro levels, as user experience and the economic policies of large platforms create an intertwined and complex usage environment. This requires bridging even further the gap between what we have traditionally called production studies, reception studies, and textuality or discourse studies. The need for an environmental, integrative, contextualising perspective, but also one firmly grounded in empirics, is evident in the authors' contributions. Hence, the need for operationalising smaller, workable concepts to complement the "big concepts" is emphasised, as well as an orientation towards processualism and materialism, complemented by phenomenology and semiotics. It is a great challenge to connect the experience of an ordinary human being, a user of technology, with the political, economic, and technological framework of media infrastructure, devices, content, and business.

Interdisciplinarity

Third, interdisciplinarity appears nowadays as a natural paradigm of conducting research on mediatisation. On the one hand, we are dealing with interdisciplinarity related to the formulation of research problems and research questions, where research requires application of knowledge and theories coming from media studies and other disciplines, and where input from media studies is not just an add-on to research questions formulated in other fields of expertise. On the other hand, there are requirements for methodological interdisciplinarity where other disciplines, such as psychology, can be successfully integrated in the study of different spheres of mediatised life. The demand for non-mediacentric research means in practice the convergence of knowledge. The study of niche areas such as militarism (Horbyk, in this volume) or fashion (Rocamora, in this volume), in particular requires a competent dialogue between different disciplines.

In the context of interdisciplinarity, the conflict arising from the analytical separation of different spheres of life from the realm of the media appears important. In some cases, even such an analytical separation is a great challenge (Frandsen, in this volume). Cross-fertilisation concerns an increasing number of scientific disciplines, hence only knowledge integrated at different levels can be complete. Research that addresses pressing issues such as digital threats and risks even forces close cooperation with, among others, technical sciences and IT (Grenz, in this volume).

Many authors thus see mediatisation studies as a diverse field with many cognitive paths leading into it. Mixed methodologies are particularly desirable here. This undoubtedly requires interdisciplinary cooperation; for example, between computer science and information systems studies, law, and especially history, which offers the possibility of capturing *longue durée* transformations. Also mentioned as enrichments for mediatisation studies are science and technology studies, feminist studies, design anthropology, and new materialism. An innovative proposal is also to go in the direction of art as well as engineering and creative practice, including research on mediatisation "present in the minds of people" who create media, both technology and digital content. Similarly, reflection on the "circuit of mediatisation", the articulation of mediatisation not only in production but also in distribution and consumption, is needed. Finally, mediatisation studies with a political orientation have the potential, according to one author, to "bridge the gap between critical research and media/technology policies and regulation".

Further mediatisation studies thus require a diversity of approaches. It seems that the typology made by Knut Lundby in his chapter on the different dimensions of the mediatisation of religion is simultaneously a universal catalogue of different approaches in mediatisation studies that complement each other: actual and potential, intended and unintended, global and local; profound and superficial. Each approach is different, but each brings new value to the rapidly changing field of mediatisation studies. Further developments also require both synchronic and diachronic studies. The often-called-for long-term comparative, longitudinal studies are still desirable, but at the same time social reality is changing so rapidly and further processes determining the shape of the media and technosphere must be identified and recognised on an ongoing basis; for example, in relation to phenomena such as "financialisation" and "algorithmic mediations" (Grohmann, in this volume). Ethical challenges are also relevant in this context. In the face of an increasing number of threats and risks and even "non-intended side-effects of successive mediatisation" (Grenz, in this volume), which certainly include environmental effects (Kannengießer & McCurdy, in this volume), a dynamic response based on an efficiently conducted research process is necessary. Researchers of mediatisation are in this respect burdened with a kind of responsibility, but they can also be said to be well equipped to contribute with improvements to existing research ethically.

The authors, regardless of specialisation, see similar inequalities in their research projects; hence the suggestion to go beyond purely Western perspectives (Europe and the United States), towards the Global South and underrepresented regions, as well as socially marginalised groups. The representatives of mediatisation studies currently face the challenge of focussing on "ordinary" individuals, everyday life, and the consequences of the use of technology, not only in the context of the high risk that contemporary society and the world are burdened with, but also in the context of threats and untapped opportunities to articulate them and thus change reality. Therefore, it can be assumed that for researchers, intellectual contribution to the canon of knowledge about contemporary transformations is not everything. Research is also guided by ethical, social, political, and sometimes environmental duty. One of the authors pointed out, however, that this does not mean developing a theory that will cover everything and solve all problems. It means creating a framework and a map for operationalising a concept that will rise to the challenge of exploring the latest, and even at the moment unimaginable, media-related phenomena. The dynamics of transformation are accelerating, and we must be conceptually and methodologically prepared for its increasing pace. Building and transforming the research field together can allow it to remain, as one author wrote, a "safe haven" from which to understand media change.

Conclusion

Viewed from a meta-analytical reflection on the chapters, one can say that different parts of the diverse research field contribute to mediatisation in their own specific way depending on the matter subjected to analysis. In some spheres, tradition, history, and local context are of great importance; in others it is the global dimension and new conceptualisations that matter more. From the previous chapters it emerges that some changes in terms, concepts, and methodology are necessary in mediatisation studies, as well as in interdisciplinary collaborations. The development of new areas and themes, as well as new approaches, are needed in the context of dynamic transformations of reality. The research niches might be sources of new practical, discursive, and research inspirations, and also the integration of European and non-European; Anglo-Saxon and dissenting perspectives are needed. Furthermore, by reflecting on other difficulties, challenges, and shortcomings of the theory and approach, the research area has a chance to develop, to face up to well-established criticism and to chart new paths of development. Therefore, there are important contributions to this overarching debate to be found in all eleven chapters of this book, pointing to new demands and solutions by which researchers can develop further avenues to advance the research field.

Reference

Krotz, F. (2007). The meta-process of "mediatization" as a conceptual frame. *Global Media and Communication*, 3(3), 256–260.

Index

For Product Safety Concerns and Information please contact our EU
representative GPSR@taylorandfrancis.com
Taylor & Francis Verlag GmbH, Kaufingerstraße 24, 80331 München, Germany

www.ingramcontent.com/pod-product-compliance
Lightning Source LLC
Chambersburg PA
CBHW070328270326
41926CB00017B/3801

9 7 8 1 0 3 2 3 4 9 4 2 8